The **BIG BOOK** *of*
REINCARNATION

The BIG BOOK of REINCARNATION

EXAMINING THE EVIDENCE THAT WE HAVE ALL LIVED BEFORE

ROY STEMMAN

Hierophant publishing

Hierophant Publishing
8301 Broadway, Suite 219
San Antonio, TX 78209
888-800-4240
www.hierophantpublishing.com

Cover photo collage: © istockphoto.com/sharply_done and enjoynz
Text design by Jane Hagaman

Library of Congress Control Number: 2011941641

ISBN: 978-0-9818771-6-7

10 9 8 7 6 5 4 3 2 1

This book is dedicated to the memory of Ian Stevenson, MD,

whose pioneering work in reincarnation research

features prominently in its pages

Contents

Part Four: Implications

Introduction

What this book sets out to do is answer two questions that every thoughtful individual will have asked themselves at some time in their life: do we live after we die, and if so, will we be reborn on earth? As you will soon discover, there is a huge body of evidence that has been accumulated over the past fifty years that suggests very strongly that life does continue beyond death, and that, in some instances at least, individuals have been reborn with memories of their previous earthly existence.

That simple statement has enormous implications, which, if accepted, would have an impact not only on most religious beliefs but also on a wide range of social issues, such as abortion and euthanasia. It also raises fundamental questions about the very nature of our consciousness and the possibility of a spiritual dimension interacting with the world in which we live.

Those who actively explore this fascinating subject can be divided into two groups, reflecting very different sources of past-life memories:

First are the scientists who investigate reports of children who begin talking about a previous life at a very early age. I refer to such cases as "spontaneous" because they arise naturally, without prompting or searching. Often these youngsters are able to provide names of people, places, and significant events in that former life. However, those memories usually fade after a few years, and so the handful of researchers specializing in this research need to learn of them as quickly as possible. They need to get to the children while they can give more information and their family members and others can provide eye-witness reports about what has already been said and what investigations have taken place. Gathering quality data in such circumstances, where long distances have to be travelled and lengthy translations made, can be extremely challenging, so I have the utmost respect for those who undertake this research. As well as meeting the leading researchers within this book, you will find their full details in appendix 1, where I provide not only their academic credentials but also comments on some of their findings.

Second are those individuals who use techniques that enable adults to explore their subconscious in the hope that they can go back in time to a former life. Most use hypnosis to induce this state of mind, though there are other methods. The vast majority of these individuals are therapists, though a few are simply interested in looking for evidence of reincarnation. "Past-life regressionist" is the most appropriate term to apply to those using such skills for either purpose. Again, you will find references to a number of past-life regressionists and therapists throughout the book, but I also include a list of a number of leading figures in this field in appendix 2.

I should observe at this point that the scientists studying reincarnation are generally skeptical of regressionists' results, arguing that the mind has a fantastic ability to invent and fabricate apparently credible stories. That's an area that I cover in some depth, along with an examination of alternative explanations for claims of reincarnation.

Last, I must assure you that it is not my purpose to convince you that reincarnation occurs for all of us. I don't know whether that is the case. I am satisfied, however, that some of the cases I cite are sufficiently evidential to conclude that reincarnation is by far the best explanation to accommodate all the known facts. What I have set out to do is to share the wealth of information about reincarnation that is available, presenting it in a way that is easy to comprehend, exploring in the process the questions and issues that are likely to be uppermost in readers' minds.

If even one of the cases discussed convinces you that it provides acceptable evidence of reincarnation, that realization could give you a whole new perspective on life—and death—in which case, your soul's journey is about to take you on an exciting new path of discovery.

—Roy Stemman
June 2011

Part One

The Past

Chapter 1

The Origins of Rebirth

Belief in reincarnation is far more deeply entrenched in Western civilization than some orthodox religions might care to acknowledge. Dismissed by many as a New Age fad that will fade with time, its popularity nevertheless suggests that in matters relating to religion and spirituality, growing numbers of people are prepared to mix and match the beliefs and teachings that most appeal to them, regardless of the dictates of the religions to which they profess allegiance or in whose churches they worship.

In 2003, the National Study of Youth and Religion, Wave 1, survey[1] in the United States revealed that virtually half of the 3,290 English- and Spanish-speaking teenagers, ages thirteen to seventeen, and those parents who participated either definitely believed in reincarnation (453 = 13.4%) or thought it was possible (1,210 = 35.9%), compared with an almost equal number who did not believe (49.4%), with just a little over 1% not having an opinion.

Six years later, a poll by the Pew Research Center's Forum on Religion and Public Life (published December 2009)[2] gave us a more up-to-date insight into the views of Americans over eighteen years old on the same topic. "Though the US is an overwhelmingly Christian country," the report comments, "significant minorities profess belief in a variety of Eastern or New Age beliefs. For instance, 24 percent of the public overall and 22 percent of

Christians say they believe in reincarnation—that people will be reborn in this world again and again." It breaks those figures down further: roughly 10 percent of white evangelicals believe in reincarnation, compared with 24 percent among mainline Protestants, 25 percent among both white Catholics and those unaffiliated with any religion, and 29 percent among black Protestants. The title of the Pew Forum report—"Many Americans Mix Multiple Faiths"—says it all, and its summary points out that many blend Christianity with Eastern or New Age beliefs such as reincarnation, astrology, and the presence of spiritual energy in physical objects. It reports ". . . sizeable minorities of all major US religious groups say they have experienced supernatural phenomena, such as being in touch with the dead or with ghosts."

We already know that at least half of the world's population, as followers of the teachings of Hinduism, Buddhism, Jainism, and various other Eastern religions, accepts reincarnation. Now, it seems, a quarter of the rest of the global family—assuming the American statistics are mirrored in other Western countries—may also share that view.

How have we come so far? Indeed, have we gone too far? There will certainly be those who recoil in disbelief at the "muddle-headedness" of such large numbers of people refusing to be confined to the teachings of their churches or the guidance of religious leaders on the subject of reincarnation. Perhaps this "rebellion" is because belief in the existence of a soul that can return to earth to experience many lives has been around for far longer than most of the major religions. So, let us start this exploration of a subject that clearly fascinates or is relevant to billions of people by examining reincarnation from a historical perspective.

Dualism—the conviction that we each have a spirit or soul that separates from the body at death and continues to exist in another world or dimension—has probably been expressed in one form or another since the dawn of civilization. Hominids began disposing of their dead in significant ways as long as three hundred thousand years ago, though there is no evidence to suggest that these practices had a spiritual dimension. Eventually, burials were introduced that included interment of various useful items with the deceased, though we can only speculate on their purpose and what funerary rituals may have accompanied them. Even simple possessions alongside a body in a grave suggest, as one expert puts it, "concern for the dead that transcends daily life." With the passage of time, the artifacts that were buried with the dead—particularly those who were eminent in their culture—increased in number and value and were clearly thought to play an important role in assisting the passage from one life to the next. Such rituals even included human sacrifices. But when did people start believing that, instead of spending eternity in the afterlife, the soul might be reborn and live one or more further lives on Earth? The evidence suggests that the concept has been around since modern civilization's earliest days.

Reincarnation and karma are important aspects of the teachings of **Hinduism,** which originated in India and is often described as the world's "oldest living religion." It had no single founder but grew, instead, out of diverse traditions whose roots extend back in time to the historical Vedic religion of Iron Age India, also known as Brahmanism. It does, however, have scriptures and philosophical texts from a variety of authors, probably recorded between 800 and 400 BC, which contain guidance and teachings that in earlier times had been handed down orally for many centuries. Of these, the Upanishads—mystic doctrines regarded as "the supreme work of the Indian mind"—provide its fundamental teachings. The Bhagavad Gita is perhaps the best known outside of Hinduism, being considered one of the most important texts in the history of philosophy and literature. The Upanishads deal in depth with the soul, karma, reincarnation, and nirvana, as well as self-realization through yoga and meditation. Hindus, however, make a semantic differentiation between "rebirth," which is for humans, and "reincarnation," which is for gods.

Reincarnation and karma are also cornerstones of **Jainism,** another ancient Indian religion, which has coexisted alongside Hinduism for thousands of years, while retaining its independence. Though its origins are different, it shares many of Hinduism's concepts—so much so, that some incorrectly view it as a branch of that religion. One notable difference is its focus on nonviolence as being necessary to enable a soul to realize its true nature and make spiritual progress to the point at which it achieves liberation from the cycle of rebirth. That, in turn, leads to Jains being strict vegetarians. Jainism's view of karma is also very different from Hinduism's, interpreting it in terms of natural laws rather than moral laws, and also prescribing two methods of shedding past karma: one passive, the other active. Historians date Jainism's origins to somewhere between the ninth and sixth centuries BC, though its own doctrine teaches that it has always existed and always will. Even though it has far fewer followers than other major religions—an estimated ten to twelve million—it has always exerted an influence on other beliefs, notably Hinduism and Buddhism, and on the cultures in which it flourishes.

It is highly likely that the young prince Siddhartha Gautama, who was born around 563 BC, would have been exposed to some aspects of either Hindu or Jain teachings, possibly both, before he experienced his own spiritual enlightenment while meditating beneath a bodhi tree in Lumbini in modern-day Nepal. We know him today, of course, as the Buddha. Instead of becoming a king or chieftain, he chose to follow a spiritual path devoted to teaching others how they too could achieve nirvana and liberate themselves from the cycle of suffering and rebirth. The Buddha lived and taught in the northeastern part of the Indian subcontinent, but his teachings gradually reached out around the ancient world, splintering into two major branches of **Buddhism**—Theravada and Mahayana, from which the Tibetan version derives—as well as having an impact on many other traditions that have their roots in his teachings. It was, undoubtedly, the first world religion and by the middle of the twentieth century could also claim to be the largest, with 520 million adherents. That number doubles to over one billion if we include East Asian traditional religions, which mix forms of Buddhism with other influences, such as folk religion, Taoism, and Shamanism. While Buddhism's teachings are complex and difficult to comprehend for many Westerners, with its pantheon of Buddhas, Bodhisattvas, and lesser deities, one concept—karma—which it shares with other Eastern religions, seems to have infiltrated the global consciousness. In simplistic terms, this is a universal law of cause and effect, driven by our good or bad thoughts and actions, the results of which we will experience either in this life or another. Karma has been described as the force that drives *samsara*—the cycle of suffering and rebirth—but even within Buddhism there are different interpretations of how this takes effect.

It was not until the hieroglyphics of the ancient **Egyptians** were deciphered, following the discovery of the Rosetta Stone in 1799, that we began to fully understand the beliefs that surrounded life and death for the three thousand years during which that particular civilization thrived. It emerged that running parallel to the development of Jainism and Hinduism was another culture focused on preparing oneself in this life for an existence in the next world. As well as building great pyramids and subterranean tombs for their dearly departed and perfecting the process of mummification, the Egyptians also recorded in great detail, in the Book of the Dead, the journey they believed the *ka* (body double) and *ba* (personality) took from this life to the Kingdom of the Dead into which they would be reborn. What is not widely acknowledged is that some of the earliest references to reincarnation are to be found in the Book of the Dead. The nineteenth-century French Egyptologist Theodule Deveria,[3] for example, explained: "The *sahou* was not truly the mortal body. It was *a new being* formed by the reunion of corporeal elements elaborated by nature, and in which the soul was reborn in order to accomplish a new terrestrial existence under many forms. . . ." According to James Bonwick,[4] in his *Egyptian Belief and Modern Thought* (1878), the Book of the Dead is full of allusions to the doctrine of reincarnation. He explains that chapters 26 to 30 relate to the preservation of the heart or life for this purpose, adding: "Absurd as this notion [of reincarnation] may appear to a modern European, there can be no doubt that it ranks among the very oldest entertained by man."

The Greeks also had a word for it: metempsychosis. It can be defined as either reincarnation—from one human body to another—or transmigration, which can also include a soul moving from a human to an animal existence, or vice versa. At the same time that Buddha was teaching reincarnation in India, around twenty-five thousand years ago, Pythagoras, the Greek philosopher and mathematician, was founding a religious movement, **Pythagoreanism,** based on esoteric and metaphysical beliefs that also included reincarnation. Of this there is little doubt, but we have to rely on the words of others as Pythagoras seldom wrote anything down. We therefore do not know what may have influenced his thoughts, though Egyptian beliefs or even Indian religions may well have played a part. Plato, student of Socrates and one of the founders of Western philosophy and science, who died around 347 BC, provides us with much information about Pythagoras and also refers to reincarnation in his writings, though whether he was an advocate of rebirth is open to question. On the other hand, a set of religious beliefs and practices known to us as **Orphism,** which were embraced by the ancient Greek and Hellenistic world as well as by the Thracians, can be traced back to the sixth century BC. The soul's immortality and the need for it to experience many lives before being released from the "grievous circle" were cornerstones of Orphism and are reminiscent of Eastern beliefs, from which they may have emanated.

Readers may not expect me to make any reference to the Abrahamic religions, such as Judaism, Christianity, and Islam, on the basis that they do not teach reincarnation. But, as we are about to see, that is not entirely true. Abraham, who lived almost four thousand years ago, is recognized as the father of the Hebrew nation who followed God's calling and led his people to a new land. He is referred to as "our Father" in Islamic and Jewish traditions and is also considered a prophet of Islam. He is the father of the Israelites in Jewish tradition, and Christians regard the coming of Jesus Christ as the fulfillment of God's promise to Abraham. Although this would appear to leave no room for reincarnation, there is ample evidence to suggest otherwise.

As the religion, philosophy, and way of life of the Jewish people, orthodox **Judaism,** which claims a historical continuity extending more than three thousand years, does not teach rebirth. But a number of sects have done so, at various times in its long history, such as the anti-rabbinical Karaites in Baghdad, in the eighth century, who taught that every soul needed to pass through a series of earthly incarnations. Eight centuries later, Rabbi Luria attracted many followers with his mystical interpretation of Jewish teachings that included acceptance of reincarnation. He was followed in the eighteenth century by the Eastern European Rabbi Israel ben Eliezer (who became known as the Baal Shem Tov), who established Hasidic Judaism to focus more on spirituality and joy than the laws that dominate orthodox Judaism. The teachings of Hasidicism include the ability of souls to reincarnate and learn from experiences in different lives, as indeed does the Kabbalah, a school of thought that exists outside the traditional Jewish scriptures, but which is enjoying increasing popularity, particularly among non-Jewish celebrities. *Gilgul* (cycle) *neshamot* (souls) is the Kabbalistic concept of souls passing through various incarnations, depending on their particular task in each lifetime.

Orthodox **Christianity** offers no support for reincarnation concepts today, but there is evidence to suggest that was not the case in its early days.

The prolific Christian writer and theologian Origen Adamantius (AD 185–254) wrote in *Contra Celsum*: "The soul, which is immaterial and invisible in its nature, exists in no material place without having a body suited to the nature of that place; accordingly, it at one time puts off one body, which is necessary before, but which is no longer adequate in its changed state, and it exchanges it for a second." As one of Christianity's most distinguished early scholars, Origen—who is believed to have been Egyptian—is credited with being largely responsible for the coalescence of Christian writings that became the New Testament, an event that took place long after he had died. He also developed doctrines that reflected Pythagorean and Platonist influences, but were also presumably based on his deeper interpretation of scriptures, arguing in favor of "the fabulous preexistence of souls." He was not alone among the early church fathers. Justin Martyr (AD 100–165) and St. Clement of Alexandria (AD 150–220) expressed similar views. But the Fifth Ecumenical Council, meeting in Constantinople (AD 553), is believed to have decreed otherwise, having declared Origen's views on the preexistence of souls anathematized—cursed. There are scholars who put a different interpretation on this ruling, issued in the name of Emperor Justinian, but the effect has certainly been to remove debate on reincarnation from the orthodox Christian arena. That has not, however, stopped some leading Christians from taking a different view.

Similarly, **Islam** does not teach rebirth, and there is probably only one passage in its religious text, the Qur'an, which was revealed to Muhammad by the angel Gabriel in the seventh century, that could be quoted in its support: "God generates beings, and sends them back over and over again, till they return to him." However, Islam's mystical and esoteric tradition, **Sufism,** is very much in favor, teaching that orthodox Muslims are misinterpreting passages in the Qur'an as being about judgment and resurrection whereas they really describe the continuous cycle of reincarnation.

And for the **Druze,** an Islamic sect whose history dates back more than fourteen hundred years, reincarnation is a fundamental teaching. Some scholars see a blending of Judaism, Christianity, and Islam, tinged with Gnosticism, Tibetan Lamaism, and the Magian system of Persia, in its beliefs. This surprising and colorful mixture might be explained by one of the claims that are made for it, namely that it came into being when Hemsa, the uncle of Muhammad, went to Tibet in 625 in search of secret wisdom. He then reincarnated in the eleventh century as H'amsa, the founder of the Druze, and is said to have been reborn successively ever since as the chief Druze hierophant.

There is no question that **Sikhism,** another religion that originated in India, 500 years ago, also confirms the reality of both reincarnation and karma. Its founder, Nānak, taught that we are each born with different temperaments, which are the result of past karma. Self-identification with the body and its environment is what keeps us on the whirling wheel of *samsara*—of births and deaths.

The mid-nineteenth century saw the birth, in quick succession, of three religions that have a bearing on this discussion. **The Bahá'í Faith,** which believes that God reveals his will periodically through divine messengers, such as Abraham, the Buddha, Jesus Christ, and Muhammad, came into being after Siyyid Ali-Muhammad of Shiraz, Persia (now Iran), announced on May 23, 1844, that he was "the Báb" ("the Gate")—the promised Mahdi, the redeemer of Islam, who would stay on earth for seven, nine, or nineteen years (depending on various interpretations). The Mahdi doctrine is common to both Shi'a and Sunni Muslims. As it happened, the Báb remained on earth for a little over six years. His claim and teachings were so strongly opposed by both Persia's Shi'a clergy and the government that they persecuted and killed thousands of his followers—Bábis—before a firing squad executed him on July 9, 1850. The Báb is claimed to have been Elijah and John the Baptist in previous lives. In 1863, one of his followers, Bahá'u'lláh, claimed to be the fulfillment of the Báb's promise that God would send another messenger, and the Bahá'í Faith was born. Bahá'u'lláh is also said to have proclaimed that he was the reincarnation of Imaam Husein, the martyred grandson of the prophet Muhammad. Its core principles are the unity of God, the unity of religion, and the unity of humankind, and it has an estimated five to six million followers in over two hundred countries and territories. But the story does not end there. In 1909, Salim Moussa Achi was born in Jerusalem, and shortly afterward his family moved to Beirut, Lebanon, where he became known as a miracle worker at the age of twenty-one and wrote under the name Dr. Dahesh. He is said to have claimed to be not only the reincarnation of the Báb but also of Jesus Christ.

Just four years after the Báb announced that he was the Mahdi, an American family was coming to terms with a very different revelation. On March 31, 1948, three months after they had moved into a house in Hydesville, near Rochester, New York, the Fox household was disturbed by strange rapping sounds. They discovered these knocks would respond to their questions, and using a simple yes-no code, they established that the spirit responsible claimed to have been murdered in the house. From that modest beginning, **Spiritualism** was born, and the Fox daughters went on to become well-known mediums, though controversy has always surrounded their alleged abilities. Spiritualism spread rapidly around the world, attracting many high-profile supporters and apparently opening up direct communication with the next world. So, does it offer an answer to the perennial question: Do we reincarnate? Disappointingly, it depends on whom you speak with. Some spirit guides teach that rebirth is a universal law and we *all* live many lives, while others declare that souls do *not* reincarnate. This raises as many questions about mediumship and spirit communication as it does about the reality of reincarnation. One explanation offered is that these spirit guides are on different planes, depending on their spiritual development, and that what they tell us is true as far as their own experiences are concerned—just as aliens returning to their home planet in two spacecraft after a visit to Earth would describe very different scenarios if one had made contact with humans living in Antarctica and the other had encountered the inhabitants of a tropical jungle.

However, the spirits who spoke with French teacher Hippolyte Léon Denizard Rivail in Paris in the 1850s had no doubts on the subject of reincarnation. Not only did they assure him that reincarnation occurred, but he was also informed that, in a previous life, he had been a Druid named Allan Kardec. He liked the name and decided to make it his *nom de plume* when writing about spirit communication, to separate his Spiritualist interests from his educational endeavors in high schools, which included running free courses for underprivileged children. Kardec collected and collated a wealth of information about the spirit world and the spiritual nature of man by compiling a list of over 1,000 questions that were put to spirits speaking through different mediums. His first work on the subject, published in 1857, was *The Spirits' Book*, followed by several others, including *The Book on Mediums* and *The*

Gospel According to Spiritism, which together form the Fundamental Works of Spiritism. Today, **Spiritism** has an estimated 20 million followers, the majority in Brazil.

Reincarnation is a dominant theme of these books, which teach that each incarnation has a purpose, occurring in a place and within a family that it deserves and in conditions that allow the soul to correct past mistakes and grow spiritually. Suffering in one form or another is likely to be the consequence of behavior in previous lifetimes. This philosophy is akin to those of Eastern religions, but Spiritists maintain that theirs is based on Christianity and that Jesus Christ's teachings are a model of moral perfection. However, Spiritists do not see Jesus as the Son of God, but as a highly evolved soul who went through many incarnations to share his spiritual knowledge with others. Indeed, Spiritists also argue that Jesus taught the reality of reincarnation, and their doctrine is based on the Bible, where such knowledge is conveyed metaphorically. Kardec died in 1869, and his tomb in the famous Père Lachaise cemetery in Paris is now a place of pilgrimage for Spiritists from around the globe. Above the chamber in which he and his wife are interred are these words: "Naître, mourir, renaître encore et progresser sans cesse, telle est la loi." ("To be born, die, again be reborn, and so progress unceasingly, such is the law.")

An even newer religion for which belief in past lives is significant is the **Church of Scientology,** the creation of science fiction writer L. Ron Hubbard, which came into being in 1952, based on his research and writings on Dianetics, a term he coined to describe a set of ideas and practices regarding the metaphysical relationship between the mind and the body. Reincarnation, says its website, is not part of Scientology, but the Church ascribes to this definition of it: "to be born again into the flesh or into another body." This is necessary since, as it goes on to explain, "Today in Scientology, many people have certainty that they have lived lives prior to their current one. These are referred to as *past lives,* not as reincarnation. Past lives is not a dogma of Scientology, but generally Scientologists, during their auditing, experience a past life and then know for themselves that they have lived before." Hubbard, who died in 1986, made a clear distinction between past lives remembered under hypnosis and those recalled by Scientologists going through an auditing process, which uses an E-meter, an electronic device that "detects areas of spiritual charge and stress." It is during this procedure, when they are encouraged to enter into an "engram"—"a mental image picture which is a recording of an experience containing pain, unconsciousness, and a real or fancied threat to survival"—that past-life memories are said to occur. Hubbard's book *Have You Lived before This Life?* (1989) provides forty-one fascinating case histories from a 1958 experiment in London in which, it is claimed, "the actuality of past lives was scientifically explored." Scientology has attracted many celebrities to its ranks, but it and its founder remain controversial. While Scientology is legally recognized as a tax-exempt religion in the United States and some other countries, it does not enjoy comparable status in the United Kingdom, France, and Germany. Whatever one's views on Scientology, it cannot be ignored that its auditing procedures are regarded by some as "the oldest known form of regression therapy."

As we have seen, belief in some form of reincarnation has permeated most cultures for many thousands of years, and there are numerous other examples I could have explored. It seems to me that a good case can be made for the global belief in reincarnation originating in just one culture and then influencing its neighbors. An impressive recent contribution to the debate from Peter Kingsley[5] argues that Western civilization was shaped by the influences of Mongolian and Tibetan shamanism. Belief in reincarnation could have developed as a way of coming to terms with suffering and justice, offering victims hope of a better future life, and threatening abusers with punishment for their crimes in their next existence. But that is mere speculation. There is another possibility that might explain why belief in reincarnation is so widespread. It could simply be that throughout time there have been individuals in every culture who have been born with memories of a past life that have proved, on examination, to be accurate. Tibetan Buddhists, for example, not only believe their important spiritual leaders, such as the Dalai Lama, the Panchen Lama, and the Karmapa, will be reborn to continue their work, but that possible candidates for that role must be questioned and tested to confirm that they are a true reincarnation. The Druze also have a long tradition of going in search of their previous-life families, and there have been similar cases in other cultures.

Chapter 2

Sands of Time

However the widespread belief in reincarnation came about, for millions of people in the twenty-first century it is a fact of life—and death. The biggest challenge for a researcher in this field is separating reality and fantasy. So many vying influences can be at play in claimed cases of reincarnation that an investigator needs to have a good understanding of human psychology, memory, and the role of the subconscious—particularly in hypnotic regression cases—if he or she is to get close to the truth.

A sense of history is also essential, for the civilizations that nurtured belief in reincarnation could continue to exert an unexpected influence over many of the world's citizens today. Reincarnation might even explain why belief in rebirth is so strong in the twenty-first century: those who accept it today do so because it was also part of their belief system in previous lifetimes. Certainly, previous existences seem to bleed through and color the lives of some individuals in a surprising way.

Let me cite Ancient Egypt as an example. Most of us are fascinated by the period in history when pharaohs ruled that country, built massive pyramids, and buried their dead in elaborate tombs with lavish trimmings to assist in their journey to the next world. But what is it that draws some people just to a particular period of Egyptian history, such as the troubled seventeen-year span when Akhenaten was pharaoh and attempted to change his people's religious beliefs? In the fifth year of his reign, the pharaoh changed his name from Amenhotep IV to Akhenaten and built a city whose modern name is Amarna for the worship of Aten, the sun deity. The legendary beauty Nefertiti was his queen and DNA testing in 2010 has also shown the pharaoh to be Tutankhamen's father.

While leading tours to Egypt, writer and lecturer Daniel M. Kolos had clients who confided to him about their Egyptian past-life memories. Surprisingly, the majority focused on Akhenaten's reign—a period that had always particularly fascinated Kolos for no obvious reason. Accepting that living previous lives in that period may have left a deep impression on many individuals, Kolos decided to stage an "Amarna Reunion" in the early 1990s. The difficulties and disagreements that arose in organizing the event most likely mirrored the discontent and turmoil that existed during Akhenaten's reign, as the original proposal was scrapped but then replaced with mini reunions in Toronto, San Francisco, and Michigan. Describing one of the reunions as a "psycho-drama," Kolos wrote:

> "Akhenaten" spoke of his vision and the ancient trials and tribulations he had to endure in order to succeed. Nefertiti and others wept throughout the weekend at the great sadness they remembered. Kiya, Akhenaten's second wife, relived her own death, being stabbed in the neck. She immediately began purging and took to her bed for two days. One of the princesses accused me of being a humorless, strict priest whose job was to enforce Akhenaten's will. I met a dancer as well as a royal confidante, neither of whom trusted me then and refused to back me now. The conference drew many healers, and much of the pain dissipated as forgiveness and unconditional love replaced it. For some, memories of a past life became like an old movie that has already been acted out. It remained either for entertainment or for learning.[1]

I don't know whether further Amarna Reunions took place, but I see that Daniel continues to make objective contributions to debates on the subject on an Internet forum website dedicated to the Amarna period. What his entertaining account failed to do, however, was to persuade me that the people involved were actually recalling past lives rather than simply fantasizing. So, in early 1995, I decided to join a Power Places Tour that might give me a better insight into connecting with the past. It was an opportunity to explore Egypt in the company of others who were fascinated by reincarnation and the possibility of investigating their past lives, and I was added to the list of speakers for the initial conference in Cairo. Many of us then set off down the Nile for a luxury cruise aboard the *Nile Goddess,* which took us majestically to Philae, Luxor, and Karnak to see tombs and temples that had survived for thousands of years, both in physical terms but also, it seems, in the subconscious minds of many of my fellow travelers. "Come to the Great Pyramid," said Power Places' advertisement, "and open yourself to spiritual discovery, understanding, and growth." Assisting in that aim were a team of past-life regression therapists, including Janet Cunningham, who is now president of the International Board of Regression Therapy, and Dr. Ron Jue, a founder of the Professional Institute for Regression Therapy. They held group and one-on-one sessions away from the main conference and also on the Nile cruise between stopovers, as well as regressing each other as part of their exploration of possible Egyptian incarnations. It transpired that Jue had been both a pharaoh and a priest in the life he recalled, though he had grave reservations about admitting that to

me because he works with many people "who use personalities to foster grandiosity," and he was concerned that the memory of a pharaonic incarnation that had surfaced during this trip might give that impression to others. It was all very fascinating and life-affirming for many of the participants, but it was clearly not an adventure that would convince a skeptic.

A big disappointment for me on that journey was that militants were in control of an area that included the tomb of Seti I at Abydos, in the Valley of the Kings, and it was deemed too dangerous for us to visit. My interest in seeing

Dorothy Eady/Omm Seti

the tomb palls into insignificance when compared to that of Dorothy Eady, who was born to Irish parents in the United Kingdom in 1904, and whose empathy and fascination with ancient Egypt began in early childhood. When visiting the British Museum as a young girl, she would rush around kissing the feet of Egyptian statues, and when told it was time to leave she responded: "Leave me . . . these are my people." Dorothy felt she wanted "to go home" but was uncertain where home was until she started seeing an ancient building with huge columns in her dreams and recognized it later when she saw a photograph of the Temple of Seti I. Then, when she was fourteen, Pharaoh Seti "appeared" to her and from then on she began piecing together glimpses of a past life in which she had been Bentreshyt, a novice priestess. In that incarnation, Dorothy realized she had broken the rules and started a secret liaison with the pharaoh. Worried that it would be discovered, she took her own life. Distraught, Seti I vowed to find her again . . . and apparently did so, in south London, three thousand years later. Dorothy Eady spent much of her teenage years studying Egyptology and being taught to read hieroglyphics by the keeper of Egyptian antiquities at the British Museum, Sir Ernest Wallis Budge. She eventually moved to Egypt at the age of twenty-nine, having married an Egyptian student, and they had a son whom she named Seti, much to her husband's annoyance. Following the Egyptian custom that women are not called by their first name, she was known as Omm Seti, meaning "mother of Seti." Based in Cairo, Dorothy became the first woman ever to work for the Egyptian Antiquities Department, but when her marriage failed she went "home" to Abydos, where she lived in a small peasant house and worked as a guide. She spent the rest of her life, through to her death in 1981, devoted to the temple and its upkeep, worshipping the Egyptian gods and communicating in various ways with the pharaoh she had loved and left in a previous existence.[2] In 1937, just a few years after Dorothy Eady's arrival in Egypt, a remarkable book by another English woman—Joan Grant—was published to critical acclaim. *Winged Pharaoh* rapidly went into new editions as reviewers described it as "glowing," "in a class apart," and, according to the *New York Times* book critic: "a book of fine idealism, deep compassion, and a spiritual quality pure and bright as flame." The well-crafted novel told the story of Sekeeta, a pharaoh's daughter who had become co-ruler of Egypt with her brother on her father's death and had taken a Minoan sculptor Dio as a lover who had left her with child as he did not want to be the pharaoh's favorite. Their son, Den, had succeeded Sekeeta as pharaoh. The book was praised for its accuracy and the amount of research that had gone into it. Eventually, however, Joan Grant revealed that she had not needed to research the story: it was autobiographical. She had been Sekeeta, and that past lifetime was recalled by a process she described as "far memory." From childhood, she had experienced vivid dreams that proved, in some cases, to be of events that were happening elsewhere in the world at that very time. She had also developed psychometry, the ability to "read" an object's past simply by holding it. It was during such an experiment on September 13, 1936, when she and her first husband, Leslie, were staying with a friend, that she was given a turquoise blue scarab that their host's brother had brought back from Egypt.

Joan Grant

Suddenly, she went "out"—she described this later as "changing level"—and began talking about life in Egypt, with Leslie taking rapid notes. After an hour she heard Leslie calling her name and came back to normal consciousness. It proved to be the first of 200 sessions in which Joan Grant dictated daily the words of Sekeeta. "The funny thing is," she said later, "that it didn't come out in chronological order. But when we came to spread it all out on the floor, we found it fitted together perfectly and needed no rewriting."

Leslie Grant, who had trained as a lawyer but then moved into archaeology, was not keen for his wife's dictated book to be published because he was certain it contained historical inaccuracies and that the period in which it was set was also wrong. But an enthusiastic publisher persuaded them that it should go into print, and over seventy years later it has appeared in over fifteen languages and, like most of the other fifteen "far memory" books Joan Grant produced, is still in print today.

Is *Winged Pharaoh* really a record of life in ancient Egypt, or simply a romantic historical novel? British author Jean Overton Fuller, a poet and artist of note who also specialized in writing biographies, spent a long weekend with the Grants in 1944 after she had told them the book was "a landmark in my life." Fuller went on to study the Egyptian "far memory" book in depth, and her findings were published as an *Occasional Paper of Theosophical History*. Fuller's research into hieroglyphics and Egyptian history shed considerable light on the contents, as well as corroborating facts that some experts, and even Joan's husband, had dismissed as incorrect at the time.

Denys Kelsey and Joan Grant

Why was it that Joan Grant could remember that Egyptian existence in such detail? Her explanation was that "far memory" was known and developed in those ancient times. Those who received the necessary training, like Sekeeta, had to remember at least ten of their own deaths, and their graduation required them to be shut in a tomb for four days and nights, during which they underwent seven ordeals. It appears to have been a gift she brought with her into the twentieth century, and with it the ability to remember many other lives. She claimed to recall dying at least forty times, often in violent or tragic circumstances, but said rebirths were more painful and frightening than passings. The other remembered lives about which she wrote included another Egyptian life, one thousand years later; a wandering sixteenth-century minstrel in Italy; a prostitute on the streets of France; an accused witch who was burned alive; an Native American girl; a Greek runner; and an English woman, Lavinia. She also recalled a death at the guillotine, twice committing suicide, dying in a joust from a spear through the eye, twice being bitten by snakes, and bleeding to death after ordering her Roman court physician to cut her wrists.

In addition to her "far memory" books, Joan Grant's other great contribution to reincarnation studies was the work she did with her third husband, Denys Kelsey, as a pioneer of hypnotherapy and regression therapy, which I will be dealing with in some detail in a later chapter. Their combined intervention helped many overcome fears, phobias, and illness.

In 1935, two years before *Winged Pharaoh* was published, another reincarnation-inspired book centered on an Englishwoman's unusual talents appeared in UK bookshops. *After Thirty Centuries,* written by Frederic H. Wood, a Blackpool-based doctor of music, told the story of his research into trance communications received through schoolteacher Ivy Carter Beaumont, who believed herself to have been Vola, a temple dancer in the reign of the eighteenth-dynasty pharaoh Amenhotep III (1406–1370 BC), in a past life. When she went into trance, a Babylonian princess named Nona spoke through her, in English. Nona explained she was actually Telika-Véntiu, one of the pharaoh's harem, who had married Amenhotep and had drowned while escaping from Egyptian priests. The medium—whose identity was concealed behind the name "Rosemary" in the book—had been Nona's Syrian handmaiden and companion in that life. What made this colorful account different from other reincarnation or spirit communication stories was that, as she emerged from trance, Beaumont began repeating Egyptian words she had heard. This seemed to be a demonstration of the ability to spontaneously speak an unknown language, a phenomenon known as xenoglossy. Wood, who had been researching Beaumont's mediumship since 1931, wrote these sounds down phonetically, gradually compiling over two thousand words, phrases, short sentences, and whole paragraphs. The significance of this was that Egyptian hieroglyphics were a mystery to modern man until the Rosetta Stone's discovery provided a key that unlocked our understanding of Egyptian writing. But how the language was spoken remained a mystery. Here, it seemed, as a result of a reincarnation link between this world and the next, was a way that might enable hieroglyphics to be translated into speech.

The breakthrough seemed to come when Alfred J. Howard Hulme read *After Thirty Centuries* and asked the author if any Egyptian words had been spoken. Wood not only confirmed that they had but also sent his phonetic interpretations. Hulme, who claimed to be a "professional Egyptologist," translated them into both English and hieroglyphics, praising Princess Nona's "infallible use of Egyptian grammar" and declaring: "It is difficult to show and explain to the ordinary reader the purely technical and most convincing features: such as period characteristics, survival of archaism, grammatical accuracy, peculiar terms, ordinary elisions, figures of speech, etc., but they are intensely evidential." And he claimed that these captured words and phrases had "completely restored the spoken language of Ancient Egypt." The two men collaborated on *Ancient Egypt Speaks* (published, incidentally, in 1937, the same year as Joan Grant's *Winged Pharaoh*), in which they outlined the way in which they had worked with the medium, revealing that Beaumont had also demonstrated *responsive* xenoglossy. Hulme had sent questions in Egyptian, written phonetically, which Wood put to the medium, who then answered in Egyptian, which Wood wrote down phonetically and sent back to Hulme for translation.

Wood followed this collaboration with *This Egyptian Miracle* in 1940. In that book Wood takes up the reincarnation theme, revealing that Nona had told them that Beaumont was incarnating on Earth for the last time. He added, "I myself have still another cycle of life to complete, according to my guides; and I shall return as a Teacher in the Far East when China, now in the birth pangs of a new era, has risen to a position of world-dominance."

Readers at that time probably found the spoken Egyptian language claim far easier to believe than the prediction of China's future growth to a world power. But they would have been wrong. Hulme turned out to be an artist, not the "professional Egyptologist" he claimed to be, and investigators could find no evidence of him ever studying at Oxford, despite the "Hons. Cert. in Egyptology" qualification he was said to have achieved at the famous university. Wood and spinster Ivy Carter Beaumont, on the other hand, were undoubtedly sincere in their beliefs and almost certainly were experiencing glossolalia (speaking in tongues), *not* xenoglossy, which means that the rare 78 rpm gramophone recording I possess of her speaking in "Egyptian" is, in fact, just gibberish, and the past lives of Nona and Vola are equally fictitious. In this case, the claim to have recovered a long-forgotten language failed to live up to that promise. There are, however, more recent cases of xenoglossy that are not so easily dismissed, as we will see in later chapters.

It is likely that Pulitzer Prize-winning author Norman Mailer, best known for his *The Naked and the Dead,* read books by or about Joan Grant and Dorothy Eady during the eleven years he spent researching and writing his monumental *Ancient Evenings* (1983). Reincarnation is one of its themes and Mailer read one hundred books on related subjects to ensure the authenticity of his novel, which is set in the nineteenth and twentieth dynasties (1290–1100 BC). His interest in the subject was triggered by Ernest A. Wallis Budge's translation of *The Egyptian Book of the Dead*. It was Budge, incidentally, who taught Eady hieroglyphics at the British Museum. In an interview with Melvyn Bragg in the *Sunday Times* magazine, Mailer says that ". . . any culture whose eschatology was founded on such a notion as reincarnation was congenial to me." Mailer expected *Ancient Evenings* to be his crowning glory, but it received a mixed reception, with one critic saying it had been difficult to review and even more difficult to read.

Trying to unravel such complex stories to determine which has the ring of truth and which is suspect is not an easy task. But scholars trying to decipher or understand ancient cultures face similar challenges. I particularly like the story of two eminent scientists, Sir Cyril Burt and Professor William McDougall, both of whom were actively interested in psychical research, who had an unexpected encounter with ancient Egypt during a research project. While Burt was still an Oxford University undergraduate (he later became emeritus professor of psychology at the University of London), he and McDougall, the renowned American psychologist, conducted research into hypnosis on a blind philosophy student. Under hypnosis, the young man began speaking in an unusual voice and claimed to be an Egyptian carpenter. He told them he had to carve tablets "in the hollow tomb of the King in his Den" and went on to describe the tomb, mentioning a god with a bright, white crown.

Some months later, the two researchers read about excavations that had recently been carried out by Sir Flinders Petrie (arguably Britain's greatest Egyptologist), who had been investigating the cenotaph of King Semti, whose "Horus name" was Den. They realized some of the details of his findings matched those described by the Oxford student. (Den, incidentally, was the son Joan Grant claimed to have given birth to in her life as Sekeeta.) The white crown mentioned by the entranced student was to be found on a tablet, worn by Osiris, and descriptions of the chamber also appeared to correspond. When questioned, the student said he knew little about ancient Egypt, except what appeared in the Bible. His blindness limited the possibility of him having subliminally taken in information from a written source. The two researchers then involved Petrie in their analysis of the case, examining telepathic or clairvoyant explanations for what had taken place. Strangely, the possibility that the hypnosis had actually regressed the blind student to a previous life appears not to have been considered or entertained by any of them. Because this case did not come to light until some time after McDougall's death, no more information ever became available and no further attempt seems to have been made to glean more information from the "ancient Egyptian carpenter," speaking through an English student. Even an archaeologist of Petrie's standing seems to have overlooked the opportunity to dig deeper to see what other buried information might be retrieved.[3]

Scholars may also have overlooked another reason why ancient Egypt seems to resonate so strongly with many people in the twenty-first century. According to Robert Bauval and Adrian Gilbert, belief in reincarnation was central to the Egyptian religion. In their book *The Orion Mystery*—which claims the three Great Pyramids at Giza mirror the position and brightness of the three stars in the constellation Orion's belt—they argue that belief in reincarnation influenced all aspects of their culture. Their interpretation of Egypt's ancient texts suggests that each pharaoh was seen as a reincarnation of Osiris. Those individuals living today who had a past incarnation in that period would therefore find it easy to accept and understand if it came to the surface.

The biggest discovery of all time—if it exists—would be finding the fabled Hall of Records whose existence beneath the Pyramids of Egypt was predicted by "sleeping prophet"[4] and past-life reader Edgar Cayce (considered by many as the greatest American psychic of the twentieth century) in the 1920s and 30s. I will be discussing Cayce and his involvement with reincarnation research in a later chapter, but I cannot depart from Egypt at this juncture without recording his impact, not only on belief in past lives but also on Egypt itself. After all, more than sixty-five years after his death, hundreds of thousands of people around the world are convinced that Cayce's higher consciousness had incredible access to hidden knowledge, ranging from the medical conditions of individuals who consulted him, to insights into ancient civilizations and the way they evolved. Even more relevant to our discussion is the fact that Cayce's self-induced trance readings, most of them carefully recorded at the time and preserved by the organization that promotes his work, also revealed what were claimed to be the previous incarnations of Cayce and those who came to him for guidance. It took Cayce, a devout Christian, some time to come to terms with many of the statements made during those readings.

The entranced Cayce said that in a previous existence he had been Ra-Ta, the high priest of Atlantis, and had escaped the destruction of the lost continent along with others, reaching the Nile Valley in Egypt in the eleventh millennium BC. Many of those who received life readings from Cayce learned that they, too, had lived with him in Atlantis and ancient Egypt, as well as in more recent times. While his own focus was on using his psychic gift to heal people, by diagnosing ailments and prescribing treatments, it is the astonishing predictions contained in a few of Cayce's readings that have caught the public's imagination, giving him the status of a modern Nostradamus and leading to the setting up of thirty-five centers around the world to study the readings. They cover a wide range of topics, including forecasts of catastrophic earth changes and the twentieth-century discovery of a Hall of Records containing the history of humanity until the demise of Atlantis. There were, Cayce claimed, three identical repositories of this ancient knowledge, each containing thirty-two inscribed stone tablets and other artifacts: one off the Sphinx's right front paw; another off the west coast of Bimini; and the third in Guatemala, having been moved from its original hideout in Yucatan. Access to the Egyptian Hall of Records was via a chamber under the Sphinx, from which a passageway led to the room containing the records.

It has to be said that the dates on which some of these events were supposed to occur have now come and gone without fulfillment, but that has done little to dampen the enthusiasm of Cayce's followers, who appear to include Bauval and Gilbert: they quote from his readings in *The Orion Mystery* and point out that Cayce's chronology of Egypt's development corroborates their own theory, which differs from the accepted history. Though the Egyptian Hall of Records was *not* discovered by the end of the last century, as predicted, Cayce's supporters point out that ground-penetrating radar readings *have* detected a chamber beneath the Sphinx, which has yet to be explored. All this conjecture about reincarnation, Atlantis, and the Hall of Records does not appear to go down well with Dr. Zahi Hawass, head of Egypt's Supreme Council of Antiquities, who claims that theories put forward by Bauval, Gilbert, and others are obscuring his country's culture. "They are stealing our history," he says. "I call them the pyramidiots." An Egyptologist with the flamboyance of Indiana Jones, Hawass has become a controversial figure, particularly since the 2011 revolution that toppled President Hosni Mubarak, who had appointed him to the Egyptian cabinet as Minister of Antiquities in January that year, as part of a government shake-up that failed to keep him in power.

Hawass has publicly acknowledged[5] that a crucial event in his life took place at the Sphinx when he met "my life-long friend and colleague Mark Lehner . . . [who] was an amateur archaeologist and a follower of the beliefs of Edgar Cayce." He continues: "Mark told me this story [of Cayce, Atlantis, and the Hall of Records] more than thirty-five years ago. In 1977, along with some other archaeologists, I met Cayce's son, Hugh Lynn Cayce, who tried to convince me that his father was telling the truth. . . . I quickly concluded that these stories did not make any sense at all, but Mark and I did begin to think that we ought to study more Egyptology." So, it seems, Edgar Cayce's claims had an indirect influence in leading Hawass into his very successful, high-profile career. In fact, it was much more direct than that. Cayce's father helped Hawass get his PhD in archaeology with a Fulbright Scholarship at the University of Pennsylvania, and Joe Jahoda, a member of Cayce's Association for Research and Enlightenment (ARE) since 1953, who was one of three hundred ARE members on a tour of Egypt when that meeting took place, used to fly up to the university each Friday to take the homesick, hungry Egyptian student out for a good dinner and conversation.

Hawass used an episode of the *Chasing Mummies* TV series, which aired in 2010 on the History Channel, to dismiss the claims of Cayce and others, including a recent revelation from English paranormal researcher Andrew Collins that he had discovered an extensive cave and tunnel system beneath the Giza plateau. Having first declared that he knew all about this system, Hawass subsequently took a TV camera crew into the caves (access was through a known tomb) and was clearly astonished that its bat-infested and spider-ridden tunnels were so extensive. However, the cave complex appeared to be an entirely natural, self-contained formation, so he confidently declared the case, and the caves, closed as far as being the hiding place of Cayce's Hall of Records. The Egyptologist also showed the cameras where he had drilled at an angle in several places around the Great Sphinx to determine if the chamber that appeared to be present on ground-penetrating radar really existed beneath the world-famous monolithic statue. He found nothing.

However, many believers say the archeologist protests too much and that he is, in fact, in league with the ARE to keep the location and contents of the Hall of Records a secret until its contents can be safely removed. The Internet abounds with reports by people who claim to have seen and filmed objects being removed from the vicinity of the Sphinx at night. These conspiracy theorists point to the fact that the ARE has been sponsoring and conducting research at Giza since 1957 in cooperation with the Egyptian authorities and Dr. Zahi Hawass in particular. Indeed, Hawass has been a speaker at three of ARE's recent annual Ancient Mysteries Conferences held at its USA head-quarters in Virginia Beach and, as I write, both he and Mark Lehner are billed to appear at the October 2011 event. Confirmation that his dismissal of the Cayce readings is all smoke and mirrors might also be read into a headline in ARE's *Venture Inward* magazine: "Zahi Hawass: More 'Cayce' than He Appears."[6] The writer John Van Auken, an ARE director and regular contrib-utor to its publications, as well as an Egypt tour leader, tells us that despite his public utterances, Hawass always appears in private to be open-minded about the possibility that Cayce was right. He adds: "However, while here in Virginia Beach [October 2010], I met with Zahi and Joe Jahoda and showed them how their drilling [beneath the Sphinx] had not been deep enough or at the correct angle to reach the Cayce chambers and the Hall of Records. Using the image carved on the Dream Stela of Tuthmoses IV (circa 1401–1391 BC) that sits between the paws of the Sphinx, I showed how it reveals an opening some 121 feet (37 meters) beneath the Sphinx. The recent drilling only went to a depth of 37 feet (11.3 meters) and at an angle that would have taken the drill over the top of the chamber rather than down into it. Without so much as blinking, Zahi turned to Joe and instructed him to get a new drill that will go 121 feet, then assured me that his team will drill again."

Egypt has a long history of tomb robbery. Perhaps Hawass is merely hedging his bets to be sure that, even if his judgment is wrong about Cayce, no one else gets to the hidden chamber before he does. There are certainly plenty of others in the race, including six men who were duped into believ-ing they could tunnel their way into the Hall of Records from a house in the village of Nazlat el-Samman, adjacent to the Giza plateau. In September

2009, having dug down to a depth of 15 meters, the house collapsed on top of them. It took rescuers four days to reach the men, by which time they were all dead. That's a very high price to pay for a treasure hunt inspired by an entranced man who claimed to be the reincarnation of the high priest of Atlantis.

While most of us associate Egypt with the time of the pharaohs, that country also gave rise, one thousand years ago, to a mystical religion that went on to take root in several Middle Eastern countries and still has around one million adherents today. The Druze and their beliefs are largely unknown to the rest of the world but, as I discovered when I visited some of their communities in Lebanon, reincarnation is the cornerstone of their religion, and every family seems to have a past-life story to tell—often with surprising results.

Chapter 3

Intricate Relationships

War-torn Beirut still bore the brutal scars of years of violence when I first visited the Lebanese capital toward the end of 1997. I was there with a film crew to make a documentary in the series *To the Ends of the Earth* for Channel 4 TV, a major public-service

All these children remember past lives

television broadcaster throughout the UK, about children who claim to remember past lives. Titled "Back from the Dead," it focused on the Druze people, many of whom live in villages in Lebanon's Chouf Mountains and for whom reincarnation is far more than an abstract religious concept: it plays a major role in their lives. I had already come across some impressive and well-documented cases of reincarnation among the Druze, mostly from twentieth-century researchers who had spent time in their communities. I knew, however, that with a film crew in tow, and a producer and director who had to make the investigation visually as well as intellectually captivating, the opportunity to do *real* research was not going to arise. But I relished the chance to meet Druze people and hear about their past-life experiences, as well as making a TV program that would encourage viewers to examine the concept of rebirth.[1]

Before heading for Lebanon, I needed to know more about the origins of the Druze and the reasons why reincarnation was so significant to them. I discovered they are an Islamic offshoot which originated in Egypt a thousand years ago—in 1009 to be precise—when al-Hakim bi-Amrih Alla announced in Cairo that he was the earthly incarnation of God. Not surprisingly, this upset the Shi'a, an Islamic sect, because his claim challenged the supremacy of the prophet Muhammad, leader of the Muslims. But al-Hakim was far from being a nobody with big ideas; he was, in fact, the sixth Fatimid caliph and the sixteenth imam of the Ismaili branch of Shi'a Islam. The Fatimids, an Arabo-Berber caliphate whose power centered first in Tunisia and later in Egypt, ruled over an extensive area of north Africa and the Levant for several decades. Robert Benton Betts, in *The Druze,* tells us that the general picture that emerges of al-Hakim, who had succeeded his father at the age of eleven in 996, "is of a brilliant megalomaniac who dreams of uniting the Islamic world under his own aegis at whatever cost—a goal toward which all his political moves, internal reforms, even the creation of a new religious movement with himself as the divine center, were aimed." It seems that al-Hakim was tapping into various religious ideas that were already beginning to gain popularity. In May 1017, al-Hakim issued a decree naming a close associate, the Iranian-born Hamza ibn-'Ali ibn-Ahmad, as the imam of "the Monotheists" (Unitarians) and granted him the freedom to preach a new reformist doctrine. As such, Hamza is considered the founder of the Druze sect of Islam and

Roy Stemman

Druze funeral

the main author of its manuscripts. But what did it teach and where did those ideas come from? The thousand-year-old origins of the Druze faith remind me, in some respects, of modern New Age religions. Here's what the Druze Heritage Foundation[2] has to say about its beliefs:

> In order to understand the Druze faith, we must step back to consider the evolution of Islamic approaches to the Qur'an. As Muslims came into greater contact with Greek philosophy, Persian thought, Indian mysticism, and Jewish and Christian theology, they began to interpret the literal message of the Qur'an in order to gain insight into its deeper ramifications. This new approach to Islam became more distinctive as Muslims increased their acquaintance with Sufism. An interaction between Greek rationalism and Oriental mysticism, which was intensified by the emergence of Sufi sages, especially in the ninth and tenth centuries AD, prepared the way for the emergence at the beginning of the eleventh century of the Druze movement as an offshoot of the esoteric Ismaili approach to Islam. Adherents to the movement believed that a third and last stage of Islam had begun: namely, al-haqiqa, "self-realization," as true a feeling of unity with the One as is humanly possible.

As one observer[3] put it: "The people of the Druze religion are like no other. They seem to belong to many religions but are yet different. Their beliefs are similar to many, but there are those few beliefs that keep them distinct." That is certainly true of reincarnation, for as well as being contrary to what most Islamic sects believe, the way in which they perceive it to operate is unlike any other religion. I will be discussing this in a later chapter. Druze beliefs were radical at the time they were introduced, including the equality of men and women, monogamy, the abolition of slavery, and the separation of church and state. This made them unpopular with other sects and when al-Hakim mysteriously disappeared around 1020, possibly having been murdered, his imam, Hamza, also went into retreat and delegated his responsibilities to others. The Druze became more secretive about their beliefs and many took to the hills, literally, emigrating to remote mountainous regions of Lebanon, Syria, Jordan, and what was to become Israel. Their fears culminated, in 1043, in their leaders' decision to cease preaching and to admit no new members. Despite that, in the twenty-first century it still has between seven hundred thousand and two million adherents worldwide, and is now far more open about its beliefs.

Having absorbed these elementary facts about this extraordinary but complex group of mixed-race people, being largely of Arab descent but also with Iranian, Kurdish, and European heritage, I now turned my attention to what they believed about the existence of a soul and its ability to pass from one body to another at death. I knew, in particular, that the foremost scientific investigator of reincarnation, Ian Stevenson, MD, professor and chairman of the Department of Psychiatry at the University of Virginia since 1957, had emphasized their importance with this observation: "I think it no exaggeration to state that the belief in it forms a larger part of the whole religion of the Druzes than it does of the religion of any other group believing in reincarnation. Druze parents nearly always encourage their children to tell them what they can remember of their previous lives." When Stevenson produced the third volume in his series of case studies suggestive of reincarnation[4]—*Lebanon and Turkey*—in the 1970s, he also made these comments in his introduction:

> Although my associates and I have so far only investigated seventy-seven Druze cases of the reincarnation type in Lebanon and Syria, there are grounds for believing that more cases will be found there than in any other part of the world when funds and workers suffice to identify and investigate them. The persons helping me in Lebanon and I have been quite unable to follow up the many leads we have received to other cases awaiting investigation. This is partly due to their abundance, partly due to lack of time, and partly due to my preference for focusing attention on a small number of cases that can be thoroughly studied.

In 1975, five years before his book was published, civil war broke out in Lebanon, involving among others the Palestine Liberation Organization and Christian Phalangists; followed a year later by the arrival of thirty thousand Syrian troops, ostensibly to restore peace; and then an invasion of South Lebanon by Israeli forces in 1978. The war continued, after various pauses, until it officially ended on October 13, 1990. During that time, between one hundred fifty thousand and two hundred thousand people are believed to have perished, most of whom were civilians and many of them Druze. For a decade and a half, Lebanon had not been a suitable place for the academic study of reincarnation, particularly by a foreign researcher. Ironically, the hostilities had created a new generation of youngsters who claimed to have vivid and often violent memories of their deaths in a former life during the war, and I was about to meet some of them.

I also had a good understanding of the impact such a belief had on families, having read one of the best newspaper features I have seen on the Druze. Written by Sue Fishkoff and published by the *Jerusalem Post* in 1995,[5] "Endless Cycles" recounted a number of impressive reincarnation case studies. The most striking of these, for me, concerned Aiz Nouhad Abu Rokon, a nineteen-year-old from the town of Usfiya, a Druze village in northern Israel where Abu Abdullah, one of three religious leaders chosen by Caliph al-Hakim in 996 to proclaim the Druze faith, is buried. "Not only does Aiz claim to remember his previous incarnation as a Lebanese Druze who was killed on a deserted road near Baalbek in February 1975," Fishkoff wrote, "but he's very close to an eleven-year-old Usfiya boy named Adib Kamal Abuassi, born November 15, 1983, who both believe is Aiz's own father, Nahoud, an IDF soldier killed in battle in Lebanon two weeks before Adib's birth."

At the age of three, Aiz told his parents that his name was Ali Badawi and he had been a truck driver in Hatbiya, South Lebanon. Then, at the age of six, he walked up to a middle-aged woman he saw in the street and said, "You're Nebiya, my wife." He then described her husband's death on a snowbound road near Baalbek. Driving alone, he had been stopped by a couple of thugs who demanded money and his vehicle. When he refused, they shot him in the shoulder and stomach and buried him by the side of the road. Nebiya, wife of murdered truck driver, Ali Badawi, was astonished. She had been visiting Usfiya when the chance encounter with her husband's reincarnation occurred. The child's statements left her in no doubt about his past-life identity and she remained in touch with Aiz and his family. Then, when he was thirteen, she invited him to visit her in Lebanon. His voice began to shake and tears filled his eyes as he told the journalist, six years later, what happened when he arrived at the house. "I stood on the front steps and called out to my daughter Leena, who was five when I died. I walked into the house, and I knew it all so well. I went to the closet and looked for my clothes, all my little treasures. Everything was as I remembered, and the family was incredibly moved to see me again." The family all accepted him as Ali's reincarnation, so when Leena got married three years later, Aiz—then aged sixteen—stood in for her father during the ceremony.

Just as Aiz had entered into the lives of the Badawi family as the reincarnated husband and father, so Adib Abuassi walked into his life. Aiz's father, Nahoud Abu Rokon, was killed on November 1, 1983, while serving in the Israeli Defense Force border police. Three years later, a small boy entered the Abu Rokon home in Usfiya, pointed to a picture of Nahoud taken shortly before his death, and said to Aiz, "I'm your father." The child's mother, Nabilla, testifies that as soon as he could talk, Adib Kamal Abuassi would ask for someone named Aiz. "I thought he meant someone in our village of Shfaram, but when we brought him to the house, Adib said he wasn't the right Aiz." Then he added: "Aunt Efat knows my Aiz." Nabilla spoke with her sister, Efat, a teacher in Usfiya, who said she had a young boy in her class named Aiz. Having obtained the family's phone number, Nabilla called the Abu Rokon home and Adib practically tore the phone from her hand, shouting into it that he wanted to speak to Aiz right away.

The Abuassis arranged to visit the Abu Rokon home, much to Adib's excitement. "He told us exactly how to get to the house," his father told Sue Fishkoff. Once inside, Adib went to the closet and declared the clothes inside to be his. Adib joins in the recounting of the event: "I told Aiz's mother I'd left one cigarette in the pack I had on me when I died. She looked in the jacket, and found it." Adib and Aiz often relate to each other as father and son, despite the reversal in age. So, when they were sitting together in Aiz's home, the elder of the two (Aiz, then aged twelve) answered his mother sharply. Without thinking, Adib (aged three) smacked his teenage "son" in the face for speaking to his (former) wife in such a way. Aiz took it in his stride. "I felt, he's my father, he has the right."

Sue Fishkoff asks her readers: "Is he a little boy? Or a man-child? When asked about his feelings for Aiz's mother—a middle-aged woman he regards as his wife—Adib blushes slightly, then says with a grin, 'I remember everything. I still love her.'" Since those early days, the Abuassis have given in to Adib's constant requests to see Aiz and have moved, together with his siblings, from Shfaram to Usfiya. "I got tired of driving him here all the time to see Aiz," Kamal Abuassi explains. It seems, then, that they have no doubts about reincarnation.

"How do you explain a two-and-a-half-year-old child who can direct us to a house in a town where he's never been, go to a closet and pick out another man's clothes as his own, recognize 'friends' by name before he meets them, look at a photo of 'himself' with his wife and know the date it was taken on the Golan?" Kamal responds. "These are just facts. Can you explain it?"

Such intricate relationships are, I was to discover, more common than I suspected, though two stories I had picked up from media sources should have left me in little doubt. The first, published in a 1988 edition of *Al-Quds,* a Jerusalem newspaper, reported that Muhammaad Zayd Salim, a Druze member of the Israeli Defense Force, had been convicted of desertion by a Tel Aviv military court. His defense was that in a past life he had been a Syrian soldier who was crushed to death by one of his army's tanks. As a result, he could not bear to be near one in his present life. The newspaper account of this event did not say what sentence was handed down by the court. It reminded me, however, that the years of Middle East conflicts had posed a particular problem for some Druze families. Because they have settled principally in Lebanon, Syria, Jordan, and Israel, families often have relatives living in two or more of those countries. And since many young males served in the armed forces of those countries, there were times when members of one family found themselves on opposite sides in battle, even brother against brother in one case that was related to me. Druze, incidentally, have a reputation for bravery in battle, largely because their belief in reincarnation means they have no fear of death.

Past-life memories have also been used as justification in a Druze murder trial. According to South Africa's *Cape Times*[6] a Lebanese teenager, Amin Kanj Torbey, sixteen, confessed to patricide in a Beirut court. He had killed his father, he told the judge, because he believed his father had murdered him in a previous incarnation. Again, no verdict was given, but if his defense had been accepted, I am sure it would have made news around the world.

There was also an Agence France-Presse report in 1998 about a boy called Ramzi who was attending a wedding near his home in one of the Middle East countries—the abbreviated report I read failed to name it. Seeing a Kalashnikov rifle fixed to a wall next to a man's portrait, he declared: "That's me,

Issam Muzannar. I was killed in an Israeli air raid." To prove his story, he asked for help to dig up a secret cache of ammunition buried under an olive tree in the garden. "Three cases were uncovered with the first dig of the spade," the agency report added. Some stories, I concluded, were almost too good to be true.

Druze spiritual leader
with Roy Stemman (right)
and Chris French

For my first visit to Lebanon, I was accompanied by pipe-smoking Roland Littlewood, professor of anthropology and psychiatry, University College of London (UCL)—his role was to be the on-screen skeptic and mine to be the promoter of reincarnation in a documentary entitled *Back from the Dead.* Though in reality, I was expecting to be quite skeptical of some of the cases we would encounter. Unfortunately, after filming for several days in the Chouf Mountains overlooking Beirut, Roland had a stroke and we had to abandon filming—before we had reached the crucial final segment, when he and I would discuss the pros and cons of the cases we had encountered. I and the film crew had to pack our bags and return to the UK, leaving the professor to recover, over Christmas, at the American University's Medical Center in Beirut. A few months later, we all headed back to Lebanon, but this time with a new skeptic, Chris French, who is now professor of psychology at Goldsmiths, part of the University of London. The result of our adventure, in which we could barely scratch the surface of the past-life cases we were introduced to, has since been screened around the world, and in a later chapter I will be discussing two of the cases that were featured prominently. Right now, I'd like to share with you some of the stories we encountered that never made it into the final cut of *Back from the Dead.*

One of the most fascinating episodes was our visit to a school in the Chouf Mountains, which was run by the Druze for children in their community who either were orphans, came from poor families, or had single parents. Of the nine hundred children who attend the school, some twenty-one—a little over 2 percent—who claimed to remember past lives were ushered into a classroom to meet us. Time permitted just a couple of quick interviews with the most promising candidates, and our subsequent checks on the facts they had provided showed they were either wrong or only partially correct. Wherever their memories came from, they appeared not to be emanating from a previous life. The same could not be said, it seems, of Laura Sabieddine, a shy girl who told us about her life and death:

> I was sixty years old and illiterate when I died. My husband used to fix watches. I helped in planting plants . . . in agriculture. I used to wait outside for my son to return from the war. My daughter Fatima used to tell me to go inside and not to wait outside. I thought he had been killed in the war. When my son came back and I saw him, I had a heart attack and died. I told my parents about my past life, but they did not believe me at the beginning. But then I recognized the car of my past-life son and I used to tell them, "This is my son." And when I saw my past-life daughter in the school bus I called her, and I said to my mother, "This is my daughter." I wanted very much to get to know her.

Fatima Abu Hamdan and her past-life mother, Laura Sabieddine

As she told me this story, a middle-aged woman sitting by her side nodded in agreement. Fatima Abu Hamdan is the daughter Laura remembers from her past life. She is also a head teacher at the school. Laura continued: "For me, my daughter is not a teacher, but I see her as a teacher in the school. The story is passed and is finished and is now an incident in the past."

Fatima Abu Hamdan readily gave her side of the story:

> I was one of six children, and my mother used to love us very much. She was extremely emotional. During the civil war it was very

difficult to go from Beirut to the mountain and my little brother was in Beirut and the militias made a checkpoint and were arresting people from the mountain who were coming back. My mother heard about this and she panicked. She thought she would die before she saw her son, but then her son arrived and everybody was extremely happy. They were saying, "You see, he's back, he's back." But the moment she saw her son she embraced him and suddenly had a heart attack.

Then our neighbor, a few years later, said, "There is a young girl called Laura. She says she is your mother in her past life." I did not believe her in the beginning because there was nothing sure about the story. One day I was passing on the school bus in front of this young girl and she started to call me by my name, "Fatima, Fatima." Then my brother passed by Laura's house in the car and she started calling him by his name. He stopped and asked her if she knew him and she told him about her story. After that, she started coming and seeing us often. Then I wanted to take care of her and here we are.[7]

Alleya and her pupil, Sami Erayes

It had not taken me long to find a past-life story almost as complex as that of Aiz, which I recounted earlier. But it was soon topped by the story told to me by Alleya, one of the other teachers at the school. She confided that when she was younger she had a teacher, Rifat Mlafat, who became her lover. Her parents frowned on the relationship and they were not allowed to marry.

"We were about to be engaged, but many problems between my relatives and his relatives prevented us from this marriage," Alleya told me. "We loved each other very much. He went into the Lebanese war. He was killed, and I was very sad, but I have something. I am happy because I hoped I would meet him in his new life. Then I heard here at the school that he was coming to learn."

Standing at her side as she tells me this story is a tall and equally happy-looking, immaculately dressed teenager, Sami Erayes. Looking up at him, Alleya adds: "When I asked his name, he told me and spoke of many things about his previous life, and I was sure he was the same person with whom I had a relationship." At this, Sami takes up the story: "I was a teacher. When I was in the Lebanese War, I and my cousin were involved in a mission. My cousin was shot and I carried him, but then I was also shot. When I was reborn l remembered my life as Rifat and spoke about those days. But now, as I get older, my memories are not so strong."

Now, of course, their roles are reversed to an extent. The pupil is now a teacher and her former teacher and lover is now a pupil at the same school. It reads more like the plot from a romantic novel, but this is real life for the Druze in Lebanon. They were clearly comfortable in each other's company and happy to talk about their former relationship. I decided, however, that it would be taking investigation into reincarnation a step too far to ask whether they were likely to resume their former liaison.[8]

Dr. Sami Makarem

One of the many victims of the Lebanese Civil War, in which kidnappings and killings were all too common, was the Professor of Druze Culture and Islamic Studies at the American University of Beirut, Dr. Sami Makarem,[9] whom I was able to interview during my visit. A militant group had taken him hostage and put him up against a wall, their guns pointing at him. The author of *The Druze Faith* thought he was about to die. But his belief that he would be reborn meant that he could face their bullets without fear. "It was almost metaphysical," he told me. "It made me know how helpful is the belief in reincarnation. There was no fear. I was, in fact, looking forward to a new life." Fortunately, he was released unharmed.

But it was my meeting with Dr. Abdel Abu Assi,[10] a Druze general practitioner, that provided me with a view of reincarnation from a very different perspective. Sitting across the desk from him in his surgery, I asked about the impact of past-life memories on those he treats. Was it unusual to come across children who remember a previous existence, I wondered, and had most of them met a violent end to that life?

"No, it's not unusual," he smiled. "In fact, it's usual, particularly in this area where the whole people believe in reincarnation. So it's a matter of fact. Most of the people I have met with, who know something about their past lives, have been killed in one way or another. These children usually remember their past lives more vividly than people who died naturally. On the other hand, they are often very difficult to handle, that's why people come to me with these complaints. They tell me this baby always cries and is difficult to handle; he sleeps very briefly, he cries and we don't know what he wants. After examining the child I find he is healthy; he doesn't have any

Roy Stemman

Dr. Abdel Abu Assi

organic problems. Then I try to find out if it's anything from his past life that's coming with him."

To illustrate his approach, he told me about a four-year-old boy who was very hard to handle at school and at home:

He was saying very many words and names and his parents did not know what they meant. They thought it might be a remembrance of a past life so they came to me and asked whether I could help. So I said, "First of all, let us face this problem: this child is telling you that he knows something about his past life. Let us take some more information from him." So I started asking him more questions. "What do you mean by this name?" "Why do you mention this name more often?" And so, he started telling me more and more things until I knew that he was talking about his death in his past life and how much suffering he had before he died. He died a violent death. He was engaged to a girl and the girl's father was very much against the marriage, and so he killed them both. This child could remember everything that happened before they were killed. I stressed to these parents that they should take him to the place he was mentioning. They did, and immediately his behavior changed 180 degrees. His schoolteacher came to thank me because this child is now normal: he's always smiling, whereas he never used to smile before, and he has started to give more attention to the lessons. She treated him at first as if he was a hyperactive child or autistic, but he was normal.

I wondered whether meeting up with his or her previous-life family resulted in an improvement in a child's behavior. Dr. Abu Assi responded:

Yes—in almost all of the cases. Even in those which were somehow hard and tough on the parents of both lives, it alleviates many of the child's problems. It's very important because these children are usually hard to handle and difficult until they meet someone who relates to them from their past life. So I am in favor of this type of meeting. In time the memory will start to fade and he will not be so demanding about meeting his parents, brothers, or sisters. Even if he has met them, he will no longer be as anxious to see them—that desire will also fade.

Lastly, I asked the doctor if he had ever treated a person whom he recognized as being a patient in two lifetimes.

Yes, exactly. I have one person I have treated in two consecutive lives. This was a girl from Alay whose name was Dada. She was eleven years old when she went with her parents on a picnic to one of the forests nearby. During the picnic she was shot accidentally by a hunter who was looking for goats. He slipped, the gun went off, and she was hit in the chest. She did not die immediately but managed to stay alive until her father got her to the American University Hospital in Beirut. While they were putting the intravenous line on her she died. Four or five years later, this Dada, who was reborn in a nearby village, heard my name while her mother was talking with her aunt. She said, "I want to go and see this doctor." Her parents said to her, "You are afraid of doctors. Last week we took you to a doctor and you screamed."

But she replied, "This doctor I want to meet."

So they brought her to me, and when she entered this door she said, "Dr. Assi, I know you. You used to treat me for this," pointing at her throat. "I used to have many sore throats. You remember?"

I said, "No, I don't remember. Just tell me who you are." She said, "They call me [name withheld], but I am Dada."

I fetched the medical records of Dada and put them in front of me and started asking her questions and this child knew everything. She even knew about her death: that she had been shot in the chest and what her father had done to fetch her to the hospital. She said, "The lady in white was sticking a needle in my arm, and I don't remember any more." So I phoned Dada's parents and asked them when exactly she died, and they said the nurse was putting an intravenous line in the arm in the emergency room, and then she lost consciousness and didn't respond any more. That was something really unbelievable. This young lady still comes to me whenever she has any problems. She thinks that I am her super special doctor because I have treated her in two consecutive lives.

I had to admit that, whatever one makes of the Druze and their religious beliefs, their culture had given rise to some fascinating real-life relationships that were crying out for a much deeper analysis than I or my skeptical partners on the TV documentary had time for. The experience also confirmed that reincarnation is about much more than living one life after another. It can also weave a tangled web of emotions as those caught up in past-life revelations learn to come to terms with their implications.

Such complex interactions based on reincarnation are not unique to the Druze. Let us now turn our attention to Tibet, where the very future of that country and its people has for centuries revolved around the rebirth of its leading Buddhist lamas.

Chapter 4

The Baby and the Buddha

Over eight hundred years ago, Buddhists in Tibet introduced a unique system of political and religious governance that has survived, despite innumerable obstacles, into the twenty-first century. At its core is belief in reincarnation. While some systems of regulation, such as monarchies and dictatorships, are designed to give control to a single family, the Tibetan approach places that responsibility into the hands of *souls* who reincarnate, time after time, to continue their mission. The most famous reincarnated leader in recent times, of course, is the Dalai Lama, who Tibetans believe is currently in his fourteenth incarnation. His role is changing, however, as a result of a long-running dispute with China, which led to his escaping from brutal Chinese oppression in Tibet, along with thousands of others, in 1959. The Dalai Lama and the Tibetan government-in-exile are now based at Dharamsala, India, where they are grappling with growing Chinese interference in the reincarnation institution.

Buddhism had reached Tibet by the mid-seventh century, and it became the state's official religion within one hundred years. By the mid-twelfth century, the Kagyu sect of Tibetan Buddhism (now known as the Black Hat) was well established, with its leader Düsum Khyenpa—the first Karmapa—founding various monasteries, including his main seat at Tsuphu, and establishing an oral tradition of instruction that continues to this day. Shortly before his death in 1193 at the age of eighty-four, Düsum Khyenpa made predictions

Roy Stemman

17th Gyalwa Karmapa

about future Karmapas. He even wrote a prediction letter that provided details of his next incarnation, which he gave to his main disciple, Drogon Rechen, whom he selected as the next lineage-holder until such time as his reincarnation was found, confirmed, and became old enough to continue the work that his death had interrupted. His next incarnation was as Karma Pakshi, a child prodigy born to a noble family in eastern Tibet. He was brought to Tsuphu monastery to receive instruction, and we are told that he learned the Kagyu tradition very rapidly, which is not surprising to believers since, in his previous life, he had been instrumental in formulating it. In 1284, Rangyung Dorje was recognized as the third Karmapa—the reincarnation of Karma Pakshi, who had died the previous year. And so the Kagyu institution of reincarnate lamas—"tulkus"—succeeding to their monastic and religious seats has continued for over eight hundred years and has spread to other branches of Buddhism, including the Gelugpa sect (Yellow Hat), not only in Tibet but elsewhere in the world. Today, the Yellow Hat sect is the largest, and its leader, the Dalai Lama, the world's most influential Buddhist. The Dalai Lama title is, in fact, a Mongolian expression meaning "broad ocean" and is not used in Tibet, where he is usually referred to as Gyalpo Rinpoche ("Precious King") or, by family members, as Kundun ("Presence").

Gedun Truppa (1390–1474) and Gedun Gyatso (1475–1542), both Gelugpa monks, were declared the Yellow Hat sect's first and second Dalai Lamas posthumously. It was not until Sonam Gyatso was confirmed as the third soul boy in this series of reincarnations in 1546 that the Dalai Lama title was bestowed at the time of his recognition and confirmation—a procedure that has been followed ever since. One of Sonam Gyatso's greatest achievements was the introduction of the Yellow Hat sect into Inner Mongolia, with the support of Altan Khan, leader and prince of the Tumed Mongols. This ruler was so impressed with the sect's Buddhist teachings that he agreed to terminate the uncivilized Shamanist custom of a wife sacrificing herself to her deceased husband. The close bond that developed between the Mongolian leader and the third Dalai Lama resulted in an unexpected change of location for the latter's next incarnation: the fourth manifestation of the Dalai Lama was born in 1589 as Yonten Gyatso, the great-grandson of Altan Khan. He was first identified by native Mongols and then by the third Dalai Lama's private treasurer as well as Inner Mongolian princes and princesses. However, it required the confirmation of a delegation from the Yellow Hat's three great monasteries before the first non-Tibetan Dalai Lama was confirmed and enthroned in 1603. The delegation is said to have deliberated long and hard before reaching a decision, which is not surprising, since an attitude of critical skepticism is encouraged within Tibetan Buddhism to promote abilities in analytic meditation. Tibetans are fond of quoting a Sanskrit saying to the effect that one should test the Buddha's words as one would the quality of gold. This approach is particularly necessary when confirming the identities of tulkus.

An important development occurred during the incarnation of the fifth Dalai Lama, Lozang Gyatso, which came during a particularly bloody period in Tibet's troubled history. The leader of one of the Oriat Mongols' four major tribes, Gushi Khan, invaded his rivals' territory of Qinghai, killing an army of forty thousand in the process. The Yellow Hat sect was very popular in that region, and Gushi Khan had respect for its two principal tulkus, the Dalai Lama and Panchen Lama, whose lineage dates back to the 1400s. The sect was virtually at war with the Black Hat sect, which wanted to stamp out the Yellow Hat. In 1641, after consultation with the Panchen Lama, the fifth Dalai Lama persuaded Gushi Khan to lead his army into Tibet, which he did successfully, making him leader of Tibet's three regions. He, in turn, placed both the political and religious power of running Tibet into the hands of the Dalai Lama, ending the Kagyu sect's supremacy and resulting in a redistribution of its wealth and assets. Statistics compiled in 1733, incidentally, show the Yellow Hat then owned 3,477 monasteries in which 316,230 monks served.[1]

The system of searching for the reincarnations of senior lamas has remained largely intact ever since, with a regent being appointed as a caretaker during the years when the newly reborn lama is growing up, until he reaches an age when he can take on the role's full responsibilities. Let us now fast-forward more than three centuries, to the period soon after the death in 1933 of the thirteenth Dalai Lama, Thubten Gyatso. Following tradition, those close to him looked for signs that would indicate where to search for his reincarnation. While the final verification of tulkus is not dissimilar to the methods used by modern researchers investigating cases suggestive of reincarnation, the preliminaries are almost mystical. Three search parties were organized to search for him the following year—to allow time for his soul to enter a developing embryo—and that quest began in earnest in 1935, when the embalmed head of the thirteenth Dalai Lama is said to have given an important clue. While his body sat in state, its head turned from looking south toward the northeast, providing an indication that his soul was now reborn in that region. Other signs followed, including a regent's vision in a sacred lake of the letters Ah, Ka, and Ma, and of a three-storied monastery with a gold and turquoise roof, from which a path led to a hill. He also had a vision of a small farmhouse. These clues were sufficient for one of the search parties to head northeast and particularly to Amdo, a historical Tibetan province that is now part of China's Qinghai province, which the regent felt sure was indicated by the first letter he had seen in the lake. The second letter was possibly a reference to Kumbum, whose monastery fitted the description given by the regent. On their way, they called on the Panchen Lama, who historically plays a significant role in identifying a newborn Dalai Lama, and vice versa when a Panchen Lama's reincarnation needs to be confirmed. He provided them with the names of three boys and where they could be found. This is not unusual: Searches for reincarnated senior lamas often culminate in the identification of a number of likely candidates who must then be tested by those closest to the previous incarnation to determine which one is the tulku. In addition to the names provided by the Panchen Lama, the searchers also carried with them a drawing produced by the regent, based on his lake vision, depicting a farmhouse with strange guttering. When they found it, in the village of Takster, they chose not to reveal their purpose, simply asking the poor family who lived there if they could stay the night. They were welcomed inside. The party's leader, Kewtsang Rinpoche, pretended to be a servant and spent much of the evening observing and playing with the youngest child in the house, Lhamo Thondup, who had been born on July 6, 1935. Despite his disguise, the four-year-old recognized the rinpoche, calling him "Sera lama"—a reference to Kewtsang Rinpoche's monastery. The search party left the next morning but returned a few days later, this time as a formal deputation carrying a variety of objects, some of which had belonged to the thirteenth Dalai Lama and others which would appeal as playthings to a young boy. In every case, Lhamo Thondup identified possessions he had owned in his previous life, saying, "It's mine, it's mine." In her moving account of his early life, the Dalai Lama's mother tells us that during the search party's brief stay, her son had spent three hours with them that evening. "They later told me that they had spoken to him in the Lhasa dialect and that he had replied without difficulty, although he had never heard that dialect before." Even though there were other candidates, they had found the fourteenth Dalai Lama—subject to official confirmation. When they learned this, his parents understood the significance of two of his behavioral traits: He always demanded to sit at the head of the table, and a favorite occupation from early childhood had been to pack things into a bag, as if going on a long journey, saying, "I'm going to Lhasa." The Dalai Lama's chief residence was the Potala Palace, in Lhasa, and when Lhamo Thondup and his family were eventually taken there in October 1939, after a three-month journey, he also correctly identified the drinking bowl and false teeth he had used in his previous life.

There are those who argue that taking small children away from their parents at an early age and indoctrinating them with religious teachings is extremely cruel. The Dalai Lama admits that separation in those early years, after being recognized as a very important tulku, had made him unhappy. Now, of course, those difficult days are a distant memory and he is recognized around the world as he fights for the rights of Tibet and its people against the might of China. By the time he was enthroned in November 1950 at the age of fifteen and given the name Tenzin Gyatso, Chinese Communists had already begun incursions into Tibet, and six months later a delegation sent to Beijing to convince the Chinese leadership not to invade the country was forced at gunpoint to sign an agreement that returned Tibet to the motherland. For nearly a decade, the young Dalai Lama did his utmost to prevent a military takeover of his country. His decision to flee Tibet came a few days after a pro-independence uprising in Lhasa was crushed by Chinese troops and was based on an instruction he received on March 17, 1959, from the state oracle. He escaped the country disguised as a soldier, accompanied by the oracle and a small escort, including his immediate family members. They eventually took up residence at Dharamsala, to which others also fled, where they have established a government-in-exile. Tenzin Gyatso, the fourteenth Dalai Lama, continues to fight tirelessly to preserve Tibet's culture, beliefs, and human rights. But his high-profile stance against China has had unexpected repercussions for his people and particularly for the institution of reincarnate lamas.

Unable to eradicate or suppress the deep-seated beliefs of Tibet's Buddhists, the People's Republic of China decided to exert control by meddling in the actual process of reincarnation, even though as a communist state, and therefore atheist, it ought not to be interested in the workings of a religious system that promotes the existence of souls that live many lifetimes. The reason for this interference, of course, has nothing to do with religion or spirituality and everything to do with politics—not only Chinese politics but also Tibetan—because the Dalai Lama has been both the religious and political leader of Tibet since 1641. In a cat-and-mouse game that has been played out between the two for the past half-century, China has found a physically nonconfrontational way of achieving its goal: a takeover bid to determine the outcome of the reincarnation process of leading tulkus. It was forced to play its hand soon after the Dalai Lama issued a statement on May 14, 1995, proclaiming that the tenth reincarnation of the Panchen Lama—who had died at the age of 51 on January 28, 1989—had been found and recognized. He revealed him to be Gedhun Choekyi Nyima, the son of nomads, born on April 25, 1989, in the Lhari district of Nagchu, Tibet, adding:

> In accordance with the historical and spiritual relationship between the Dalai Lamas and the Panchen Lamas, the Search Committee for the Reincarnation, primarily represented by the Tashi Lhunpo Monastery in exile in India and various groups and individuals from all the regions of Tibet, as well as from outside, have approached me to perform the examination and divination to determine the reincarnation.
>
> I have taken upon myself this historical and spiritual task with a strong sense of responsibility. Over the recent years, I have with great care performed all necessary religious procedures for this pur-

pose and have made supplications to the infallible Three Jewels. I am fully convinced of the unanimous outcome of all these recognition procedures performed strictly in accordance with our religious tradition. . . .

The search and recognition of Panchen Rinpoche's reincarnation is a religious matter and not political. It is my hope that the Chinese Government with whom I have kept contact regarding this matter through various channels over the recent years will extend its understanding, cooperation, and assistance to the Tashi Lhunpo Monastery in enabling Rinpoche to receive proper religious training and to assume his religious responsibilities.

That hope was short-lived. China immediately branded the Dalai Lama's choice as illegal and void because he had failed to seek China's approval. Gedhun Choekyi Nyima and his parents promptly disappeared and have not been seen since. China, which had been conducting its own search, then announced its list of candidates for the role of eleventh Panchen Lama, eventually bestowing that title on Gyaincain Gyaltsen Norbu, the son of two Communist Party leaders, after the drawing of his name from a golden urn, China's preferred selection method. So, Tibetan Buddhism now has two Panchen Lamas: one, whose whereabouts is unknown, selected by Tibet's leading tulku, the Dalai Lama, and a second, who is paraded by China as the public face of Buddhism. The importance of having its own Panchen Lama, of course, is that when the Dalai Lama dies—he celebrated his seventy-sixth birthday in 2011—its own Panchen will be used to help identify and recognize a candidate chosen by the Chinese as the reincarnate fifteenth Dalai Lama. In fact, the Chinese government has taken other actions to ensure that outcome by introducing a new law, which came into effect in March 2011, that requires Buddhist monks in Tibet to seek permission from the Chinese communist regime for reincarnation. Ironically, its introduction was described by the Chinese authorities as "an important move to institutionalize management of reincarnation," but its effect will be to ban the rebirth of either the Dalai Lama or Panchen Lama *outside* of China. However, the Dalai Lama has side-stepped that issue by retiring as political leader of the Tibetan government-in-exile—something he has openly discussed for many years—to further democratize the 145,000-strong Tibetan refugee community.

Formally ending a three hundred seventy-year tradition allows his political successor to be freely elected. As for his role as spiritual leader and his future incarnations as the Dalai Lama, he has offered a number of alternatives, all designed to defeat China's intentions. He could, he has suggested, identify his own reincarnation before he dies, so that there would be no argument about it. He might be reborn as a woman. He could even return in the body of a foreigner. Or a referendum could be held on whether he should be reincarnated at all. What is certain, he says, is that he will *not* reincarnate on Chinese soil. How this will pan out in the future is difficult to predict, but it does astonish many observers that while the Dalai Lama is doing his best to remove religion from his country's politics, China is determined to inject politics into its religious institutions. And the result, almost certainly, will be that in a decade or so, there will be two Dalai Lamas.

Nowhere else on this planet does reincarnation play such a pivotal role in the fate of a nation, and it is inevitable that it is the major tulkus whose words and actions make the headlines. Yet the process occurs at all levels of Tibetan Buddhism, and much to the surprise of many people, it seems to be adept at choosing youngsters, sometimes before they can speak and often from humble origins, who become highly capable leaders. It's a phenomenon noted by Ngawang Zangpo, who translated and wrote an introduction to Jamgon Kongtrul Lodro Tayé's nineteenth-century study, *Enthronement: The Recognition of the Reincarnate Masters of Tibet and the Himalayas.*[2] During the course of his studies under the guidance of Tibetan meditation masters, Zangpo met nearly one hundred men and one woman who were acknowledged as reincarnate masters. "Whether one chooses to believe in reincarnation or dismisses the idea as nonsense," he wrote, "I believe anyone would be struck by these individuals. If the outstanding qualities they seem to share—uncommon compassion, patience, vigor, wisdom, humor, loving-kindness, goodness, and often genius—are due to a selection system capable of recognizing prodigies before they are able to talk, it is a system that deserves serious study." The translater explains that his involvement in the book was the result of an announcement by the Dalai Lama in 1991 that a child Zangpo had known practically since his birth—"a 'little buddha' in diapers"—is the reincarnation of Kalu Rinpoche, the Tibetan meditation teacher and spiritual guide with whom he had studied from 1912 until his death in 1989.

Similar examples of reincarnation are to be found elsewhere in the world, reflecting Tibetan Buddhism's global development and the widening search for reincarnate masters, which means that as well as embracing its teachings, some Westerners and their families have had to learn to cope with the enormous implications of belief in rebirth. Jeffrey Miller, a Jewish New Yorker, for example, but also a student of Tibetan and Zen Buddhism for nearly thirty years, became Lama Surya Das, regarded as "the most highly trained American lama". Tenzin Sherab, a young Canadian living in Montreal, is officially recognized as the reincarnation of Geshe Jatse, an eminent Tibetan sage and meditator, who had died in his cave in Tibet over thirty years earlier. Both seem to have adjusted well. Sometimes, however, a reincarnated lama chooses a different path. Osel Hita Torres, a Spanish boy identified as the reincarnation of Lama Thubten Yeshe, who established the Foundation for the Preservation of the Mahayana Tradition (FPMT) at a very early age, appears to have struggled with his new role. He no longer allows people to call him Lama Osel, and while still accepting his reincarnated status and maintaining his association with FPMT at a friendly distance, he is pursuing a creative career in cinematography.

Other Buddhist tulkus seem to embrace their new incarnation with welcoming hands even though their identification results in hardship or loss for those around them. The mother of the fourteenth Dalai Lama has provided us with a very moving account of the three-month trek that she and other family members had to endure, along with a huge entourage, as they made their perilous way from Kumbum to Lhasa, across parched landscapes and territory renowned for banditry, in order to deliver her son to the Tibetan capital so that his reincarnated soul could continue its spiritual mission. Such is the power of belief among Tibetan Buddhists. But even they understand the need for the search party to assess the evidence of a past life to be sure that they have found the right candidate.

It's a process that has captured the imagination of many researchers, as they probe the possibilities of rebirth in their attempt to understand the mysteries of our existence and answer the perennial question about consciousness: What, if anything, happens to us when we die?

Chapter 5

Pioneering Spirits

Buddhism's leaders apply strict verification rules to ensure their tulkus are correctly identified. For millions of others around the world who believe in reincarnation, the need for positive confirmation of a past life does not have the same urgency. Those who claim to have memories of a previous existence soon learn that some of their friends and family will believe them while others will not. For most people—apart from those few who are determined that their claims be accepted—it matters not whether others regard their memories as real or fantasy because their opinions will have no influence on their present lives. No long trek to Lhasa awaits them in order to become a world-famous spiritual leader—just the continuation of what is likely to be a far more mundane existence in their current incarnation. But by the nineteenth century, some individuals were beginning to realize that *if* past-life claims could be proved, resulting in scientific evidence for the existence of a soul capable of surviving death and returning to live again in a new body, then that would have enormous implications for the whole of mankind. Their research, and the influence of several charismatic thinkers and philosophers, helped lay the foundations for the incredible growth of interest in reincarnation that was seen in the twentieth century. This may, in part, have been due to a general willingness to explore new spiritual horizons.

Whatever the cause, it was certainly accelerated by the gradual realization that almost anyone appears to be able to retrieve "memories" of past lives. That came about with the discovery of various techniques—such as mesmerism, somnambulism, and hypnosis—that could change an individual's level of consciousness and seemingly give access to deeply buried memories.

It's not a new idea. Almost two centuries before the birth of Christ, Patañjali, the Indian codifier of the Yoga Sutras (Hindu scriptures relating to the practice of yoga), provided techniques that were beneficial, including one verse (3.18) that reads: "By self-control on the perception of mental impressions, knowledge of previous lives arises." The theory being, of course, that in an altered state of consciousness, memories of previous incarnations could surface from the subconscious and be retained in the conscious mind.

For some individuals, special techniques to recover past-life memories are not necessary—they are born with the memories. Indeed, such cases are a global phenomenon, affecting mostly young children and following a recognizable pattern, providing in the process some of the strongest evidence for reincarnation on record. An early case that displays all of these characteristics was recorded by Lafcadio Hearn (1850–1904), a European writer with an international following who was best known for his books about Japan, particularly its legends and ghost stories. In his *Gleanings in Buddha-Fields: Studies of Hand and Soul in the Far East* (1897) he included a translation of a series of old Japanese documents that he described as "very much signed and sealed, and dating back to the early part of the present century," which were in the library of Count Sasaki in Tokyo. Copies had been made for Hearn so that he could translate them.

The case concerns a Japanese boy, Katsugoro, a farmer's son born in 1815. At the age of four, while playing with his elder sister Fusa, he asked her where she had come from before her present birth. She thought the question foolish, but Katsugoro said he could remember. His name had been Tozo, and he lived in Hodokubo with his parents, named Kyubei and Shidzu. When his grandmother later questioned him about this, Katsugoro told her that until the age of four he could remember everything about his former life, but those memories were now fading. He still remembered, however, that his father, Kyubei, had died when he was five years old, and a man named Hanshiro had taken his place in the household. Tozo died a year later of smallpox, and his body had been placed in a jar and buried on a hill. The boy then asked his grandmother to take him to Hodokubo to visit his former father's tomb, which she did. On arriving at the village, Katsugoro raced ahead and, on reaching a particular building, declared to his grandmother, "This is the house" and promptly ran inside. The grandmother followed and her questions elicited the information that the owner's name was Hanshiro, his wife was Shidzu, she had a son Tozo, who had been born in 1805 and died in 1810, and whose father was named Kyubei. All of the child's statements were confirmed. Glancing out of the house, Katsugoro remarked that the tobacco shop across the road, and a tree, had not been there when Tozo had been alive, which was also true.

This, of course, is anecdotal evidence. We have only the grandmother's word for it, and we must assume Hearn's translation from the original Japanese is accurate. Nevertheless, as we will see in the next chapter, it is strikingly similar to modern cases suggestive of reincarnation.

For some reason, in Western culture few children claim to remember past lives, assuming that they have lived before. The possibility of uncovering such memories from the mind's deepest recesses was, however, a concept that excited several European researchers. French physician Abroise-August Liébeault (1823–1904), for example, experimented with the idea more than a century ago, using various methods of suggestion. Liébeault influenced the "Nancy (Suggestion) School" and is regarded by many as the father of modern hypnotherapy. He studied clairvoyance and mediumship, and his writings on psychic phenomena illustrate the overlapping interest that existed at the time between hypnosis and the paranormal.

By the end of the nineteenth century, another Frenchman, Gabriel Delanne (1857–1926), had published several influential books on spiritual subjects and is noteworthy for introducing a scientific approach to the study of psychic phenomena—particularly reincarnation. His mother was an active medium and his father, Alexandre, a close friend of Spiritism's founder, Allen Kardec. Among Delanne's books, all based on personal experience and scientifically conducted research, are *Evidence for a Future Life, Documents for the Study of Reincarnation,* and, finally, *Reincarnation.* The Spiritist philosophy, which embraced a strong belief in past lives, spread rapidly from its Parisian roots to become a worldwide movement due largely to the work of Kardec and Delanne.

At the same time as Liébeault and Delanne were researching and writing about their experiences, the redoubtable Ukrainian-born Helena Blavatsky (1831–1891) was demonstrating her psychic powers and formulating a spiritual philosophy that culminated in 1875 in her establishing the Theosophical Society in New York (it later moved to India). Reincarnation plays a significant role in Theosophy's teachings due to the strong influence of Buddhism.

Another psychic who made a big impact at the end of the nineteenth century was Hélène Smith (1861–1929)—real name Catherine-Elise Muller—the daughter of a Hungarian merchant. She exhibited a variety of psychic phenomena and was investigated by, among others, Théodore Flournoy, professor of psychology at the University of Geneva, who showed particular interest in her ability to go into trance and describe her past lives, which included being a Hindu princess and Marie Antoinette. She also appeared to have the ability to see and describe distant places. It was that gift that led to Flournoy writing the book that made her famous: *From India to the Planet Mars* (English ed. 1900). Hélène Smith not only gave details of a civilization living on that planet but also used her gift for automatic writing to produce examples of the Martians' written language, which she translated into French. The book was well-received but, to be fair to Flournoy, he was not a gullible investigator, attributing much of what she "saw" to infantile imaginings.

One of the most famous of nineteenth-century mediums, Daniel Dunglas Home (1833–1886), was among the many Spiritualists who were outspoken in their criticism of past-life claims and would have endorsed Flournoy's conclusions. Home declared: "I have met a dozen Marie Antoinettes, six or seven Marys of Scotland, a whole host of Louises and other kings, about twenty Great Alexanders, but never a plain John Smith. I would like to cage the latter curiosity."

Meanwhile, French investigator Albert de Rochas (1837–1914) had become one of the best-known psychic researchers. An outstanding military engineer, superb administrator, and scholar, it was occult and psychic studies that really captivated him. The subjects he researched included reincarnation, spirit mediumship, telepathy, telekinesis, and somnambulism. De Rochas's many books about his experiences include two on reincarnation that were published shortly before his death: *Les Vies Successives* (Successive Lives) in 1911 and *La Suspension de la Vie* (The Suspension of Life) in 1913.

His techniques were unusual because he found he could induce a trance-like state in a subject by making longitudinal passes with his hands, sending the individual back in time, who then remembered earlier experiences in this life and then beyond, "into the grey," and back farther into a previous existence. By making transversal passes with his hands, he was able to bring the subject back through those various recollections into the present. However, no attempt seems to have been made to verify whether these past-life memories had any factual content.

By the beginning of the twentieth century, our focus switches to the United Kingdom, which was becoming far more amenable to the concept of reincarnation. Among the believers was Travers Christmas Humphreys, QC (1901–1983), a British barrister who was a Buddhist and a Theosophist, both of which proclaim reincarnation as a fact of life—and death. Humphreys was called to the Bar in 1924 and in the same year became founding president of the Buddhist Society of London, now the oldest and largest in the UK. He was involved as a prosecutor in numerous murder trials, including that of Timothy Evans who, after being hanged for a crime he did not commit, was posthumously pardoned; and Ruth Ellis, the last woman to be hanged for murder in England. Later in his career he became a judge at the Old Bailey. His belief in reincarnation was apparently based on far more than Buddhist and Theosophist teachings. Humphreys was convinced he had been sentenced to death some thirty-three hundred years earlier during the reign of Egypt's Rameses II for making love to a girl priest—a Virgin of Isis—who had sworn to refrain from sex in order to honor the goddess. With such a past-life memory, it is perhaps not surprising that he believed it was karma that made him a prosecutor, just as it was karma that led criminals to commit crimes.

In the same year that Humphreys opened the Buddhist center in London, the intrepid Belgian-French explorer Alexandra David-Néel (1868–1969) arrived in Lhasa with a companion, both disguised as pilgrims. She was the first European woman to visit the Tibetan capital and managed to stay for two months before suspicions about her true identity were raised. A Buddhist and a Spiritualist, she learned the language and returned to Tibet in 1937, writing fascinating accounts of her experiences, including various meetings with reincarnated lamas. She produced over thirty books about

Eastern religion, philosophy, and her travels, often published simultaneously in French and English. They include *My Journey to Lhasa* (1927), *Magic and Mystery in Tibet* (1929), and *Immortality and Reincarnation* (1961). Christmas Humphreys, incidentally, wrote a foreword to her *Buddhism: Its Doctrines and Its Methods* (1978).

Another Oriental traveler was Alexander Cannon (1896–1963), a British-born doctor who was one of the earliest hypnotherapists and researchers. Some of his claimed experiences are so sensational that the accuracy of his accounts must be viewed with suspicion. For example, in his book *The Invisible Influence* (1933) he tells us that he, his porters, and their luggage were levitated over a chasm in Tibet. As a result, the London County Council, for whom he worked as a psychiatrist and research scientist at a mental hospital, dismissed him on the grounds that he was unfit to practice, though he appealed successfully and was reinstated. In recent years there have been reports that King Edward VIII was one of Cannon's patients, shortly before his abdication in 1936, and also that the hypnotist was a spy and Nazi sympathizer.

What is of interest to us, however, is Cannon's contribution to the evidence for reincarnation that emerged as he used hypnotism to treat his patients' ailments. In *The Power Within* (1952), whose subtitle was *The Reexamination of Certain Psychological and Philosophical Concepts in the Light of Recent Investigations and Discoveries,* he tells us:

> For years the theory of reincarnation was a nightmare to me and I did my best to disprove it and even argued with my trance subjects to the effect that they were talking nonsense, and yet as the years went by one subject after another told me the same story in spite of different and varied conscious beliefs, in effect until now, well over a thousand cases have been so investigated and I have to admit that there is such a thing as reincarnation. It is therefore only right and proper that I should include this study as a branch of psychology, as my text bears witness to the great benefit many have received psychologically from discovering hidden complexes and fears which undoubtedly have been brought over by the astral body from past lives.

However reticent we may be about taking Alexander Cannon at face value—he did, after all, adopt various fancy titles, such as Kushog Yogi of Northern Tibet and Master-the-Fifth of the Great White Lodge of the Himalayas—there's no getting away from the fact that he appears to have been a pioneering spirit as far as the exploration of past lives through hypnosis is concerned, as well as being one of the first to apparently use those past-life memories for therapeutic purposes.

Coincidentally, this was something Joan Grant (1907–1989)—whose far memory abilities I described in some detail in chapter 2—began exploring at around the same time as Cannon, together with her third husband, Denys Kelsey, a psychiatrist. Her first books, published in the 1930s, were based on her recollections of former lives he claimed to have lived in Egypt. But in *Many Lifetimes* (1968), she and Denys looked back on the lessons they had learned about past lives and their therapeutic value in dealing with a variety of conditions. Their trailblazing work is also commemorated in *Speaking from the Heart: Ethics, Reincarnation and What It Means to Be Human,* a collection of essays, poetry, and lectures compiled by her granddaughter Nicola Bennett, together with Jane Lahr and Sophia Rosoff. Denys Kelsey elaborated further on their experiments in *Now and Then* (2007), illustrating their findings for the first time with actual case studies.

At the same time as Alexander Cannon and Joan Grant were using very different techniques to recover past-life memories from their subjects in England, a dramatic case of reincarnation was being investigated in India with scientific rigor. It concerns Shanti Devi, a girl born in 1926 who claimed she had been named Lugdi in her previous life. She had been married at the age of ten in that life to Kedarnath Chaube, the owner of a cloth shop in Mathura, with a branch shop in Hardwar, and her first child had been stillborn. Worried about the outcome of her second pregnancy, by which time Lugdi was crippled with arthritis, Kedarnath took her to the government hospital at Agra, close to the Taj Mahal, where a son was born on September 25, 1925. But Lugdi's condition deteriorated and nine days later, at the age of twenty-six, she died.

No such fate befell Babu Rang Bahadur Mathur who happily survived the birth of a daughter, whom she named Shanti Devi, on December 11, 1926, in Chirawala Mohulla, Delhi. It became obvious by the time Shanti Devi was four years old that she was different from other girls her age.

She spoke of her husband, calling herself Chaubine (Chaube's wife) and describing certain characteristics of his appearance. She also spoke of her children and said she had lived in Mathura. A distant relation, Babu Bishan Chand, who was a teacher in Ramjas High School at Daryaganj, a neighborhood of Delhi, took an interest in Shanti Devi's claims and said he would take her to Mathura if she told him her husband's first name—something she had refused to do because it was an Indian custom not to refer to a spouse by his name. Lured by this offer, she whispered the name Pandit Kedarnath Chaube. Bishan Chand made enquiries, established that such a person existed, and wrote him a letter detailing all the statements made by Shanti Devi. Kedarnath replied, confirming most of her statements and suggesting that one of his relatives, Pandit Kanjimal, who lived in Delhi, be allowed to meet the girl. When they met, Shanti Devi recognized him as her husband's cousin, described her previous home in some detail, and told him where she had hidden some money. She assured the visitor that, if taken by train to Mathura, she would be able to find her way to her former home.[1]

Impressed with what he had heard, Pandit Kanjimal persuaded Kedarnath to visit Shanti Devi in Delhi. He did so, accompanied by his son and his present wife, but he posed as his elder brother. Shanti Devi blushed and stood aside when introduced to him. When asked why, she responded, "No, he is not my husband's brother. He is my husband himself." Then, turning to her mother, she said, "Didn't I tell you that he is fair, and he has a wart on the left side cheek near his ear?" When her mother began to prepare a meal for the visitors, Kedarnath was astonished to hear Shanti Devi say, correctly, that her past-life husband's favorite dishes were potato parathas and pumpkin squash. Later, they spent some time alone talking and Kedarnath then declared his acceptance of Shanti Devi as the reincarnation of Lugdi because she had told him things no one except Lugdi could have known.

News of the extraordinary case soon spread and reached the ears of Mahatma Gandhi, the Indian political and ideological leader, who not only met with her but also invited her to stay in his ashram. Gandhi appointed a committee of fifteen prominent people, including parliamentarians, national leaders, and media representatives, to study the case. On November 24, 1935, they accompanied Shanti Devi on her first visit (in this life) to Mathura by rail. Their subsequent report testified:

As the train approached Mathura, she became flushed with joy and remarked that by the time they reach[ed] Mathura the doors of the temple of Dwarkadhish would be closed. . . . The first incident which attracted our attention on reaching Mathura happened on the platform itself. The girl was in L. Deshbandhu's arms. He had hardly gone fifteen paces when an older man, wearing a typical Mathura dress, whom she had never met before, came in front of her, mixed in the small crowd, and paused for a while. She was asked whether she could recognize him. His presence reacted so quickly on her that she at once came down from Mr. Gupta's lap and touched the stranger's feet with deep veneration and stood aside. On inquiring, she whispered in L. Deshbandhu's ear that the person was her "Jeth" (older brother of her husband). All this was so spontaneous and natural that it left everybody stunned with surprise. The man was Babu Ram Chaubey, who was really the elder brother of Kedarnath Chaubey.

Shanti Devi then instructed the driver on how to get to her former home, pointing out various changes that had taken place in the area since she had lived there, all of which were found to be correct. Later, she asked the driver to take them to a second house in which she and Kedarnath had lived for several years. She recognized various people, including her former mother and father; answered test questions; located a well hidden beneath a stone; and showed the committee members where she had hidden money on the second floor of her home. No money was found, but Kedarnath later confessed that he had found and removed it after Lugdi's death. The august committee concluded that Shanti Devi was indeed the reincarnation of Lugdi.

Although it happened eighty years ago, Shanti Devi's story is significant, according to reincarnation researcher Dr. Kirti S. Rawat, because it remains "one of the most thoroughly investigated cases, studied by hundreds of researchers, critics, scholars, saints, and eminent public figures from all parts of India and abroad from the mid-1930s on." Dr. Rawat conducted his own investigation, which resulted in a further piece of evidence that was not revealed to the committee. It occurred when Kedarnath, his wife, and son visited Delhi to check Shanti Devi's story, and they stayed for one night in the home of his friend Pandit Ramnath Chaube. During that visit, Kedarnath asked the nine-year-old Shanti Devi, in front of his wife, how she had become pregnant when she was so riddled with arthritis that she could not even get up. "She described the whole process of intercourse with him," Dr. Rawat says, "which left Kedarnath in no doubt that Shanti was his wife Lugdi in her previous life." Dr. Rawat confirmed this story with other sources and then, just four days before her death at his last meeting with Shanti Devi, who never married in this life, he mentioned it to her and got the response, "Yes, that is what fully convinced him."[2]

Our journey into the past is coming to an end. We have now arrived well into the twentieth century, which many see as a turning point in Western culture's attitude towards reincarnation that is so positively reflected in opinion polls. It is now time to move firmly into the present to examine the explosion of interest and activity that surrounds the still highly controversial subject of past lives. And what better way to start than by dropping in on Morey Bernstein, an American businessman, as he conducts a hypnosis experiment with housewife Virginia Tighe in Pueblo, Colorado. What happens next will astound people around the world as the voice of Bridey Murphy, apparently silent for almost sixty years, begins to relive her former existence.

Part Two

The Present

Chapter 6

Out of Her Mind

Some would say Virginia Burns Tighe, a twenty-nine-year-old housewife from Pueblo, Colorado, must have been out of her mind when she agreed to assist a friend, Morey Bernstein, with his hypnosis experiments. However, what *came* out of her mind has challenged experts ever since, after what was meant to be no more than an evening of home entertainment became a worldwide sensation. While in trance, Tighe had transformed magically into Bridey Murphy, an Irish woman who had been born in County Cork at the very end of the eighteenth century. The story of Bridget (known as Bridey) Kathleen Murphy's apparent reincarnation could be described as the case that launched a thousand past lives. Though not the first such case on record, it caught the public's imagination like no other, before or since, and undoubtedly encouraged many others to explore past-life hypnotic regression. Yet it is a story that is still hotly debated today, more than half a century later, and one that is often mistold.

Depending on which book you read, you will find the Bernstein-Tighe-Murphy experiment either lauded as compelling evidence of reincarnation or dismissed as a blatant fraud. There is no doubt on anyone's part that during six hypnotic sessions, recorded on reel-to-reel tape and preserved to this day, Virginia Tighe spoke in an Irish brogue as if she were a woman who had lived one hundred years earlier. But questions remain about the source of that information, which included the names of people and places that were later verified by investigators. For believers, the explanation of how she acquired that data is simple: it was already in her mind, since Virginia Tighe *was* Bridey Murphy—they are the same soul. That was too much for many people, particularly those whose religious beliefs or scientific training made no allowance for the possibility of rebirth. So the mind of Virginia Tighe became a battleground, though fortunately she was protected from the glare of publicity for a while by the pseudonym Ruth Mills Simmons.

Variously described as "a tractor dealer" and "a business executive of wealth and board member of four of Pueblo's leading firms," Morey Bernstein had been skeptical of hypnosis until a visiting colleague demonstrated its powers. Once hooked, he began exploring its potential with willing subjects. With his wife, Hazel's, encouragement, he quickly discovered which one of their social circle attendees was the best candidate for further research. Of the group, Virginia Tighe, the wife of an insurance salesman, proved to be the most responsive to his hypnotic suggestions. She regressed back easily to events early in her life—though she and her husband were largely disinterested and could probably find better ways of spending an evening. Bernstein had been astonished by Alexander Cannon's book *The Power Within,* in which the British psychiatrist revealed he had taken many patients back to previous lives using hypnosis. It fascinated the Pueblo businessman, and he was determined to explore the possibility himself. And so on November 27, 1952, having identified his best subject, Bernstein decided, unannounced, to ask Tighe, while in trance, to go back to her birth . . . and then farther back in time to a previous life. Bridey Murphy emerged immediately, as she did on five subsequent occasions through to the final session in October 1953.

The story she told began with her birth on December 20, 1798, as the daughter of a barrister Duncan Murphy and his wife, Kathleen. She lived at "The Meadows," outside of Cork, had a brother Duncan, who was two years older, and a younger brother who had died as a baby of "black something." During these sessions Bridey began to take on a stronger Irish brogue, and her speech became more personalized. Bridey said she had gone to a day school during the week, run by a Mrs. Strayne. This seems to have continued until she was about fifteen. Mrs. Strayne's daughter Aimee married Bridey's brother Duncan. Bridey, from a Protestant family, then married Sean Brian Joseph MacCarthy, whom she called Brian, the son of a Roman Catholic barrister, John MacCarthy, in Cork and also again in Belfast, although this fact was kept from Bridey's parents. The second ceremony took place in the room of Father John Joseph Goran (or Cormon, or Corman) rather than in the church. He was a priest at St. Theresa's Church, Belfast, which was located off Dooley Street, about five minutes away from where they lived. The couple stayed with Brian's grandmother Delilinan.

Asked to recall details that might help verify her story, Bridey said there was a shop called Farr's that sold foodstuffs; a shop called Cadenn House that sold garments for ladies; and a greengrocer called John Carrigan. In addition, she was asked about the currency used, and referred to pounds, tuppences, and sixpences. Bridey was also asked to say Irish words and explain what they meant. She spoke of "brates"—a little wishing cup—and a "tup"—somebody who was a bit of a "rounder." Her use of the word "lough" was also interesting. She mentioned the names of rivers and lakes, using the same word to describe both. Though "lough" is now used in Ireland only to refer to a lake, at the time Bridey claimed to have lived, it was used for both. During the fourth session Virginia/Bridey sneezed and asked for a "linen" (meaning handkerchief). She also named places of interest, such as Carlingford, which she said was near Belfast, and a place called Mourne, which was close. She spoke of a port at Calway, a county called Limerick, and a place called Munster. She recalled a trip to Antrim she had taken when young and another to Baylings Crossing. Her husband, Brian, wrote for the *Belfast NewsLetter*, probably on legal matters, and taught at Queen's University. Asked if she could remember anybody else at the university, Bridey recalled three names: William McClone, Fitzhugh, and Fitzmaurice. The couple also had friends called Kevin and Mary Catherine Moore. She said she had enjoyed dancing—particularly the "Morning Jig" and the "Sorcerer's Jig"—and revealed she could play "Londonderry Air," "Sean," and "The Minstrels' March" on the lyre. Bernstein planted a post-hypnotic suggestion that Tighe would dance a jig when she came out of trance, which she duly did.

There was much more, as Bridey recounted other events in her life, through to her death in 1864 after falling down the stairs at her home in Belfast, Northern Ireland. Enough, in fact, to fill a book, which Bernstein eventually—though somewhat reluctantly—started to work on at the urging of William J. Barker, a columnist and feature writer for the *Denver Post*'s Sunday magazine, *Empire.* The young journalist had heard about the experiments from his brother-in-law, who was a friend of Bernstein, and although skeptical, persuaded the *Post* to let him investigate it further. By then, Bernstein was busy setting up an investment company in New York and was an infrequent visitor to Colorado, so it was not until September 1954 that *Empire* became the first publication to publish the Bridey Murphy story, over three issues. It created quite a stir. Meanwhile, Bernstein had arranged for an Irish legal firm, librarians, and others to conduct independent research to check out some of Bridey's information, but on seeing the results he felt they had hardly scratched the surface. So, publication of his book, *The Search for Bridey Murphy,*[1] on January 1, 1956, still left many questions unanswered. The most important, of course, was whether the mind of the hypnotized Virginia Tighe had manufactured the story, using snippets of information it may have gleaned from some obscure sources and inventing the rest. Crucial in evaluating that possibility was the need to check every name and date provided by Bridey Murphy against historical records or accounts. Barker, the journalist who first broke the story, was about to make a major contribution in that respect, due in part to a newspaper circulation war that broke out around the book's publication. The *Chicago Daily News* had bought syndication rights and sent its London correspondent, Ernie Hill, to Ireland for three days to investigate. His search for corroboration of Bridey's story was largely unproductive, resulting in a negative report.

William J. Barker, on the other hand, had far more success during the three weeks he spent in Ireland for the *Denver Post.* The result was an impressive, impartial nineteen-thousand-word account of his Irish adventure, published by the newspaper as a separate twelve-page supplement, and later widely reprinted by other US and Canadian publishers. All of this boosted the sales of Bernstein's book and the newspapers that fought over the story, but it did little to settle the burning question: Had Virginia Tighe lived a previous life as Bridey Murphy? The major problem in answering that question was that records of births, deaths, and marriages in Ireland did not exist until after 1864 (the year Bridey died), making verification of some statements almost impossible. On the other hand, investigation has shown that much of what she spoke about *was* accurate, even to the names of some of the individuals she referred to and the shops she mentioned. Nevertheless, to this day we cannot be certain that Bridey Murphy was a real person. The jury is still out, though you would not think so from some of the sensationalized accounts that appeared at the time and continue to be regurgitated by editors and reporters too lazy to check the facts. Take for example the *Chicago Tribune*'s obituary of Robert J. Smith, who died at the age of eighty-five in October 2010, under the headline, "Former reporter and *Tribune* editor helped debunk *The Search for Bridey Murphy.*" It said that as a young reporter he had "discovered a woman named Bridey Murphy who had lived in Chicago, across the street from Tighe, when she was a child" and had broken the story in the *Chicago American.* What the obituary does *not* tells its readers is that this and other claims made by the Chicago newspaper were checked out by the *Denver Post* and found to be far from the truth. A woman named Bridey Corkell *did* live across the street at one of the locations. However, Tighe never spoke to the woman, though she did know her children. Whether the woman's maiden name was Murphy has not been revealed, but interestingly one of her sons, John, just happened to be the editor of the *Chicago American.* The *Denver Post* also showed many of the other claims to be wrong or unsubstantiated, but the damage was done and *Life* magazine made it worse by repeating the *Chicago American*'s errors without reviewing or referring to the *Denver Post*'s rebuttal.

Another false claim was recently peddled by staff writer Barry J. Whyte at *Irish Central* (www.irishcentral.com). After recounting the "Bridey Murphy-mania" story[2] he added: "That's when Bernstein admitted he'd suggested it all to Virginia while she was under. But by then, of course, the book had become a bestseller, Bernstein was rich, and the country was seized with reincarnation fever. Morey Bernstein made Bridey Murphy, then made a fortune." The suggestion that Bernstein fed the information to the entranced Tighe is patently absurd. All six sessions were not only witnessed by others but were recorded. I posted a comment at the end of Whyte's story, asking him where he got that information. He has never replied nor has the editor responded to my follow-up email pointing out the error.

All of the above, and much else, is dealt with in a thoroughly revised and updated 1965 version of *The Search for Bridey Murphy*[1]—known as the "counter-attack edition"—containing supplemental material from the reporter who broke the story, William J. Barker. This includes chapters responding to skeptics and also an account of his own research in Ireland. Among those who have also spoken in defense of the Bridey Murphy communications, or at least refute the suggestion that cryptomnesia (forgotten memories) can explain them in their entirety, are philosopher Curt John Ducasse and parapsychologist Dr. Ian Stevenson.

Ian Stevenson

Ducasse, former chairman, Department of Philosophy at Brown University, and past president of the American Philosophical Association, made a full-scale study of the case, giving the results in a paper, "How the Case of the Search for Bridey Murphy Stands Today," published in 1960, and his book, *A Critical Examination of the Belief in a Life after Death* (1961), in which he says that "Neither the articles in magazines or newspapers . . . nor the comments of . . . psychiatrists hostile to the reincarnation hypothesis, have succeeded in disproving or even establishing a strong case against the possibility that many of the statements of the Bridey personality are genuinely memories of an earlier life of Ruth Simmons [Virginia Tighe] over a century ago in Ireland." Stevenson, Carlson Professor of Psychiatry at the University of Virginia, Charlottesville, agreed with Ducasse's verdict in a paper[3] that was later published as a book, *Twenty Cases Suggestive of Reincarnation*[4] in 1974, observing: "What some critics of the case provided were *suppositions* of possible sources of the information about Bridey Murphy, not *evidence* that these had been the sources." Since then, English skeptic Melvin Harris has suggested[5,6] that Virginia Tighe may have retained information subconsciously from the 1933–34 world's fair in Chicago, which featured an Irish village. She was ten at that time.

Virginia Tighe died in 1995, having stood by the genuineness of the hypnosis sessions throughout her life but still undecided about the reality of reincarnation. Morey Bernstein died four years later, never having claimed to have proven reincarnation, but certainly having opened countless minds to the possibility. He was already a successful businessman when Bridey Murphy entered his life, and he became a philanthropist whose Bernstein Brothers Foundation funded many parapsychological researchers in later years, including Dr. Ian Stevenson. Hazel Higgins, the wife of Morey Bernstein—they divorced in 1963—was a firm believer in reincarnation and in destiny. "I think it was one of those things that was meant to happen," she said just a couple of years before her passing in 2007. "I think it was great. I'm sorry it didn't change more people. I think if they believed in reincarnation, it would help in many respects." Hazel had proved to be a good hypnotic subject in her former husband's experiments but was never able to retrieve a previous life.

Few Puebloans have much interest in the town's paranormal past these days, though a handful of dedicated enthusiasts have done their best to ensure its historical association with Morey Bernstein and Bridey Murphy is not forgotten. John Smith, a retired university chemistry professor and lover of Pueblo lore, was entrusted with many of Bernstein's papers; having been sifted, sorted, and collated to make them more accessible to future generations, they now reside, along with the reel-to-reel tapes and other memorabilia, in the Pueblo County Historical Society's collection. Smith has also lain to rest the suggestion that the book made Bernstein's fortune. "He was a millionaire before this broke," he told the *Pueblo Chieftain* newspaper.[7] "He almost exclusively refused enticements; he refused all offers. He split royalties from the publisher with Virginia Tighe."

Local businessman Bret Bezona has good reason to be enthusiastic about Bernstein's legacy: he lives in the house on North Elizabeth Street in which at least one of the most productive of the Bridey Murphy sessions took place, and where Bernstein almost certainly wrote *The Search for Bridey Murphy*. Among the items he discovered when he bought the property in 1999 was an old Royal typewriter on which it is likely the bestseller was written. From that moment, Bezona became a collector of memorabilia relating to the case, so who better to remind us why the Bridey Murphy case has probably contributed more to the debate on reincarnation than any other.

"The book's initial print run in 1952 had been an optimistic ten thousand, but within two months, two-hundred thousand copies were in print, and it spent twenty-six weeks on the *New York Times* bestsellers list," Bret Bezona explains.[8] "It was reissued in 1965 and was eventually published in thirty languages in thirty-four countries. It was also made into a movie, *The Search for Bridey Murphy,* in 1956, though that didn't have the same impact as the book. I believe the total number of copies sold, in various editions and languages, must be around ten million. No wonder *Time-Life,* three decades later, confirmed that few other books had seized the imagination of America as firmly as Morey Bernstein's volume. It also permeated other creative arts, particularly music. There were at least half a dozen songs, including tunes recorded by Stan Freberg and Peter Nero. There was even a group called the Bridey Murphys."

Will we ever know whether Bridey Murphy had once enjoyed a separate existence, one hundred years earlier, or were the results of the hypnotic trances just the colorful creation of Virginia Tighe's subconscious? We'll probably never know, and there are still those who believe the case should not be closed until we can be sure that all of its elements have been exhaustively researched. After all, as historian and archivist John Smith once said, "no mystery is closed to an open mind."

Chapter 7

Fears and Phobias

Chase Bowman was five years old when it first became obvious that he had an apparently irrational fear of loud noises. It was 1988 and his parents, Carol and Steve, were hosting a big Fourth of July party at their home in Asheville, North Carolina. The party ended with the guests taking a short walk to a municipal golf course from where they had a superb view of the town's annual Independence Day fireworks display. As soon as the sound of exploding fireworks started reverberating off the hills, Chase—who had been eagerly anticipating the color and excitement of the display—started to cry. No amount of comforting and reassurance stopped his tears, and in the end his mother took him home, leaving Steve with their nine-year-old daughter, Sarah, and party guests to enjoy the fireworks to the end.

Even when they got back to the house, away from the noise, Chase continued sobbing deeply. When his mother asked him if the noises had scared him his hysteria grew worse. There was nothing more she could do but rock him gently in her arms until the sobbing stopped and he fell asleep.

This episode was forgotten for a month until the family visited the town's indoor swimming pool. Chase loved the water, yet as soon as they arrived inside the noisy pool area, he began crying hysterically. He grabbed his mother's hands and pulled her towards the door, refusing to listen to reason.

Later, Carol Bowman realized that the sound of the diving board reverberating off the bare walls of the pool building might have sounded to Chase's ears like the booming of the firework explosions. But she was still at a loss to understand why her young son should react in this way.

Such fears and phobias affect the lives of huge numbers of people. An estimated more than six million Americans suffer from specific phobias, ranging from the common (and perhaps understandable) fears of snakes, spiders, and heights, to the more irrational terrors that an encounter with open spaces, being touched, knees, the moon, rain, and foreigners can induce in some people. There are medical terms for all of these and numerous others, including the unlikely "phobophobia," which, as its name implies, is a fear of phobias!

Theories about the causes of this form of mental illness are many, ranging from genetic memory to long-forgotten traumatic childhood experiences, and various forms of treatment are used to either rid sufferers of the condition entirely or minimize its impact. These often involve assisting the patient in identifying an event early in their life that gave rise to the irrational fear, but sometimes no cause can be found. In the case of Chase Bowman, his parents could think of nothing in his young life that would have produced such an emotional response to loud noises. The opportunity to delve deeper came a few weeks later when a skilled hypnotherapist, Norman Inge, was staying as a houseguest with the Bowmans while conducting past-life regression workshops in Asheville. While the family was enjoying afternoon tea and laughing at Inge's stories, Carol mentioned Chase's irrational fear. The hypnotherapist suggested an experiment to which both mother and son readily agreed. That moment, she says in her book *Children's Past Lives,* "was a turning point in my life."

On Inge's instructions, Chase climbed onto his mother's lap, closed his eyes, and began describing what he saw when he heard the loud noises that frightened him. Nothing, Bowman writes, could have prepared her for what she was about to hear.

> Young Chase immediately began describing himself as a soldier—an adult soldier—carrying a gun. "I'm standing behind a rock. I'm carrying a long gun with a kind of sword at the end." My

heart was pounding in my ears, and the hair on my arms stood up as
I listened. . . . "What are you wearing?" Norman questioned. "I have
dirty, ripped clothes, brown boots, a belt. I'm hiding behind a rock,
crouching on my knees, and shooting at the enemy. I'm at the edge
of a valley. The battle is going on all around me."

All this came from a child who had not shown any interest in war games
and had never owned a toy gun. He continued:

> "I don't want to look, but I have to when I shoot. Smoke and
> flashes everywhere. And loud noises: yelling, screaming, loud
> booms. I'm not sure who I'm shooting at—there's so much smoke,
> so much going on. I'm scared. I shoot at anything that moves. I
> really don't want to be here and shoot other people."

There were more surprises in this and later memories that Chase
described, including the fact that he had been black in that life. Despite his
mother's skepticism, later research showed that there were black soldiers who
fought in the American Civil War. Chase also said he was shot in the wrist,
taken to the field hospital where his wound was bandaged, then sent back to
man a cannon. His description of the hospital also tallied with accounts of
that time, but it was his sister, Sarah, who remarked that the wrist in question
was the one on which he had suffered eczema since he was a baby. Whenever
he became upset or tired he would scratch that wrist until it bled and Carol
often had to bandage it to prevent him from scratching it further.

His mother writes:

> To our astonishment and relief, within a few days of his regres-
> sion to the lifetime of a soldier, his mother writes, the eczema on
> Chase's right wrist vanished completely, and it has never returned.
> Chase's fear of loud noises also totally disappeared. Fireworks,
> explosions and booming sounds never scared him again. In fact,
> soon after the regression Chase began showing an intense interest
> in playing the drums. Now he's a serious drummer, filling the house
> with loud booming sounds every day.

When daughter Sarah was nine years old, Carol and Steve discovered that Sarah had lived with an inexplicable fear for as long as she could remember but had kept it to herself. She was terrified of fire, particularly the thought of being trapped in a burning house. It emerged after Sarah went to stay the night with a friend, Amy, who lived down the street—something she had done many times before. The girls stayed up late watching a movie that showed scenes of burning houses, at which point Sarah became upset. And when someone in the film was killed in a fire, she became distraught, crying so uncontrollably that Amy's mother had to take her home in the middle of the night. Discussing this reaction with her parents later, Sarah confessed she had always been so frightened by the thought of their house catching on fire that she had packed a bag with her favorite Barbie dolls and some clothes and kept it hidden under her bed. This fear was totally out of character for their normally self-assured daughter.

Having seen the dramatic result that Norman Inge had produced with her brother, Chase, Sarah asked Inge on his next visit if he would try the same experiment with her. He sat her at the kitchen table, then told her to close her eyes and describe what she saw when she felt the fear of fire. Sarah began describing in detail a two-story house in which she saw herself as a girl of eleven or twelve and, under Inge's guidance, moved forward in time to the point where the fear became a real event, and she was caught up in the terror of her predicament. Her graphic account tells of flames and smoke everywhere as she runs into her parents' bedroom, but they are not there. Their beds are made and there is no sign of them. "Why don't they get me out?" she pleads. She is trapped in a room until her ordeal comes to an end when a burning beam crashes to the floor. Her soul then leaves her body and floats above the burning house. Looking down, she sees her distraught and helpless parents and brother watching as the house burns. That scene brought consolation to Sarah, who now realized that her past-life parents had loved her and would have saved her if they could. She also lost her fear of fire and unpacked the bag she had kept ready for such an emergency. But, adds her mother, her daughter is still very careful when she lights a match!

Carol Bowman's son and daughter are now grown up and prospering in Philadelphia and New York City, and Carol has become a respected regression therapist who has helped other people's children overcome similar fears.

Her main focus is working with adults, but she is surprised that similar techniques to those used with Chase and Sarah—which did not involve hypnosis or suggestion—are not used more often to assist young children with fears and phobias.

Of course there are skeptics who will dismiss the Bowman children's accounts as the colorful imaginings of young, impressionable children, and certainly there is no evidence to verify that they actually led the former lives they described—apart from the healing of those traumas and the disappearance of their phobias. To the doyen of investigators in this field, Dr. Ian Stevenson, phobias were a recurring theme in many of his scientific papers and books. He even wrote a paper[1] dedicated to the subject. "Phobias in Children Who Claim to Remember Previous Lives" focused on 387 cases of children who claimed to remember a previous life. More than one third (141 = 36%) exhibited phobias that, in Stevenson's words, "nearly always corresponded to the mode of death in the life of the deceased person the child claimed to remember."

Stevenson points out that strong fears occur frequently in children. For example, research has shown that 90 percent of Californian children between the ages of two and fourteen had experienced at least one specific fear, and he cites similar statistics from other sources, including historical ones.

"A child who claims to remember a life that ended in drowning may have a phobia of being immersed in water; one who claims to remember a life that ended in stabbing may have a fear of bladed weapons, and so on." Most of the phobias occurred in relation to violent deaths of all kinds. They occurred much less frequently in the cases of children who remembered natural deaths. In a series of 240 cases in India, phobias occurred in 53 (39%) of the 135 cases with violent death, but in only three (3%) of the 105 cases having a natural death. "Nevertheless," Stevenson tells us, "noteworthy phobias do sometimes occur in the latter type of case. One child who remembered the life of a man who had gorged himself on yogurt that had evidently been contaminated and then had died of severe gastroenteritis (perhaps with peritonitis) showed a marked aversion for yogurt."

Another fascinating case quoted by Stevenson concerns a Sri Lankan child who manifested a phobia before she had even spoken about the previous life from which it seemed to derive. As a baby, she struggled so much against being bathed that it took three adults to hold her down for this. Also, before she could speak, at the age of six months, she displayed a marked phobia of buses and cried when transported in one. When she could speak, she described the life of a young girl who had lived in another village, who had been walking on a narrow road that crossed flooded paddy fields. A bus had come along, and this girl, stepping back to avoid it, had fallen into the floodwater and drowned.

Stevenson offers other examples of sensory association between objects that were significant in a claimed previous life, such as the case of a young Turkish boy who said he remembered a previous life that ended when a van in which he was riding crashed against the abutment of a narrow bridge. He displayed a phobia of automobiles and also a marked phobia of the bridge where the accident had occurred, which was not far from his birthplace. Another Turkish case involved a child drowned in a river, which flowed near the subject's village. It was noticed that he avoided going near the part of the river where the drowning had occurred. An Indian child remembered a previous life in which he had been murdered near a temple by a barber and a washerman. In this life, he had a generalized fear of all barbers and washermen, and he showed marked fear when taken to the area of the temple where the murder had occurred.

As we will see, the cases involving phobias apparently linked to past-life events form just one avenue of exploration for researchers attempting to provide proof that reincarnation is a reality. For those whose lives have been blighted by the fear that phobias introduce into their lives, recalling an apparent past-life event that rationalizes their mental distress—whether real or imagined—has a remarkable therapeutic value, regardless of whether or not they believe in reincarnation.

Chapter 8

Children Behaving Strangely

Growing up isn't easy. Children can be a joy and watching them develop in their formative years gives parents a huge amount of pleasure. There are times, however, when their behavior puts a strain on that relationship, as they test how far they can go in getting their own way in a world dominated by adults. Every child is different, of course, and each has his or her own way of dealing with life's ups and downs. Inventive and creative, they have inbuilt psychological mechanisms that enable them to cope with many situations, such as inventing imaginary friends when real ones are in short supply. So the small percentage of kids claiming to have lived before must be treated with extreme caution, and the fact that—like imaginary friends—those claimed memories of a previous existence fade and are usually lost completely by the age of eight possibly adds weight to those reservations.

Child psychologists and most parents understand this very well. But some cases are puzzling in the extreme and have even made their way into academic journals. Readers of the *Journal of Medical Ethics,* for example, were treated to a paper by psychiatrist Dr. Amin Muhammad Gadit of Memorial University of Newfoundland, Canada, in 2009, which told of the "management dilemma" that a past-life memory case presented to his clinical practice in St. John's. A young Muslim boy, age twelve, had visited Jaipur in India, the home city of his parents, who were with him on vacation. He soon felt it was strangely familiar, and he told them he had spent a number of years there. "He identified a house where he claimed to have lived," Dr. Gadit writes, "and described the entire inner structure of the house. The local residents confirmed the existence of such a family about thirty years ago." It was an experience that left the boy emotionally disturbed, resulting in recurrent dreams about that supposed life and difficulty in relating to his parents. On their return from Jaipur the family consulted Dr. Gadit, who determined that their son was perfectly normal, apart from suffering anxiety. A multidisciplinary team, with the assistance of an imam, helped the boy come to terms with his memories "by reassuring him that there was no doubt about the truth in his history" and assuring him that "maybe everyone has past lives—the only difference is that you can remember yours." It's unlikely the medical team really believed that, since the paper's title was, "Myth of Reincarnation: A Challenge for the Mental Health Profession."

The parents of Dr. Gadit's patient probably had less to contend with than those of twenty-four children in Myanmar (formerly Burma), investigated by Dr. Ian Stevenson and others, who all claimed to have been Japanese soldiers who were killed in a previous life. This was not something their parents were likely to have encouraged. Japanese forces had occupied the country between 1942 and 1945, during World War II, ostensibly to help Burma gain independence from the British, but subsequently the Japanese took control and imposed a reign of terror on the country's inhabitants. About a quarter of a million Burmese died during the war. The twenty-four "Japanese" cases represent a small percentage of more than 750 individuals in Myanmar who claimed past-life memories that have been investigated. They do not come close to providing proof of reincarnation because the children involved gave no personal names or addresses that could assist with verification, other than the name of the city. Nevertheless, their very unusual "Japanese-like" behavior was so exceptional that reincarnation has to be considered in any effort to explain it.

Ian Stevenson and Jürgen Keil explored the alternatives in their 2005 paper[1] titled, "Children of Myanmar Who Behave Like Japanese Soldiers: A Possible Third Element in Personality." At the time of their investigations, the youngest subject was just six years old and the eldest was fifty-three. Eight of the twenty-four were female and the cases were generally found in a triangular area of upper Burma between Mandalay, Meiktila, and Pyawbwe, where most of the battles and resulting casualties occurred in 1945. What is striking is that more than half of these children (thirteen) played at being soldiers, and a fourteenth, who was female, showed an unusual interest in guns. None acted out a civilian occupation. There were, of course, also Burmese soldiers who died in the war, but the parents of these children detected Japanese traits in other aspects of their behavior. Despite this, they did not reject their offspring. The "Japanese-like" behavior displayed by one young subject included extraordinary cruelty toward animals and a tendency to violence against other human beings. This repelled his family, but their attempts to persuade him to be gentler fell on deaf ears. Another child asked for pliers to pull out the fingernails of playmates who annoyed him. (The Japanese were notorious for their torture and cruelty against the Burmese and others during World War II, and this was one of their methods.) Some of the children proudly declared themselves to be Japanese and identified with that country.

Japanese styles of clothing were also very much in evidence among this group of subjects. An eighteen-year-old boy, for example, habitually dressed as much like a Japanese soldier as he could, wearing trousers, a belt with large buckle, and boots—very different from the sandals and longyi, the loose-fitting material that is tied at the waist and usually falls to the feet, worn by Burmese men and women. Another of the twenty-four subjects did not wear a longyi until he was fifteen, and a third, whom the researchers met when he was twenty-four, was then wearing the traditional garment but still preferred wearing trousers and apparently did so whenever he could.

"Not all unusual behavior can be explained by genetics and environmental influences, alone or together," Stevenson and Keil argue. "This seems to be true of the unusual Japanese-like behavior we have described. If we can exclude other factors in the development of such behavior, the way is open to consider a possible third component in the development of personality. The word reincarnation is applicable here, although this term is difficult to define in behavioral terms. We wish to suggest that some aspects of the deceased person's personality—not necessarily all of them—are transferred in a way that cannot readily be explained by [other] alternatives."

This conjecture looks far more plausible in cases where a child's behavior and attitude are coupled with supporting evidence, including names and identification of people and places. An impressive case of this type concerns Toran (Titu) Singh.

Born around 1983 in the village of Bad, northern India, around nine miles from Agra and the Taj Mahal, he began speaking at the age of one-and-a-half, sooner than his five siblings, and early on he demanded, "Tell my grandfather to look after my children and my wife. I am having my meals here and I am worried about them." Asked by his mother who he was, Titu replied, "I am from Agra. I don't know how I came here." Later, he admonished his mother with the words, "Mummy, please don't go out in these clothes. I feel embarrassed by them. My wife had beautiful saris." He also told her: "Your house is dirty. I will not stay. My house is very big." When expected to walk or take a bus, he complained, "I used to go by car. I will not go on foot or in a bus." As he grew older, he would cry almost every day, saying he wanted to "go home."

Such complaints are not uncommon among children remembering past lives, but Titu's parents took them in their stride. Gradually, he began providing more and more information about his previous existence. He said he had a shop in Sadar Bazaar and named a brother (Raja Babu) and sister (Susheela). Titu was upset that his father, Mahavir Singh, who owned land in Bad but travelled every day to Agra to teach chemistry at a college, never took him along to visit his "home." He told his elder brother and a friend, "I have a shop of transistor radios, and I was a big smuggler and goonda (someone who uses force to get his way). I am the owner of Suresh Radio."

The brother and his friend found a shop with that name in Sadar Bazaar, Agra, and spoke to Uma Verme, the widow of its owner. They learned that her husband, Suresh Verme, who was a noted smuggler on the black market, had been shot dead in his car on August 28, 1983.

When the widow told her family about Titu's brother's visit and the claim that was being made, a group of them decided to pay an unannounced visit to the boy's home village in April 1987. Titu became very excited when he saw them approaching, recognizing his former wife, Uma; his father and mother (Chanda and Burfi); and two of his three brothers from that former life. He spoke to Uma about a trip he (as Suresh) had taken to Dolpur with their two children, whose nicknames—Mono and Tono—he also gave. Before they left, he accompanied them to their vehicle, observing, "This is not my car. My car was white." Although he had not seen one before, he played the tape deck in the car and even drove it a short distance, with the help of Raja Babu, a past-life brother, working the brake, gas, and clutch pedals. When Titu realized they were not taking him with them, he was furious, throwing his shoes at his mother and shouting, "I am not yours. You are not my mother." Later, when Titu met his past-life parents, he told his mother, "I am just passing through with these people who do not have a TV, a car, a video. I will run away with you." When his current father tried to remove him physically, Titu fought with him so strenuously he tore his shirt, hugging Chanda Singh, Suresh Verme's father, with whom he wanted to stay. Chanda placated him by saying, "Son, go. I will come see you."

All the above comes from an excellent and very detailed case study in a paper[2] by Antonia Mills, "A Replication Study: Three Cases of Children in Northern India Who Are Said to Remember a Previous Life." As well as reporting on events that had occurred earlier, Mills carried out her own investigation, which included taking Titu to meet people and visit places associated with the murdered Suresh Verme. I will be returning to the important case of Toran (Titu) Singh in a later chapter or two, with additional information.

Titu Singh's emotional response to apparently finding himself in a child's body yet with memories of an adult life provides powerful testimony to the strength of feeling that is experienced by many young children in such a situation. I have written elsewhere[3] of similar cases, such as a Sri Lankan girl, Dilukshi, who pointed out that her "real" parents *never* shouted at her. Instead, they called her "darling" or "sweet little daughter." In India, Parmod, second son of Bankeybehary Lal Sharma, a Sanskrit scholar and professor at an intermediate college in Uttar Pradesh, told his mother at the age of two-and-a-half not to cook, as he had a wife in Moradabad who could prepare their food. He also complained about the Sharma family's financial status, which compared unfavorably with his previous life. Also from India comes the case of Laxmi Barain, the spoiled son of a wealthy landowner whose inheritance allowed him to live a life of luxury and indulgence, including seeing a prostitute, Padma, regularly. When that life came to an end, he appears to have found himself reborn into poverty as Bishen Chand, who, as soon as he could speak, complained about his present circumstances. "Even my servant would not take the food cooked here," he declared. When given cotton clothes he tore them off, demanding silk ones instead. And at the age of five-and-a-half he asked his father, "Papa, why don't you keep a mistress? You will have great pleasure from her." Many years later, when Bishen was twenty-three, he met and recognized Padma, who was then aged fifty-two, and attempted to rekindle their sexual association by visiting her with a bottle of wine. She resisted his overture, reminding him, "I am an old woman like your mother." In the case of Swaran Lata, on the other hand, her new life in a Brahmin family was in sharp contrast to her previous existence, when she had been a member of India's lowest caste, the untouchables. Unfortunately, it meant that though she was a lovable child, her behavior—particularly her manners and personal habits, which they regarded as repulsively dirty—fell far short of her parents' expectations. She happily cleaned up the excrement of younger children and horrified her vegetarian family by asking for pork.

When I refer to children behaving strangely, it is inevitable that this expression will likely be interpreted as meaning "behaving badly." But behaving exceptionally well is also a strange behavior for most children, as was the case with three past-life memories reported from Sri Lanka by Erlendur Haraldsson and Godwin Samararatne in the *Journal* (1999) of the Society for Psychical Research, titled, "Children Who Speak of Memories of a Previous Life as a Buddhist Monk: Three New Cases." Sandika Tharanga (born 1979), Duminda Bandara Ratnayake (1984), and Ruvan Tharanga Perera (1987) share one thing in common: At an early age they each spoke of having led a monastic life before their present existence and exhibited behavior that was totally in character with that claim.

Sandika was born of middle-class Roman Catholic parents and started talking about having been a monk at the age of three. He began worshipping three times a day and described attending an almsgiving ceremony and then hearing a loud noise—a shot or an explosion—after which he could remember nothing more. Among his unusual behaviors were his requests to be taken to the temple, particularly on special days, and to have a Buddha image in the home to worship. He did not eat meat. Sandika's parents became more sympathetic to Buddhism because of his exemplary behavior and interests, which differed radically from their own religious life. They also noted that he was fearful of loud noises and when startled by one he would place his hand on the left side of his chest, as if in defense. He proved to be an outstanding pupil, studying at a Buddhist college, though probably to his parents' relief, he has shown no desire to become a monk in this life.

Duminda was three when he spoke about his previous life as a chief monk at the Asgiriya monastery, one of Sri Lanka's largest, frequently expressing the desire to visit the temple. His unusual behavior as a child included wanting to carry his clothes in the fashion of a monk, wanting to be called "Podi Sadhu" (little monk), going every morning and evening to a chapel close to his home, and plucking flowers to bring there and placing them in a typical Buddhist fashion. He had no desire to play with other children and expressed a desire to become a monk and to wear a monk's robe, which his mother seldom allowed him to do. Duminda enjoyed reciting stanzas (usually short religious statements) in Pali, the ancient language of Sinhalese Buddhism used and learnt only by monks. When taken to Asgiriya monastery, Duminda did not want to sit down until given a white cloth to sit on, which is the tradition for monks.

When Ruvan began speaking of his previous life at the age of two, he said he had been at Pitumpe monastery—a name unknown to his parents. He told them it was in Padukka (some twenty miles away), and he described various details that proved to be correct. He never asked for toys, only pictures of Buddha, which he collected lovingly. Ruvan was eight when the researchers met him. They learned that he sits in a lotus position when visiting the temple, without having been taught to do so; wants to wear a robe like a monk; and knows how to hold a fan when chanting. He does not want to eat at night and discourages his family from doing so (monks are not supposed to have meals from noon until next morning); he does not eat fish or meat (a few monks do not); he recites the Buddha's first sermon; can read the book of chants (Gatha pota); and wants the family to perform a puja (prayer-like ceremony of worship with recitations and offerings such as flowers and incense) in the evening and scolds them for not doing so. Probably the most impressive aspect of his highly unusual behavior was his ability, like Duminda, to chant stanzas in Pali. The researchers suggest he may have learned these from listening to them on radio or television, but his parents reject that theory. One day Ruvan's family had visited the Pushparamaya Pathawatta temple to discuss the possibility of his entering as a monk novice. He then told his parents: "I wish to stay here; you can go home." Ruvan told the researchers he was happy in the temple, does not miss home, has time to meditate, and that there is much to study. He was ordained into the temple in Rajgama in 1996.

In two of the three cases, research based on statements made by these young boys has suggested the identity of the monks they claim to have been in their previous existence. For the sake of brevity, however, I have confined my references to the unusual behavioral aspects of these cases. One of the two researchers involved in these three cases, Icelandic investigator Erlendur Haraldsson, has written several papers about the psychology of children claiming past-life memories and how it differs from children without such memories.

Ian Stevenson has highlighted some other unusual forms of behavior, which he calls philias—children's desires to eat different kinds of food or to wear clothes that differ from what is normally worn in their culture. It has also been suggested that a craving for alcohol, tobacco, or drugs in this life might be a carryover of a past-life addiction. One of his colleagues, Dr. Jim Tucker, has also produced a "Strength-of-Case Scale" designed to assess how evidential cases suggestive of reincarnation are. He divides this evidence into four broad categories, one of which is "behaviors that seem to relate to the previous life" and gives points to each item. Here are the items on his list, any or all of which—when displayed by a child or adult—could suggest that he or she is being influenced by past-life memories:

- ◇ Unusual dietary cravings or avoidances
- ◇ Unusual methods of eating or table manners
- ◇ Unusual use of intoxicants
- ◇ Unusual philias
- ◇ Unusual skills or aptitudes
- ◇ Unusual animosities
- ◇ Unusual phobias
- ◇ Behavior related to that of the opposite sex
- ◇ Desire or reluctance to return to previous family or place
- ◇ Memories of previous life expressed in play

Taken on their own, none of these can be regarded as evidence of reincarnation. But when several occur, particularly in addition to verified statements about a former life, such behavioral patterns have far greater significance.

Chapter 9

When I Was Famous

For a person who had recently watched his remains being interred, Nicholas II of Russia seemed remarkably fit and well when I met him in Chicago in 1998. He looked similar to the pictures I had seen of him in many reference books, but he no longer speaks Russian nor rules over a nation. As Donald Norsic, his life as a creative director in the advertising industry was being overshadowed by memories of a very different former existence. Two months before we sat in the warm autumn sunshine of Lincoln Park, discussing his past and present lives, Russia had finally laid to rest the brutally murdered Romanov family—the Tsar, Tsarina, and three of their five children—together with their doctor and three servants. The remains of Russia's last reigning royal family had been recovered from a mass grave seven years earlier, identified by DNA matching, then interred in a moving ceremony on July 17, 1998, at the Cathedral of St. Peter and St. Paul in St. Petersburg, where previous tsars were buried. It attracted a worldwide television audience and extensive media coverage. Friends had invited Norsic to go with them to St. Petersburg for the service, but he declined, preferring to stay in his apartment and listen to it on the radio, alone.

"I woke up from a sound sleep at the moment the ceremony started," he told me.[1] "It was six AM here. I turned on the radio, and I shared it, as it occurred, and I cried." He paused as his voice faltered, and he let out a deep sigh. "I'm feeling compelled to cry now, just remembering it. When the bells began ringing, I started crying." Those bells had been installed in the cathedral by Nicholas II in 1905. Though he spoke passionately about Russia, he had no desire to return to the country he believes he once ruled. It would, he told me, bring back too many memories and cause him great distress. The life-changing event for Norsic was seeing the movie *Dr. Zhivago*, which he did very reluctantly because he expected to be bored. "I felt as though my reality and the movie's reality changed places," he explained. He then began dreaming about his previous life, and eventually, under hypnosis, he was able to describe his coronation, the birth of his children, where he had lived, and the people who were important to him. Risking ridicule, Norsic wrote a book about his experiences, *To Save Russia*,[2] in which he lists fifty facts that he is certain were not known to him previously and to which he was not exposed before the hypnotic regressions.

So, is Donald Norsic's case one of "far memory" to an actual life lived earlier, or "tsar memory" inspired by more mundane influences? We are faced with two problems when trying to evaluate such stories. First, the possibility that the person claiming to have been famous in a previous life may simply be suffering from delusions of grandeur: a psychological way of compensating for a humdrum life. However, there was nothing dull about Norsic's life. At the time the memories emerged, he was picking up awards for his work in advertising, owned his own racing-class sloop, belonged to Chicago's most prestigious yacht club, and became fleet champion. Second, the fact that famous people's lives are so well-documented that it is almost impossible to prove that information about them could not have been absorbed by the claimant, consciously or subconsciously, from reading newspapers, magazines or books, or watching television programs or movies.

With that in mind, let me share with you, very briefly, some of the claims made by or about mostly ordinary people who are believed to have been famous in a past life. A handful are fortunate to have been famous in both lives. I'll pass no judgment, but readers who wish to do so can explore many of these cases in far greater detail on the Internet before making up their own minds. I've placed them, in no particular order, in groups that relate to either their stations in life or the aptitudes that made them special.

Royalty and Rulers

MARIE ANTOINETTE: British medium Daniel Dunglas Home, as already noted, complained in the nineteenth century that he had met a dozen women who claimed to be the reincarnation of Marie Antoinette, Queen of France. Since then, a few dozen others are likely to have emerged. The latest has been given the pseudonym "Kiera Hermine," according to a report by Paul Von Ward's The Reincarnation Experiment website,[3] while investigations into the claim continue. A book by "intuitive reincarnation researcher" Marie-Alix Ravel is promised, which we are told will be "reality cloaked as fiction."

KING ARTHUR: John Rothwell, reborn in England in 1954, is so convinced that he was once the legendary King Arthur that he changed his name by deed poll in 1976[4] and must now be addressed as "King Arthur Pendragon." A familiar and striking figure at Druid ceremonies at Stonehenge, as well as other pagan events at ancient sites, King Arthur often finds himself in conflict with the authorities, partly because he appears to believe that the rights and privileges he enjoyed in the fifth and sixth centuries should have accompanied him into his present incarnation. It should be added that his historical existence is debated and disputed by modern historians.

HATSHEPSUT MAAT-KA-RA: Singer Tina Turner, having been told by a Californian psychic that she is the reincarnation of a famous queen who ruled as pharaoh from 1473 to 1458 BC, went off to Egypt in search of the truth. Her traveling companion, novelist Moyra Caldecott, revealed[5] that Tina had been drawn to Egypt for years but "does not claim that she is who the psychic says she is. She is puzzled, curious, intrigued." As for the queen of pop, she appears to have a very down-to-earth approach to the subject, saying,[6] "We know we have lived before, and we know we have lived in Egypt before, but the details still escape us." I assume she is using the royal "we" in that quote. Turner adds: "Perhaps we are not meant to know. Perhaps if we know these things for sure, we will abandon our lives 'here and now' and try to live 'there and then' . . . the knowing will come when it comes. Don't push it."

NEFERTITI: It was an extraordinary dream that convinced Elizabeth Christensen[7] to spend at least $165,000 on twenty-three cosmetic operations, so that she would look like the woman she believes she was in a previous life. In her dream, Christensen—who lives with her security consultant husband on England's south coast—saw a beautiful but mysterious young woman who smiled at her, then vanished. She saw that face again in a magazine article about Nefertiti, the Egyptian queen and wife of fourteenth-century BC pharaoh Akhenaton. Commenting on the costly cosmetic surgery, she explained to a tabloid newspaper that she has been "transforming myself into a modern-day version" of Nefertiti. If her claim is true, she will be on nodding terms with actress Shirley MacLaine, who says she was a maidservant to Nefertiti in one of her own many former lives.

Artists

PAUL GAUGIN: Peter Teekamp[8] is a Dutch artist who has come to accept, after a series of coincidences followed by past-life regression sessions, that he is the reincarnation of French artist Paul Gaugin. He claims there are many similarities between his and Gaugin's work and style, but he kept this information to himself for two decades. During that time, he had hidden a unique "signature" in each of his paintings and was delighted when friends discovered it. Teekamp has now revealed that Gaugin included the identical hidden signature in his works, too. He also believes he has discovered a Gaugin original charcoal sketch on which the artist's famous *Tahitian Women on the Beach* (1891) is based.

MICHELANGELO: Having taken a rest from his extremely busy life as an Italian Renaissance painter, sculptor, architect, and engineer, who produced such superb works of art as the magnificent *David* and *Pietà* sculptures, Michelangelo is back on earth again and living in Las Vegas. His name is Paul-Felix Montez,[9] and he is once again a sculptor, often working on a vast scale, having produced the large horses and statues at Caesar's Palace, as well as being a movie-set and special-effects designer.

Writers

CHRISTOPHER MARLOWE: A close friend of William Shakespeare, Marlowe was a sixteenth-century playwright whose death occurred in circumstances that have always been a mystery—until now, and his reincarnation as a woman,

Brenda Harwood, who is keen to set the record straight. She first identified with Marlowe while watching a TV program that purported to show how his life ended. "I didn't die like that!" she shouted at the television. Harwood's subsequent research on his life triggered a series of flashbacks that she has put into a book, written through his eyes.[10]

Show Business

LAUREL & HARDY: Fans of the famous comedy duo will be delighted to learn that many years after their deaths they are back together and performing comedy in front of appreciative audiences. English-born Stan Laurel and Georgia-born Oliver Hardy successfully moved from silent black-and-white films to sound movies in their Hollywood career. Now they've apparently returned from the next world to New Jersey, where they were born in the 1970s, eighteen months apart, as brothers Josh and Danny Bacher[11] in a Jewish family. The fast-rising comic duo has been winning acclaim ever since they started performing together.

MARILYN MONROE: Scottish singer Sherrie Lea Laird[12] was born nine months after the sudden death in 1962 of film star and sex symbol Marilyn Monroe, and though not a Marilyn fan, she began identifying increasingly with the actress as her own musical career took off in Toronto, Canada, to which her family had emigrated when she was four. Sherrie had a number-one hit record with *No Ordinary Love* in Canada and Europe. As well as having flashbacks to Marilyn's life, she also became suicidal at the same age as when Marilyn took her life, leading her to seek help from psychiatrist and past-life regressionist Dr. Adrian Finkelstein.[13] Revelations about the actress's life and death, based on Laird's eight years of therapy, are now available in book form, *Marilyn Monroe Returns: The Healing of a Soul.*

Religious Figures

APOSTLE PAUL: Nick Bunick was a regular guy until two psychics independently told him he had lived at the time of Jesus.[14] That, in turn, led to him being regressed, producing twenty-six hours of tape recordings from thirteen sessions, in which he described in great detail the life of the Apostle

Paul. Having concluded from those hypnotic regressions that the message of Jesus and Paul has been distorted by the Church, Bunick is now trying to rectify the situation. He has told his story in *Time for Truth*[15] and promotes his teachings through a foundation with the same name.

JESUS: Sergei Anatolyevitch Torop[16] was once a traffic cop in Siberia, but today he is known as Vissarion and heads a religious movement he founded in 1990—the Church of the Last Testament—whose followers believe him to be the reincarnation of Jesus Christ. Not surprisingly, he also teaches rebirth, as well as veganism, and the impending end of the world. He is, however, not alone in believing that he is Jesus reborn. Wikipedia lists nineteen others, all living in the twentieth century, who have made similar claims, including David Shayler,[17] a former UK military intelligence agent and whistleblower who served a short prison sentence for an offense under the Official Secrets Act in 2002. Soon afterward he declared himself to be the Messiah and to hold the secret of eternal life. That revelation was followed in the news that he was now living as a woman and his transvestite "alter ego" was called "Delores Kane."

Politicians

ABRAHAM LINCOLN: Charles Lindbergh is famous in his own right for achieving the first solo flight from the United States to Europe (Long Island to Paris) in 1927. He received the nation's highest military decoration, the Medal of Honor, for this historic exploit. But in previous incarnations, according to a book by Richard Salva,[18] which quotes the great Indian master of yoga Paramahansa Yogananda, Lindbergh had first been a Himalayan yogi before being reborn as US President Abraham Lincoln. Meanwhile, to this day there is disagreement over whether Lincoln's assassin, James Wilkes Booth, died in an ambush after he killed the president or whether the body recovered at the scene was someone else's. Hypnotic regressionist Dell Leonardi[19] believes he escaped, having recorded severnty-three hours of sessions with an anonymous twenty-one-year-old in Kansas City who, under hypnosis, appeared to be the assassin and, as well as descibing how he shot Lincoln, recounted his escape from the Sixteenth New York Cavalry and subsequent life in the US, England, and France.

MAHATMA GANDHI: India's great political and ideological leader, who advocated nonviolent resistance to bring about change, was reborn in 1968—twenty years after he was assassinated. In his current life, according to reincarnation researcher Walter Semkiw, he is American civil rights campaigner and environmental activist Anthony K. "Van" Jones,[20] whose current appointments include being a senior fellow at the Center for American Progress. Van Jones was named *Time* magazine's "environmental hero" in 2008; Gandhi was its "man of the year" in 1930. Van Jones' opinion of Semkiw's theory is not known.

LYMAN TRUMBALL: The name of this US Senator from Illinois will not be recognized by most Americans, but then he did serve during the American Civil War and died over one hundred years ago (1896). He is particularly remembered as the coauthor of the Thirteenth Amendment to the Constitution that prohibited all kinds of slavery. In his current incarnation, his political actions will certainly make a much greater impact on the pages of history, for according to Walter Semkiw (whose research methods I discuss in chapter 11), he is now better known as Barack Hussein Obama II, the forty-fourth president of the United States.[21]

Others

THOMAS ANDREWS: William Barnes is a man with a mission—to clear his name. Not the name by which he is known in his present life, but the one he used in his previous incarnation when he was a Northern Irish master shipbuilder and designer. As Thomas Andrews he designed the ill-fated *Titanic* and has since been held responsible by some people for the maiden voyage disaster one hundred years ago, when she hit an iceberg and sank with the loss of over fifteen hundred lives, including Andrews. Having been haunted by flashbacks and dreams about the event for much of his life, the Arizona-based Barnes underwent hypnotic regression sessions resulting in a fascinating account of his former life. In those recollections, which took place before the release of the epic *Titanic* movie, "Andrews" defends the ship's design and instead places the blame for *Titanic*'s sinking on poor quality construction materials.[22]

ANNE FRANK: When Swedish poet and author Barbro Karlén declared[23] in a 1995 TV interview in Amsterdam that she was the reincarnation of Anne

Frank, it caused a sensation. After all, it was from an attic in that Dutch city that the young Jewish girl wrote her now world-famous diary about the ordeal she and her family endured while hiding from the Nazis. Karlén's subsequent autobiography has done little to end the controversy, and the fact that she is non-Jewish in this life is one of the issues that has been raised. There was even an unsuccessful attempt to prevent her book's publication by the son of Holocaust survivors. However, a cousin of Anne Frank, Buddy Elias, who was the director of the Anne Frank Fund at the time the book was published, is a believer in reincarnation and publicly supported Karlén, with whom he said he feels a certain "soul relationship."

When I asked Rabbi Yonassan Gershom, an expert on reincarnation, particularly in relation to the Holocaust, to write a piece about the Anne Frank/Barbro Karlén controversy for a magazine I was editing,[24] his account included this sentence: "I had already been contacted by four other people who *also* claimed to be Anne Frank, along with a plethora of Hitlers, Mengeles, and other characters from World War II."

There is, it seems, no shortage of individuals willing to claim the lives of the famous—and infamous—as their own. So, cast a skeptical eye over the preceding cases, by all means. But remember, if reincarnation is possible, then even famous and infamous people have to be reborn. And ordinary people, in some future life, may experience what it is like to be a celebrity. For, if true, reincarnation could provide us all with countless experiences on the social scale of our planet's rich and diverse cultures.

Chapter 10

Keeping It in the Family

Four-year-old Maung Pho Zaw was being taken to another village in Upper Myanmar by an uncle when a snake bit his left foot. The uncle acted swiftly to lessen the effect of the snake venom by borrowing a cheroot that a woman was smoking and applying it to the bite, which was oozing blood. He then applied a tourniquet and hurried the child to a hospital where he was rebuked by medical staff for using a folk remedy. Neither the uncle's futile attempt to help his nephew nor the intervention of the doctors at the hospital were able to save the life of Maung Pho Zaw. He died that evening.

A few months later, a neighbor told his grieving parents that Maung Pho Zaw had appeared in a dream, saying he was trying to find his way home but did not know the way. Shortly afterward, the dead boy's father also had a dream in which his son told him he had come home. Maung Pho Zaw's mother became pregnant soon after these dreams, and it was obvious to them as soon as Ma Myint Myint Zaw was born, that their son had returned to them—but as a daughter. Their certainty came from the round birthmark on her left foot, in the same position as the snakebite that had killed her brother. This was confirmed when the child was old enough to speak about her memory of that event. She talked of the snakebite and had a strong phobia of snakes, refusing to go out after dark in case she was bitten again. Interestingly, she displayed a marked masculinity from an early age, refusing to wear earrings and insisting on wearing her dead brother's clothes when she discovered them. Even when Ma Myint Myint Zaw was old enough to attend school, she insisted on wearing boy's clothes. Her parents and teachers were surprisingly tolerant of these demands. By the time she reached puberty, however, she had become more feminine. Ma Myint Myint Zaw, who was apparently once her own brother, married at the age of eighteen, and at the time Ian Stevenson researched and wrote about this case,[1] she had produced two children and was said to be a good wife and mother.

Although it is a highly unusual case, the events surrounding the birth and young life of Ma Myint Myint Zaw are by no means unique. Researchers have come across a number of cases in which the subject who claims to recall a past life is related in some way to the person who died. Indeed, in some cultures, it is a comparatively common occurrence. The view seems to be that if you are to be reborn, you might as well return to a family you know and who will welcome you back. Interestingly, even in Western cases remembered under hypnosis, subjects claim to realize that family members in their current life were also related to them in their previous existence. What is unclear, I confess, is whether the host parents have any choice in the matter. Take, for example, the following case[2] from Thailand, also reported by Ian Stevenson.

Before his birth, Thiang San Kla's parents both dreamed that his father's older brother, Phoh, had come to them and said he wished to be reborn as their child. Stevenson does not tell us what their answer was—assuming they responded in their dreams—but I suspect they may have had reservations. After all, Phoh was a notorious cattle thief who was killed by a posse of thirty villagers at Ban Ar Vud because they believed he was visiting their neighborhood to steal their cattle.

Whether they welcomed Phoh's reincarnation or not, they were left in no doubt that the wayward brother had returned when Thiang San Kla was born because the baby boy's body displayed six birthmarks, the most prominent of which was a large, ugly, raised area on the back of his head. It coincided with the fatal blow that had killed Phoh; he was struck with a heavy knife used to open coconuts or chop wood. Curiously, another of the birthmarks was on the boy's right big toe, consisting of a partly detached nail and dark pigmentation of the nail or tissue beneath it. This corresponded to a chronic infection of the same toe with which Phoh had suffered for some years before his murder. These birthmarks, together with Phoh's appearance in his parents' dreams, left the couple in little doubt that he had returned. This was confirmed by Thiang San Kla when he was old enough to speak, making a number of statements about past-life events and recognitions of persons Phoh had known, which fully convinced the family that he had returned to them. Hearing of Phoh's apparent rebirth as his own nephew, a policeman who was familiar with the cattle thief's criminal history and had investigated his murder decided to call on them. Stevenson tells us that Thiang not only addressed him by name and gave correctly the names of the people concerned with "his" murder, particularly the actual killer, a man named Chang, but also expressed a desire to take revenge.

Birthmarks are enormously important to the evidence of reincarnation and I have devoted an entire chapter to this subject (chapter 21). Though several investigators had drawn attention to birthmarks over quite a long period, it was Ian Stevenson who recognized their significance and made a special study of this physical aspect. Some cultures, however, have long accepted that birthmarks can help identify reincarnating souls, and that is certainly true of the Tlingit, Alaska's indigenous people, and similar tribes— the Haidas, Athapaskans, Eskimos, and Aleuts—for whom rebirth forms part of their beliefs. So a story that Stevenson uncovered in America's frozen north[3] is perhaps not quite as extraordinary when viewed against that cultural backdrop. It is, nevertheless, astonishing in the implications it carries for the doctrine of rebirth.

Victor Vincent, a full-blooded Tlingit, believed very strongly in reincarnation. What's more, he was certain that his deceased sister Gertrude had been reborn as her own granddaughter, also named Gertrude. In other words, Mrs. Corliss Chotkin Sr. had given birth to her own mother. So far, of course, we are dealing only with conjecture on Victor Vincent's part, though apparently Gertrude Jr. did give her family some information about her grandmother that she could not have acquired normally. Over the years, Victor had felt increasingly close to his niece, and it was on one of his visits to stay with her and her husband, in Sitka, that he told her, "I'm coming back as your next son. I hope I don't stutter then as much as I do now. Your son will have these scars." With that, he pulled up his shirt and showed her a scar on his back that was clearly the residue of an operation that had been carried out some years earlier because the small round holes of the stitches remained visible. He also pointed to a scar at the base of the right side of his nose, also the result of an operation. "I know I will have a good home," he added. "You won't be going off and getting drunk." This was a reference to a number of alcoholics in the family. Another reason he gave for wanting to return was his belief that Gertrude Jr. had been his sister, and he wanted to grow up again with her. That wish appears to have been granted when, on December 15, 1947, eighteen months after Victor's death in Angoon, Mrs. Chotkin gave birth to a healthy son, named Corliss after his father. And, just as Victor had predicted, the child bore two distinct birthmarks of exactly the same shape and in the same location as the scars her uncle had shown her when he predicted his return.

When Corliss Chotkin Jr. began to speak, at around thirteen months, his mother was assisting him to say his name correctly one day when he responded impetuously, "Don't you know me? I'm Kahkody." This was the tribal name of his uncle, Victor Vincent, and the boy spoke it with an excellent Tlingit accent. The family was so impressed that they gave him the same tribal name. Learning of this event prompted Mrs. Chotkin's aunt to reveal that she had dreamed Victor was going to live with the Chotkins shortly before the boy's birth. On a visit to Sitka docks with his mother and a foster brother who was four years older than he, Corliss spontaneously recognized one of Victor's stepdaughters, becoming very excited, jumping up and down and saying, "There's my Susie." He was two years old at the time and it was just a coincidence that they and Susie were there at the same time. Indeed, neither his mother nor foster brother had spotted her. He hugged her, spoke her Tlingit name and kept repeating, "My Susie." A similar thing happened, at the same age, when Corliss spotted a man in the street whom he recognized immediately. "There is William, my son," he said excitedly. Sure enough, Victor's son was visiting Sitka, unknown to Mrs. Chotkin. Further proof came when he was a year older and his mother took him to a large meeting of Tlingits. Looking around, Corliss picked out a face that was very familiar—his past-life wife—before his mother had seen her, declaring, "That's the old lady," (a familiar term he had always used for her) and, "There's Rose," which was her correct name. Corliss did much the same when a friend of Victor's passed his house while he was playing in the street. Mrs.

Alice Roberts was visiting Sitka, and when the young boy recognized her, he called out her pet name. He also recognized three other friends of Victor. One interesting observation, in addition to much more supporting evidence gathered by Stevenson, was that, like his uncle Victor, Corliss Jr. also had a severe stutter when young and this persisted until he received speech therapy at around the age of ten. There was no evidence of this speech impediment at the time Stevenson interviewed the Chotkins, which was in the early 1960s when Corliss Jr. was a teenager.

The Victor Vincent case is one of seven from Southeastern Alaska about which Stevenson wrote in detail in his book *Twenty Cases Suggestive of Reincarnation*.[4] Another in which the child claimed to be his own uncle concerned Jimmy Svenson, who was half Tlingit and half Norwegian. At the age of two Jimmy informed his parents that he had been his mother's brother, John Cisko, who died in suspicious circumstances. In a third case, a celebrated Alaskan fisherman, William George Sr., apparently returned as his own grandson—something he had predicted he would do. And a fourth case centered on Norman Despers, who claimed to be his own grandfather reborn.

Although they are far rarer, there *are* cases in Europe of individuals apparently reincarnating as their own relatives. The story of the Pollock twins, Gillian and Jennifer, created great excitement in the British media in the 1960s after it was reported that they were the reincarnations of their own sisters, who were tragically killed, along with another child, when a car mounted the sidewalk and ploughed into them. It was May 5, 1957, and the children were on their way to Sunday Mass in northeast England. They died instantly. Despite being a staunch Roman Catholic, their father, John, also believed strongly in reincarnation, and he prayed for proof of rebirth. So when Florence told him she was pregnant, he confidently predicted she would give birth to twins. A gynecologist who examined his wife begged to differ, but on October 4, 1958, John's prediction was confirmed with the announcement that he and his wife, Florence, had been blessed with identical twin daughters, Gillian and Jennifer.

Critics, rightly, will argue that believing the newborn girls were their dead sisters was no more than the wish fulfillment of grief-stricken parents. But the evidence suggests otherwise. For a start, John noticed a thin white line on Jennifer's forehead that was identical to one Jacqueline had on her forehead after falling from her tricycle when young. And Florence observed that a birthmark on Jennifer's left hip was of the same kind and in the same place as one on Jacqueline's body. There were no similar visible birthmarks on Gillian, which is unusual for monozygotic twins. But it was their early behavior, after the family had moved from Hexham to Whitley Bay when they were just four months old, which provided some of the most striking evidence. Ian Stevenson, who investigated this case,[5] was able to observe what happened when the twins were taken back at the age of three to the neighborhood where their sisters had died. Given free rein to walk around Battle Hill as they wished, Gillian and Jennifer knew where "their" school was, even though it was obscured by St. Mary's Church, and they correctly identified their old house as they walked by. At home, when they were presented with toys that had belonged to their dead sisters, the toys were "remembered," called by their proper names, and attributed to the corresponding twin. On one occasion, when Florence went to check that her daughters were playing happily on their own, she was dismayed to find Gillian cradling Jennifer's head and saying that blood was coming from her eyes because that was where the car had hit her.

Another unusual case with a family connection, this time involving Burmese twin boys, is also one of the earliest to be researched. The investigator was Harold Fielding Hall, a top-ranking civil servant in Burma, and he wrote about it in his book *The Soul of a People*,[6] which covers a wide range of topics relating to that country (now Myanmar). Soon after twins Maung Gyi and Maung Ngé were born in 1886, their parents moved from Okshitgon to Kabyu, so they grew up knowing nothing of the place where they were born or of its inhabitants. Soon after they began to speak, the brothers began using different names for each other. One called the other Maung San Nyein while the other was called Ma Gywin, a woman's name. Their parents remembered these were the names of a devoted couple who had been born next door to each other on the same day, had married, and had also died on the same day—at about the same time the twin boys were born.

It was decided to put their past-life memories to the test and so Gyi and Ngé were taken to Okshitgon, to the married couple's former home and the neighborhood where they had lived. Not only were they able to identify roads, places, and people who were connected to them in their past lives but also the clothes they had worn. Amusingly, the younger twin, who had been

the wife, remembered a debt that had not been repaid. Unknown to her husband, she had borrowed two rupees from a woman named Ma Thet and had
not paid it back before she died. The woman was found and confirmed the
unpaid loan exactly as the twin had remembered. Fielding Hall interviewed
the twins when they were six and still had strong memories of their previous
existence. He described the twin who recalled being the husband as a chubby
little fellow, while the brother who had been the wife was smaller with "a
curious dreamy look in his face, more like a girl than a boy."

Stories of such loving family bonds bringing souls back together again
will doubtless resonate with comedienne Joan Rivers, following the hypnotic
regression she experienced under the influence of hypnotherapist Brian
Weiss.[7] The wisecracking Rivers was hardly relaxed at the start of the session,
admitting to Weiss that she was still grieving for her mother, who had died
some years earlier, and her husband, who had passed away more recently,
having taken his own life. As soon as she went into a deep hypnotic trance,
however, Rivers began describing a life in England in 1835 where she was
taller and thinner, a gentrified woman who was also the mother of three
daughters. "One is definitely my mother," she volunteered, referring to a child
of six. Weiss asked her how she knew that, and she responded, "I just know
it's her." She then began sobbing and asked to leave that life as she realized the
daughter in question was dying. Weiss obliged by taking her farther back in
time to a life where she was a man—a farmer. As he brought Joan Rivers out
of the regression, Weiss said he knew the healing process was already beginning to work: "She understood that her precious mother, who was her young
daughter in 1835 England, was a soul companion across the centuries. Even
though they were now once more separated, Joan knew that they would be
together again, in another time and another place."

Dick Sutphen is a respected regression therapist who has helped many
individuals explore their past lives, but when he was interviewed[8] on the subject by a journalist in 1994 it was his own experience of a former life that
was the main talking point. Sutphen revealed that he enjoyed a very close
relationship with his son Hunter (his wife, Tara, describes them as joined
at the hip) and he knew they had been together in at least one previous life.

This, he said, was revealed in "one of the most vivid regressions I've ever had" when he discovered that their relationship in that life had an unexpected twist: "Hunter was a woman. I was a man. We worked in a fabric and dye mill in eighteenth-century England. After we were married, she taught me to cut patterns and sew, and we opened a tailor shop in our little house. We had a wonderful relationship. But even in deep trance, I had to laugh at my attire. I dressed fancier to walk in the park than I would to attend the Grammy Awards today."

If all these cases can be taken at face value, they suggest that soul bonds exist between many individuals and can express themselves in often quite unexpected and unusual relationships, with daughters becoming wives, wives becoming sons, and grandfathers becoming their own grandchildren. There is also a suggestion that the influence of this association extends far beyond immediate family.

Many years ago, Austrian researcher Alois Schwaiger visited the UK and shared with me his theory,[9] which he said provided scientific proof of reincarnation. He first took an interest in the subject when he was nineteen and felt that he was the reincarnation of his grandfather. His methodology involved tracing the matrilineal line (from mother to daughter) of a person claiming to be reincarnated. This is also done along the branches of the genealogical tree of the person whose life is remembered. Schwaiger claimed that at some point it would be found that they have a common ancestor. In other words, if X believes he was Y in a previous life, study of the female lines of both family trees, looking at the mother, grandmother, great-grandmother, and so on, will eventually produce a convergence at person Z, a common ancestor. He told me that he had tested this theory on twenty cases and found it to be true every time. He said he had also found it to be true in a transnational case. Applying this analytical approach to Asian cases would, however, be impossible because of the lack of records—even the birthdates of some reincarnation subjects are not known for certain.

So what is the logic behind this matrilineal theory? Dr. Schwaiger explained that within everybody there is a male and female component. At death, the male side dies but the female element of the soul returns to its origin before being reincarnated again. If true, this is clearly good news for feminists, but I must confess that many years later I am still trying to understand how having a shared ancestor, many generations before, adds any more weight to the case for reincarnation than the immediate evidence that appears to be carried over from one life to the next. I have written elsewhere[10] about Englishman Simon Jacobs who discovered he is the reincarnation of a distant relative—a case I am still investigating.

It is appropriate at this point to make reference to so-called "genetic memory." Some skeptics use the term to dismiss reported cases of reincarnation in families, suggesting that the memories of the person who died are passed on, genetically, from one generation to the next. It's an interesting idea and one that should be explored—but there is yet no evidence that individual memories can be handed down in this way. Even if it is discovered that such a biological mechanism exists, it would apply only to a miniscule number of cases in which there is a direct blood link between the person who died and the family member who appears to have inherited his or her memories. Reincarnation, therefore, would appear to be a much simpler explanation.

Chapter 11

Looks Familiar?

Let's face it, few of us are 100 percent happy when we look in the mirror. Ears too big? Nose too long? Lips too thin? Saggy jowls? Double chin? Furrowed brow? Even if we are comfortable with our facial features and what the passage of time does to them, there's probably something else we would like to change about our physical body. Some would prefer to be thinner or taller, others shorter or more muscular. Slimmer hips or longer legs would be on other people's wish lists. Perhaps in the next life?

Well, I have some bad news for those readers who hope they might have a perfect body next time around. If reincarnation researcher Walter Semkiw and others are right, when we are reborn the chances are we will look remarkably similar to how we look now. I know this seems to fly in the face of reason as well as genetics, but Semkiw claims to have some powerful evidence to support his argument, and independent research by others does suggest that aspects of our appearance, as well as our memories, might carry over from one lifetime to the next.

Actually, it's not a new idea. As far as I am aware, the first detailed collection of examples to support the look-alike theory was compiled by English author Clarice Toyne, who wrote several books about her spiritual experiences more than forty years ago. In one of these,[1] she tells of her psychic awareness and the emerging ability to "see the past lives of others" that she developed by studying not only her own reflection in a mirror, but also her lawyer husband, Wystan. Here's how she described that process:

> Then I studied the face of my husband. As I watched, several faces that still were plainly him, portrayals of his soul, flickered before my eyes. I grew to recognize that the bone-formation of face and head remained characteristic and similar. The shape of the features changed a little from century to century, especially when there was a change in race or parentage. Yet it was notably and often strikingly similar to the cast of features now worn by the soul. This disposed of the modern argument that we are simply a product of our parentage and environment. I was taught that they were ours because of what we had been and were up to the time of conception, and their effect upon us was slight.

So where was all this leading Clarice Toyne? The answer was revealed in her second book,[2] which takes us into another spiritual dimension and communication with a highly evolved spirit who revealed the past incarnations of famous people who are shown to have a striking physical resemblance in successive lives. Now, I accept that this might be a step too far for some readers, but the very concept of reincarnation requires the existence of a spiritual dimension in which souls exist between incarnations, so the possibility of some form of communication between gifted individuals and those existing in that other world cannot be lightly dismissed. In Toyne's case, that communication sometimes simply took the form of "inspiration" while at other times she heard the disembodied voice of a spiritual being she called the Teacher. Explaining the process, Toyne writes:

> I was gardening one day, planting pansies, when suddenly a name was dropped into my mind like a pebble into a well. "This was my name when last on Earth," added the Voice. Excited, I fled for my bicycle and soon was cruising down the long hill into the city, bound for the reference library.

This, of course, was in the days before computers, the Internet, and search engines. Her research in libraries and secondhand bookshops revealed an astonishing similarity in the appearances of various well-known people in their most recent lives and in what the Teacher assured her was their former incarnations. Toyne assembled these for a subsequent, illustrated book that claimed not only a remarkable physical resemblance for various famous subjects in successive lives but also striking similarities in other traits, including skills and character. They include:

Sir Winston Churchill, British wartime prime minister, who the Teacher said was Thomas Wentworth, Earl of Strafford (1593–1641), an English statesman who was a powerful minister at the time of King Charles I.

Danny Kaye, the stage name of Russian-born actor and singer David Daniel Kaminsky (1913–1987), whose success on Broadway led to his playing the title role of *Hans Christian Anderson*, a movie about the famous Danish poet and writer (1805–1875) whose fairy tales and children's stories, including *The Ugly Duckling*, are still very popular. And, according to Toyne's spiritual Teacher, that's the very person Kaye had been in a previous life.

G. K. Chesterton, the prolific English writer, journalist, poet, and philosopher (1874–1936) was none other than Dr. Samuel Johnson (1709–1784), who has been described as "arguably the most distinguished man of letters in English history."

General Charles de Gaulle, French general and later that country's president (1890–1970), had two famous previous lives, also as a French general: Louis de Bourbon, Grand Condé (1621–1686), and Joseph II of Austria (1741–1790), whose wife was the granddaughter of the incumbent King of France at that time.

Other cases quoted by Clarice Toyne and inspired by her Teacher include George Bernard Shaw (Voltaire) and Pierre Teilhard de Chardin (Blaise Pascal). I will make no attempt to express an opinion on these claims. Readers wishing to do so can easily make their own online examination of the corresponding likenesses and personalities of the individuals cited. But it *is* pertinent to ask at this point, assuming Toyne and her spiritual guide have correctly identified the past lives of these famous people, *why* is there this close resemblance in appearance? Here's the answer Toyne was given:

Because we are the product of our custom or thought, our reaction to circumstances. We forge ourselves by our way of thinking, both conscious and subconscious, and build ourselves, our bone structure upon the ray-energies thus drawn into us. We sculpture ourselves over the ages. Change is very gradual.

Harold Waldwin Percival came to the same conclusion a quarter of a century earlier. The author of *Thinking and Destiny,*[3] a thought-provoking thousand-page work that has been described as "a remarkably complete exposition of the origin and development of the universe," in which reincarnation plays an important part, dedicated his book "with love to the conscious self in every human body." It was written after he became "conscious of Ultimate Reality," but he insisted that it was for each reader to judge the truth of his statements. So, judge for yourself the following extract from that book that relates to physical appearance:

The features and form of the body are true records of the thoughts which made them. Lines, curves and angles in their relation to one another, are like so many written words which the thoughts and actions have formed. Each line is a letter, each feature a word, each organ a sentence, each part a chapter, and all make up a story of the past, fashioned by thinking and expressed in the human body. The lines and features are changed by and with one's efforts at thinking. The kind of body which is born is the kind the soul-entity had determined as a result of past thoughts.

So perhaps we all need to think beautiful thoughts to improve our appearance, though we should also remember that good looks are not the most notable aspect of some of the world's greatest achievers.

Elsewhere in his book, Percival adds:

The form and features of a person change little more from existence to existence than they do at various periods in a life on earth. Thinking changes features gradually during life. Pictures of the average person taken at corresponding periods of two or even several lives would show little difference. The physical parents may or may not be the same, but the features furnished by heredity, no matter from what parents, are the same for a string of lives, with the ordinary person.

Quite how he arrived at that conclusion is unclear, but photographic evidence *is* now increasingly being offered by others in support of reincarnation. Scottish reincarnation researcher and hypnotist Tom Barlow, for example, demonstrated this similarity impressively[4] in the case of Mrs. A. J. Stewart, an English playwright whose dreams since childhood of a bloody end to a former life culminated, at the age of thirty-eight, in the realization that she had been King James IV of Scotland, the last British monarch to die in battle (1473–1513). He had declared war on England and was killed at the Battle of Flodden when leading his men south while King Henry VIII's troops were fighting the French.

Born Ada F. Kay in Lancaster, England, in March 1929, her life had been haunted by "far memories" of that former existence, which she recorded in two books. "AJ," as she liked to be called, became a BBC scriptwriter and moved to Scotland, where she clearly felt more at home. In discussions with Tom Barlow about her former royal life, she produced two black-and-white photos, explaining that she could clearly remember, as James IV, having her portrait painted and had commissioned the photographs to show, as closely as she could, her pose and what she was wearing for the portraiture. She

A. J. Stewart and King James IV

then searched to find the painting of "herself" (or "himself") and eventually located it at Newbattle Abbey, close to Edinburgh, and had it photographed for comparison. Barlow examined them closely and made transparencies of both images to achieve a more precise comparison by overlaying one on another. He noted that the face was more elongated on one of the images, but "when the images are superimposed, not only are the eyes perfectly aligned in the direction that they are looking, but the horizontal distance between the eyes is exact. Similarly, the nose and mouth are also in vertical alignment, and when the male image is brought up to match the female features (a man's skull is normally longer than a woman's), there is total symmetry." Barlow adds, "It is also unusual that the present personality should have such a close physical likeness to the past incarnation, especially over a timescale of some 450 years."

At the First World Congress on Regression and Past-Life Therapy, held in the Netherlands in 2003, I discovered I was in the presence of none other than the soul known earlier in history as John Adams, second president of the United States. Not that Walter Semkiw, an American doctor, behaved any differently from anyone else in the pleasant Dutch surroundings, apart from expounding a passionate belief in reincarnation as one of the presenters. He has continued to do that, as author of three books—two of which are focused on what he regards as the scientific evidence for rebirth. In the first, *Return of the Revolutionaries,*[5] he presents a host of cases, supported by photographs, that show similarities in appearance between well-known twenty-first-century individuals and their previous personas. As with Clarice Toyne, the physical similarities are frequently striking, but are they enough? Among the questions his research raises are: How did Semkiw identify these past incarnations, and how sympathetic to this concept are the famous people he has identified?

It transpires that Semkiw's methods are similar in some respect to Toyne's in that he often received spiritual assistance. Initially, Dr. Semkiw—who has served as assistant chief of occupational medicine at a major medical center in San Francisco for a number of years and before that was medical director of Unocal 76, a Fortune 500 company—was skeptical about reincarnation when told by a medium in 1984 that he was John Adams reborn.[6] When he did decide to examine the idea, in 1996, "I found that I did see myself in him, based on common physical features, personality traits, and interests." He also recognized some of Adams's friends and family among people close to him. Before long, Semkiw found that "intuitions and synchronistic events" were leading him to recognize other reincarnations and the discovery that "facial architecture stays the same."

The results he produced between 1996 and 2002 were undoubtedly intriguing, but could easily be dismissed as one man's guesswork or fantasy. This was something Semkiw fully understood. In addition, he was encountering problems in establishing all the past-life matches he was looking for by his own efforts. He overcame that difficulty (as far as believers are concerned) in late 2001 with the involvement of trance medium Kevin Ryerson, who channels spiritual guides and whose name will be familiar to readers of Shirley MacLaine's books on reincarnation and spiritual exploration, including *Out on a Limb, Going Within,* and *The Camino.* Semkiw had experimented with other psychics before meeting Ryerson, but "without finding anyone who could reliably identify past-life matches." What was different about Ryerson was that the guide he channeled for this corroborative work, called Ahtun Re, was not only able to confirm some of the past-life associations identified by Semkiw but also to reveal new cases for Semkiw to investigate.

"I know I can be criticized for using a spiritual source for a portion of my case material," Semkiw writes.[7] "I counter that view with the observation that Ahtun Re has demonstrated abilities validated by objective criteria. Further, most of the matches that he has established involve prominent individuals, the majority of whom have agreed to be included in this book." In fact, 90 percent of the cases presented in his book were originally hypothesized by Semkiw or other independent researchers and only 10 percent were identified by Ahtun Re. Semkiw is now so confident of the spiritual guide's ability to confirm an individual's past lives that he checks *all* cases with Ahtun Re and publishes only those that receive his confirmation. However, we are left to guess which of his well-known subjects happily agreed to be included in his book and which have slipped in merely because they never objected. It's a heady mix of cases, including Bill Clinton, Al Gore, George W. Bush, Tony Blair, Dennis Kucinich, Oprah Winfrey, and Ralph Nader. He has since published a second book, this time in India, which includes some of the cases already mentioned but also offers a new section related to the subcontinent's political legends and film stars, including Indira Gandhi and Benazir Bhutto.

One case that Semkiw explored produced an unexpected, even sensational, result. The researcher was particularly interested in identifying other participants in the American Revolution and, to that end, had concluded that physician and politician Matthew Thornton, born in 1714 and a signatory to the Declaration of Independence, was now living in the twenty-first century as Norman Shealy, MD, coauthor of *The Creation of Health*.[8] Their facial architecture, we are told, is consistent, and Ahtun Re confirmed the match. Semkiw duly contacted Dr. Shealy, a neurosurgeon who is a renowned pain-management expert and inventor of the TENS pain-blocking unit, as well as having acted as consultant to leaders in various specialties, including the personal physicians of Presidents Eisenhower and Kennedy. Dr. Shealy's response expressed surprise at the past-life link with Thornton about whom he knew nothing. However, he revealed that he *was* aware of another past life—as John Elliotson, a prominent English physician, and he readily shared that information with Semkiw.

It came about, he said, while attending a Neuroelectric Society conference in Aspen, in 1972, during which a lecturer mentioned Elliotson's name in a reference to mesmerism. "When he said that," Shealy told Semkiw, "I felt as if someone had thrust an iceberg down my back, and I said to myself, 'My God, that's me.'" He journeyed to London the next year, and, arriving at University College Hospital where Elliotson had his office, he felt immediately at home. He learned more about his former self's interest in mesmerism and the fact that some of Elliotson's patients, in a mesmeric trance, became clairvoyant and easily made diagnoses. Incredibly, before he had heard of Elliotson, Shealy received a $50,000 grant from a Fortune 500 company, which asked to remain anonymous, "to study psychic diagnosis." He subsequently visited seventy-five individuals who were said to be excellent clairvoyants and found five who were between 70 and 75 percent accurate in their diagnoses. In summary, Dr. Norm Shealy informed Semkiw, "I have never had any question that I was John Elliotson in my last life." Armed with this information, Semkiw was able to confirm a physical resemblance between all three—Thornton, Elliotson, and Shealy.

Joseph R. Myers is a professional engineer and reincarnation researcher who sees nothing unusual in looking similar from one life to another. He believes it was a truth known to the Classical Greek philosopher Plato four centuries before the birth of Christ. Interestingly, this revelation about physical similarities came to him in a way not dissimilar to Clarice Toyne. He describes "a single elevated consciousness experience" which provided him with "the pattern for an accurate hypothesis." In this heightened state of awareness he watched a parade of gradually changing faces from a series of his own previous lives. "Each of the faces bore a striking resemblance to the previous one," he explains. "The fine lines and wrinkles indicated personalities that varied widely but the whole structure of the face changed only gradually."

It was not, however, the process that led him to discover his own previous existence as Edward Bellamy (1850–1898), socialist and author of *Looking Backward*,[9] a novel that was one of America's most popular and best-selling books at the end of the nineteenth century. It told the story of a man who travels forward in time, in a hypnotic trance, from 1887 to the year 2000 where he finds himself in a socialist utopia, a scenario that allowed Bellamy to express his views on economics and make predictions about America's financial future. This was a subject in which Joseph Myers had a deep interest, and after he had lectured on the subject, someone remarked to him that he had clearly read *Looking Backward.* He had not, but intrigued, he obtained a copy of the famous book as well as some biographies of its author. "Before I'd read two chapters, I realized that I had written it," Myers tells us. Various details in the biographies also provided meaning to flashbacks and dreams that had plagued him for many years. Having concluded that he had once been Edward Bellamy, he also noted a striking similarity in their appearances, so much so that a friend mistook a framed image of Bellamy to be a picture of Myers.

This experience gave Myers the determination to research reincarnation in greater depth, which he did with the enthusiastic support of his wife, Mary, until her death in November 2004 at the age of eighty-six. Over the years he has lectured on the subject; produced a book, *Edward Bellamy Writes Again;*[10] and built up an impressive collection of illustrated reincarnation case studies that he presented on a website, in much the same way as Walter Semkiw has done, putting the emphasis firmly on facial recognition from one life to the next. It is not, however, clear where the confirmation for these "matches" comes from in most of his cases. They include Lyndon Baines Johnson, the thirty-sixth president of the United States, and his wife Claudia "Lady Bird"

Johnson, who appear to look remarkably similar to Andrew Johnson, the seventeenth president, and his wife, Eliza Johnson. Not only do they have the same surname, but they were both vice-presidents to assassinated presidents of the United States—Lincoln and Kennedy.

But now we start running into problems because on Myers's website Walt Disney is shown as the reincarnation of Charles Dickens, and J. K. Rowling, author of the Harry Potter books, is said to have once lived as C. S. Lewis, author of *The Chronicles of Narnia*. There do appear to be some interesting facial similarities between the two, but when we turn to Semkiw's research, we are told that Charles Dickens has reincarnated as J. K. Rowling. Could they both be correct? Dickens lived from 1812 to 1870 and Walt Disney from 1901 to 1966. C. S. Lewis' life was from 1889 to 1963 and J. K. Rowling is still with us, having been born on July 31, 1965. So, while these dates work for Joseph Myers's claims, they clash with Semkiw's because, if Charles Dickens had been reborn as Walt Disney, he couldn't also have been reborn as J. K. Rowling, since she was born eighteen months before Disney's death (though overlapping lives are discussed briefly in the final chapter). This suggests we cannot take such claims at face value, as it were, without supporting evidence and the need to cast a very critical and perhaps cynical eye over the source of such assertions. I came across one probably well-meaning website,[11] which had excellent resources for anyone exploring reincarnation, but was also profusely illustrated with "case studies" that its compiler refers to as "possible matches" . . . derived after the author either "read about the people, communicated with them in writing, or met with them." What amused me was how many actors featured in her cases, due I am sure to how more accessible their images are in the search engines' databases.

Both Clarice Toyne's inspirer, the Teacher, and Kevin Ryerson's spiritual informant, Ahtun Re, explained that *they* had access to the Akashic Records. This term comes from a Sanskrit word meaning "sky," "space," or "aether" and is used in Theosophy and anthroposophy to describe a compendium of mystical knowledge encoded in a nonphysical plane of existence. "I flick through their files like a history book," the Teacher told Toyne, explaining how he was able to peer into the pasts of famous individuals.

That facility was not at the disposal of Doralice Santana, a Brazilian woman who had an unexpected vision during a hypnosis session in September 2005.

She saw herself walking down a path flanked with trees and coming across a stranger—a man with a heavy, dark mustache and dressed in nineteenth-century fashion with a wide tie and wearing a hat and coat. "He said he had been with me all my life," she explains. Although Doralice's native language is Portuguese, she knew English well enough to teach it at university level and so she understood what this unknown man was saying. She asked him who he was and he replied, "Don't you recognize me? I'm Edward."

Doralice emerged from the hypnotic trance in tears, feeling she had lost someone she loved and determined to find him. Fortunately, she had access to the modern equivalent to the Akashic Records: computer search engines. She clicked on "images" and typed in "Edward." "His face was very clear to me," she says. "I wanted to confirm whether that experience was real." Today, such a search produces almost seventeen million options on Google. In 2005 it would have been fewer, but sifting through them to find the Edward she met when in a trance was a formidable task. Undaunted, Doralice spent almost eight hours on her quest before the image of Edward Bellamy presented itself on her computer screen. Through this, she learned about the book he had written, bought a copy, and by the time she reached the third or fourth chapter was convinced she had read it before. Her curiosity about Bellamy eventually led her to Joseph Myers's website and his belief that he is Bellamy's reincarnation. Despite being unsettled by that revelation, Doralice emailed him in January 2006 and they began corresponding. Myers soon had his own vision in which he met a spiritual being "of overpowering beauty" that he believed was Doralice. He concluded that she was the reincarnation of Bellamy's wife. Their emails became more emotional and within two months Myers proposed to Doralice, and in her own words, "I couldn't say 'no,'" even though at that time they had not even exchanged photographs. They decided they would settle down together in the city of Recife, Brazil, where Doralice works as an administrator.[12]

Their story may not convince others of reincarnation's reality, but Joseph and Doralice have no doubts. They married in the United States on December 9, 2006, for what they believe is the second time—one hundred twenty-five years after they were first joined in matrimony in their former lives, as Edward and Emma Bellamy.

Chapter 12

What Sex Is a Soul?

Most of us think of ourselves as either masculine or feminine, and we probably assume our soul has the same sexuality. That, of course, can be dismissed as an absurd notion: Sex relates to our physical existence whereas the soul derives from a spiritual dimension in which sex presumably plays no part. Such an assumption may prove to be false once reincarnation research answers some of the questions that still puzzle us about the rebirth process and the nature of the soul.

Why is it, for example, that the majority of cases that are suggestive of reincarnation relate to males? In a review of 1,095 cases investigated by Stevenson,[1] 62 percent were male and 38 percent female. I have not seen statistics that analyze cases in which the subject remembers more than one previous existence, but my knowledge of such cases suggests that the lives remembered are more often in the same sex as their present incarnation. Certainly, recalling a life as the opposite sex is the exception, rather than the rule, but is far from being rare. The reason for this apparent gender fixation may have more to do with memory than it has to do with sex. Studies of past-life accounts note the very high incidence of violent deaths in the previous life, suggesting that the trauma triggers the memory of that experience and the life events preceding it. Without being able to offer any supporting evidence, I suspect that more males than females die violent deaths, either because of the nature of their work or the fact that they are more prone to kill each other, as well as usually being on the front line in conflicts. It has also been suggested that the imbalance in cases of past-life recall simply mirrors male dominance in most cultures. Yet another explanation I have seen is that men's lives are more memorable than women's and so are more easily recalled.

Those conjectures and sweeping generalizations, however, bring us no closer to understanding whether souls have a sexual orientation or are asexual. A century ago it was a topic that occupied the best brains within Theosophy, in which reincarnation is a central tenet of its doctrine. Founder Madame Helena Petrovna Blavatsky assured her followers that "the immortal spirit is sexless, formless, an emanation from the One universal BREATH" and "may reincarnate in either sex and may change from one to the other gender in different lives."[2] Some felt the need to elaborate on that. Susan E. Gay, for example, contributed a "Theosophical-Feminist Manifesto"[3] in *Lucifer,* the society's journal. In her view, men who were manly and women who were very feminine were the *least* developed souls. Writing in 1890, thirty-eight years before universal suffrage extended the right to vote to all adult women in Britain, she said that if men were to realize that at some point in the future they might find themselves incarnated in women's bodies, they might think twice about their assumption that women were "naturally" subordinate to men. That wasn't going far enough for another Theosophist writer, Frances Swiney, who wrote that all souls were essentially feminine. She conceded that they had to pass through a masculine state on their soul journey but dismissed this as a "kindergarten" period. While these views may seem extreme to twenty-first-century eyes, we should not forget that even Charles Darwin, in *The Descent of Man,* had suggested that man's "superiority" to women was a direct result of evolution.

It was a man, however, who introduced what may be seen as a more reasoned approach to the highly volatile question of the soul's sexuality. Charles Webster Leadbeater, a former English clergyman and admired writer on the occult who eventually became a leading Theosophist in the early 1880s, argued that the soul changed sex, over many lives, in order to learn lessons and evolve, but it generally stayed in the same sex for between three and seven incarnations, before changing gender. In 1898, Leadbeater and Annie

Besant (who was to become president of the Theosophical Society in 1908) conducted an investigation into the past lives of Miss Annie Wilson, Mrs. Besant's secretary and housekeeper. They claimed to trace Miss Wilson's previous lives back to before the birth of Christ. A theme that emerged in a book[4] (part of a series) based on that research, and recurs in Leadbeater's other past-life genealogies, is that individuals who work together as Theosophists in their present lives have had close relationships in the past, usually involving changes of sex. For example, Miss Wilson had been Annie Besant's son in one life and many years later in China, had been her wife. In another of their works,[5] they traced the many past lives of Jiddu Krishnamurti, the Indian boy whom Leadbeater and Besant discovered and believed would be the vehicle for the appearance of a world teacher they were expecting. Leadbeater caused outrage in Theosophical circles by claiming he had, in previous incarnations, been married to Krishnamurti and his brother, Nitya, and that Christ, in a previous incarnation, had been married to Julius Caesar.

Canadian psychologist and Theosophist Charles Lazenby offered a revision to Leadbeater's theory of having up to seven incarnations before changing gender. He believed the soul experienced six lives as the same sex, to varying degrees, and for the seventh incarnation it would "take on the coloring" of the opposite sex before living six lives in that gender. He described this transitional phase as an "intermediate sex" in which individuals' physical bodies belonged to one sex but their thoughts and desires belonged to the other. Today, the expression "being in touch with one's masculine or feminine side" is an acknowledgment that our sexual nature is far more complex and perhaps less defined than previously thought, at least in those cultures where homosexuality is now socially acceptable and where transgender individuals can receive psychological and surgical support to help them deal with the conflict they perceive between their minds and anatomy. "I've been born in the wrong body" is a statement of fact frequently made by the latter, who make that assertion without any belief in a past life or the possibility that reincarnation may have influenced the way they feel. But that's a possibility that Ian Stevenson was very aware of when he researched cases suggestive of reincarnation, particularly where the remembered life was in the opposite gender. In such cases, it is not uncommon for a child to insist on wearing clothes that would normally be worn by the opposite sex or to play games that would be associated with that sexual identity. He describes them as "sex-change" cases, by which he means they have changed sex from one life to the next, not that they have had surgery.

I mentioned briefly (chapter 8) the cases investigated by Stevenson of young children in Myanmar[6] with memories of having been Japanese soldiers occupying their country during World War II. One of these cases displays very strong sex-change behavior.

While pregnant, before the birth of her daughter Ma Tin Aung Myo on December 26, 1953, her mother dreamt on three occasions that a stocky, shirtless Japanese soldier wearing short pants was following her and saying he would be coming to stay with her and her husband. When her daughter was around four years old she was seen to be weeping. Asked why, she said she was pining for Japan. From then on, Ma Tin Aung Myo began talking about her previous life when she was a Japanese soldier stationed in the village when the Japanese were occupying Burma. She said she had been a cook and that an Allied plane had strafed the village and killed her. Interestingly, her mother, Daw Aye Tin, told Stevenson that she had known and even been friendly with a cook in the Japanese army who had been stationed in the village, but she did not know if he had been killed there.

Ma Tin Aung Myo was able to describe what she (as a male soldier) was doing and wearing when the aircraft approached, and how she had tried to avoid the bullets but was hit in the groin and died instantly. With the passing years it became clear to Ma Tin Aung Myo's parents that she was not a typical young Burmese girl. She complained that the climate was too hot and the food was too spicy for her tastes; she preferred sweet things and also liked to eat fish half raw. She also frequently expressed her feelings of "homesickness" as well as anger towards British or American people when they were mentioned in her presence. Above all, she was very boyish, asking her father to buy her a toy gun, playing at being a soldier, and playing football and cane-ball—interests not shared by her three sisters and only brother.

She also insisted on wearing men's clothing and having her hair cut in the style of a boy. Her school disapproved, requiring her to go to school dressed appropriately as a girl. When Ma Tin Aung Myo refused to obey the rules and her school would not compromise, she dropped out at around the age of eleven, which limited the work she could do in the future. When Stevenson

met her in 1974 he found that she was earning only a meager income as a
hawker of foods at a nearby railway station.

Her masculinity did not fade with maturity. Indeed, not only did she show
no interest in marrying a man but even said that she would like a wife. She
clearly thought of herself as a man and disliked being considered a woman,
even asking to be called "Maung" (the respectful name used when addressing
a boy) rather than "Ma," which is used for girls.

Like the other Japanese cases investigated by Stevenson, it is "unsolved"
because Ma Tin Aung Myo was unable to provide names or other facts about
the claimed previous life that were verifiable. The researcher tells us that she
is atypical since in most "sex-change" cases the children adjust to their anatomical sex within a few years of their past-life memories fading. But the
continuation of her gender preferences into adulthood is not unique, as is
illustrated in the following cases from Brazil and Portugal, both investigated
by Ian Stevenson.

There were two impressive cases of apparent reincarnation in the Lorenz
family, who lived in Brazil's southernmost state, Rio Grande do Sul, and
produced thirteen children. The father, Francisco V. Lorenz, was a schoolteacher who made detailed notes in each case. The first concerned a girl
named Sinhá who was lonely and deeply unhappy and eventually allowed
her health to deteriorate, dying at about the age of twenty-eight in 1917. She
had befriended Francisco's wife, Ida, and on her deathbed, Sinhá promised
Ida Lorenz that she would return as her daughter, saying "at an age when I
can speak on the mystery of rebirth in the body of the little girl who will be
your daughter, I shall relate many things of my present life, and thus you will
recognize the truth." Ten months later Ida gave birth to a daughter, Marta,
who from the age of two-and-a-half began speaking about her memories of
life as Sinhá. This, of course, is not a sex-change case, but it does indicate a
soul's ability, it seems, to return in the sex of its choice. That appears to be
also what had already happened in the Lorenz family, but this time with a
soul returning as the opposite sex.

The Lorenzes' first child was a boy, Emilio, who died in infancy. When
a daughter was born in 1902 she was named Emilia, after the boy, though
it seems unlikely that the parents believed her to be the reincarnation of
their son. Emilia was unhappy throughout her short life, apparently feeling

awkward as a girl. She told several of her brothers and sisters that if there were such a thing as reincarnation she would return as a boy in her next life. Emilia rejected a number of proposals of marriage and told her siblings she would die single. She also attempted suicide on several occasions and died in 1921 from the effects of taking cyanide. Later, her mother believed Emilia had contacted her at Spiritualist meetings, expressing regret for her suicide and promising to return, but this time as a son. The Lorenzes are said to have been incredulous that their dead daughter could be reborn as a boy, but soon after the birth of their thirteenth child, Paulo, in 1923, they had to give the possibility serious consideration.

Paulo was unlike their other sons. For the first four or five years of his life he refused to wear boy's clothes. Stevenson reports,[7] having interviewed many of the family members forty years after the events, that Paulo insisted at that young age on either wearing girls' clothes or none at all. He took to wearing boys' clothes only when a pair of trousers was made for him from one of Emilia's skirts, remarking, "Who would have said that after using this material in a skirt, I would later use it for trousers?" He showed no interest in doing what boys usually like to do, playing instead with girls and dolls. His sexual orientation slowly changed to being masculine; though, Stevenson adds, "important elements of femininity were obvious into his teens, and a strong feminine identification (for a man) persisted to the time of my investigation of the case in 1962."

Although Paulo appears to have made a rare few direct statements about having been Emilia, many of his actions mirrored those of his dead sister, and he displayed knowledge of events in her life as well as habits and aptitudes. Emilia is said to have shown "a genius for sewing" and the same was true for Paulo. He explained his sewing skills by saying he had been taught by Dona Elena (who had taught Emilia) and accurately described her house even though he had not visited it. He also recognized a sewing machine that had belonged to Emilia, declaring, "This machine was mine and I have already sewed a lot with it."

Stevenson testifies that Paulo, at the age of thirty-nine, "retained a more feminine orientation than most men of his age." The story of Paulo does not have a happy ending. He took part in political activities, and after the overthrow of the president in 1963, Paulo felt the authorities were watching him. He became delusional, felt persecuted, and killed himself (after previous, unsuccessful attempts) by pouring an inflammable liquid over himself and setting his clothes and body on fire in 1966. This, Stevenson learned later, was one of the ways in which Emilia had also tried to take her own life.

In Portugal, Stevenson investigated another unusual case, again involving a birth within the same family and with a change of sex.[8] In 1960, just before her seventh birthday, Angelina Lopes was struck by a car and killed while returning from the beach with her mother, Irma, and two sisters. Irma Lopes was distraught, and though a strict Roman Catholic, she appears to have received some comfort from a psychic who assured her that Angelina would be reborn to her, but possibly as a boy. During her short but happy life, her daughter had once expressed the wish that she were a boy. In the seventh month of her next pregnancy, Irma dreamt of Angelina, who informed her that the baby would be a boy. He was, and was given the name Alfonso; then within a month, the family moved from Loures to Lisbon. An early indication that Alfonso could be Angelina reborn was when he began addressing Irma as "Dear Mother," a term the dead girl had used, but which her sisters did not. Stronger evidence soon emerged when Alfonso, aged four, and neighbors of the Lopes family, including a son, Hernani, who used to play with Angelina, visited them from Loures. Spontaneously, Alfonso asked Hernani, "Have you kept the wooden horse?" This was a toy Angelina had enjoyed playing with. "No, I gave it to Ana," Hernani replied. "Oh yes," Alfonso responded, "to Anihas and her little son"—a correct reference to the recipients of the gift, even though Alfonso had never met them.

On a later occasion, before he had started going to school, Alfonso went into the kitchen where his mother was cooking and noticed a red checked napkin. "Look, Mama, the napkin I used to take to school with my snack. I will take it again when I go back to school, won't I?" It was the napkin that Angelina used to take to school. Soon after Alfonso's own schooling began, Irma was asked to meet with his teacher, who informed her that Alfonso was claiming to be a girl and referred to himself using feminine words when writing or speaking. When the teacher tried to correct him, explaining he was a boy, Alfonso insisted, "No, I am a girl." He had stopped doing so by the age of seven.

Perhaps the most astonishing item of evidence presented by Stevenson in the Lopes case reminds us of one aspect of the Paulo Lorenz case in Brazil.

On his return from school one day, Alfonso spontaneously picked up a drinking glass and placed it inside a stocking. Then, taking a needle, he pretended he was repairing it, saying, "Oh, I have not done this for such a long time." Angelina liked to visit an aunt who was a seamstress and would pretend she was mending stockings in exactly the way Alfonso did. Irma Lopes confirmed that no one had shown the technique to her son before he spontaneously demonstrated it.

"I have followed some of these children into their teens and young adulthood or later," Stevenson tells us. "The majority gradually accept their anatomical sex, give up cross-dressing, and become more normal in all respects. A small number, however, have not adapted so well; they have remained fixed in the gender role of the sex of the previous life and usually are correspondingly unhappy." He was also consulted by two persons wishing to undergo sexual reassignment surgery who were certain that their gender dysphoria had not been influenced in any way by their parents. "They conjectured that their strong gender preference might have derived from a previous life, although they had no memories of one." Ever cautious, Stevenson adds, "Their explanation for their condition seemed plausible, but remained without any confirmation."

Chapter 13

Celebrity Believers

It's easy to make fun of some individuals who claim they were historically famous, but what are we to make of cases involving famous people who say they recall living sometimes quite ordinary lives in a previous existence? From the long list of celebrities in front of me—of whom show business people seem to feature prominently—I am going to discard those suspected of making the claim for publicity purposes or, at the very least, not offering a shred of supporting evidence. That shortens the list quite considerably. I've added the names of some famous people who expressed a strong belief in rebirth without claiming memories of a past life, or who have undergone regressions to what appear to be previous incarnations. I should also make the obvious observation that being famous does not give an individual a greater insight into life's mysteries than anyone else. So, I am including them not because we should pay more attention to their statements, but because their claimed experiences or opinions allow us to peer through an entertaining as well as sometimes illuminating cross-cultural window on reincarnation beliefs in the twentieth and twenty-first centuries, and occasionally earlier. I'll keep them brief and present them alphabetically, by surname.

ANDY BELL: Openly gay lead singer in British pop duo Erasure, which has sold over twenty million albums worldwide, Bell has declared, "I've been a woman many, many times, but being a man is new to me."

PHIL COLLINS: The London-born Genesis percussionist and solo star is one of only three recording artists to have sold over one hundred million albums. In 2010, he revealed[1] that he had lost his life in a previous incarnation at the Battle of the Alamo. The singer is now an avid collector of all things related to the thirteen-day seige in 1863 when Mexican troops launched a bloody attack on the Army mission near San Antonio, Texas. The wife of a fellow Alamo enthusiast is said to have identified Collins's past life as John W. Smith, a Texan courier who was known as El Colorado.

LORD DOWDING: Air Chief Marshal Hugh Dowding, who led the Battle of Britain in World War II, was a Spiritualist and also a firm believer in rebirth. He spoke publicly on the subject at Theosophist meetings, and in his book *Lynchgate*[2] he declared, "I am personally convinced beyond any shadow of a doubt that reincarnation is a fact."

JUDITH DURHAM: Lead vocalist in the talented 1960s folk group The Seekers Judith eventually stepped down in order simply "to do something else." She and her husband, Ron Edgeworth, were then initiated into an unnamed faith by an Indian master and began following "the path of God realization." After Edgeworth's death, Judith was asked where she thought he was. "My wish is that Ron has had his last birth and is now with God," she responded. "But he could already be in a womb somewhere. We said our farewells and I have no wish to see him again, even though I'm still attached to him in my heart."

RALPH WALDO EMERSON: The American philosopher and poet made his feelings about reincarnation clear in this quote, "It is the secret of the world that all things subsist and do not die, but only retire a little from sight and afterward return again. Nothing is dead; men feign themselves dead, and endure mock funerals, and there they stand looking out of the window, sound and well, in some strange new disguise."

KENNY EVERETT: It is hardly surprising that the British disc jockey and TV comedian believed in reincarnation. For twelve years he was married to a Spiritualist medium, Lee, who is now a regression therapist. On a TV chat show, eight years before his death from AIDS in 1995, he said his wife had told him that in a previous life he had been her son, and before that he was a Spanish nun. In a later newspaper interview, he said: "I see death in my own philosophical way. I can't imagine I was nowhere before this. I'd like to come back living in Italy or Spain or somewhere. As long as I don't come back bald or in Bosnia, I don't mind."

PABLO ARMANDO FERNANDEZ: When asked in an interview[3] if he believed we lived more than one life, the celebrated Cuban poet replied: "Absolutely, I am convinced of it because of my own experience. If I didn't believe in reincarnation I would be ungrateful and a hypocrite. In the farthest corners of the five continents, I have found true sisters and brothers who have recognized me as an essential part of their own being. My soul chose Cuba to be born here. It is the soul that chooses the place and the family in which one reincarnates. I have experienced very strange things that have to do with karma and that is not by chance. Those are lessons which allow us to understand what we have been in other times and with whom we have been."

GLENN FORD: The Canadian-born American actor whose movie career spanned seven decades was a close friend and confidante of psychic Peter Hurkos. When approached to make a movie about the Dutch psychic, Ford decided to explore the subject in depth. As well as studying Hurkos's abilities, the fifty-four-year-old actor underwent three past-life hypnosis sessions in December 1975, during which he appeared to recall five previous lives.

HENRY FORD: The American industrialist whose Model T revolutionized transport was a firm supporter of reincarnation and was convinced he had lived before as a soldier killed at the battle of Gettysburg. In a 1928 newspaper interview[4] he explained: "I adopted the theory of reincarnation when I was twenty-six. Religion offered nothing to the point. Even work could not give me complete satisfaction. Work is futile if we cannot utilize the experience we collect in one life in the next. When I discovered reincarnation it was as if I had found a universal plan. I realized that there was a chance to work out my ideas. Time was no longer limited. I was no longer a slave to the hands of the clock. Genius is experience. Some seem to think that it is a gift or talent, but it is the fruit of long experience in many lives. Some are older souls than others, and so they know more. The discovery of reincarnation put my mind at ease. If you preserve a record of this conversation, write it so that it puts men's minds at ease. I would like to communicate to others the calmness that the long view of life gives to us."

BENJAMIN FRANKLIN: At the age of twenty-two, the philosopher, inventor, and one of the Founding Fathers of the United States of America, wrote his famous and eloquent epitaph: "The body of Benjamin Franklin, printer (like the cover of an old book, its contents torn out and stripped of its lettering and gilding) lies here, food for worms: but the work shall not be lost, it will (as he believed) appear once more in a new and more elegant edition . . . revised and corrected by the author."

LYNNE FRANKS: PR doyenne Lynne Franks, on whom the TV comedy series *Absolutely Fabulous* was loosely based, believes there is a past-life explanation for her promotional activities: "I have been told that in another life I was a female shaman, like a tribal spiritual leader, banging drums around a village. I've never thought about it before, but that's it. I'm a drum beater! . . . So I'm not going to stop beating drums; I'm going to be beating a different message."

URI GELLER: According to researcher Walter Semkiw, Uri Geller was once the famous Victorian medium D. D. Home. Whether the famous spoon bender accepts that past-life identification is unknown, but he certainly appears to embrace the concept of reincarnation. During his early career in Israel, Geller demonstrated in theaters and nightclubs, using hypnotism as part of his act. He has told[5] of an occasion when he took an Arab back in time, counting back the years "into the minus numbers." What happened next astonished Geller: "He was a Moroccan, he told me later, but when I asked him who he was, he replied in Polish, 'My name is Leopold.'" Geller says he yelled for an interpreter who translated the man's account of a past life for fifteen minutes. "I can think of nothing that explains all the details, except to admit that we live again and again. . . . He was an Arab Moslem who had been, without any doubt, a Polish Jew."

ROBERT GRAVES: The English poet took issue with those who said Christianity rejected reincarnation with these words: "No honest theologian therefore can deny that his acceptance of Jesus as Christ logically binds every Christian to a belief in reincarnation—in Elias's case (who was later John the Baptist) at least."

GLENN HODDLE: The former England football manager astonished the world in 1998, first by revealing he was using a spiritual healer to treat injured players, and then a few months later by declaring his belief in reincarnation.[6] "I think we have been here before, spiritually. It's my belief that this physical body is just an overcoat . . . I think we make mistakes somewhere down here and I think our spirit has to come back and learn. That's why there is injustice in the world. Why are there certain people born into the world with terrible physical problems and why is there a family who has got everything right, physically and mentally?" Unfortunately, the backlash from those comments led to Hoddle's dismissal as the England team's manager though he did receive support from the Dalai Lama.

VICTOR HUGO: The great French romantic novelist and poet was a regular attendee at seances while he was a political exile on the island of Jersey. There he communicated with spirits who taught the doctrine of reincarnation, though he reported[7] that animals and aliens from the planets Mercury and Jupiter also gave messages.

ENGELBERT HUMPERDINCK: The pop singer claims to have lived ninety-five previous lives, including one as a Roman emperor, though as far as I know he has made no claim to being the reincarnation of the original Engelbert Humperdinck, a German composer born in 1854 who died in 1921, fifteen years before the birth of Arnold George Dorsey, the singer's original name before he changed it officially.

THOMAS HUXLEY: "I am certain that I have been here as I am now a thousand times before, and I hope to return a thousand times," the English philosopher and zoologist wrote in *Essays upon Some Controverted Questions.*

RUDYARD KIPLING: In *The Sack of the Gods,* the English writer took a very logical approach to reincarnation: "They will come back—come back again—as long as the red earth rolls. He never wasted a leaf or a tree. Do you think He would squander souls?"

DAVID LLOYD GEORGE: The British Liberal politician who was prime minister of the United Kingdom's coalition wartime government from 1916–1922 said of his traditional Welsh upbringing: "The conventional heaven with its angels perpetually singing, etc., nearly drove me mad in my youth and made me an atheist for ten years. My opinion is that we shall be reincarnated."

LORETTA LYNN: Country and western singer Loretta Lynn recalled during a regression that she had been a Cherokee princess; an American farmer's wife; an Irish woman; an old, bedridden man; and a waiter in the 1920s. She had also been a maid to one of England's King Georges with whom she had an affair, though this led to her murder by one of the king's male confidantes who was exceedingly jealous.

SHIRLEY MACLAINE: Keeping track of the much-loved actress's many former lives is difficult. She has done more than most to promote general interest in reincarnation, having written several books on the subject,[8] but is accused by some of bringing a serious subject into disrepute. Among the claimed previous incarnations she has recalled was one as a dancer in an Egyptian harem, a maidservant to Nefertiti, a model for Toulouse-Lautrec, and the lover of Charlemagne (King of the Franks and Emperor of the Romans) by whom she bore three children. In more recent times, she claims, Charlemagne was reborn as Olaf Palme, the assassinated Swedish prime minister, with whom she had an affair.

GUSTAV MAHLER: "We all return," the great German composer declared. "It is this certainty that gives meaning to life, and it does not make the slightest difference whether or not in a later incarnation we remember the former life. What counts is not the individual and his comfort, but the great aspiration to the perfect and the pure which goes on in each incarnation."

NORMAN MAILER: The Pulitzer Prize-winning author was an expert on reincarnation and Egypt. He read one hundred books on the subjects during his eleven-year research for *Ancient Evenings,* which deals with the twentieth Dynasty of ancient Egypt. In a 1983 magazine interview[9] coinciding with publication of that book, he said ". . . any culture whose eschatology was founded on such a notion as reincarnation was congenial to me." The book's main character reincarnates three times.

HENRY MANCINI: Under hypnosis, the composer of *Moon River* and *The Pink Panther* theme tune is said to have discovered that he is the reincarnation of nineteenth-century Italian composer Giuseppe Verdi, whose works include *Rigoletto, La Traviata, Aida, Otello,* and *Falstaff.* Before that he had been an engineer for the building of the Great Pyramid at Giza and an officer in the court of Montezuma, the last Aztec emperor in Mexico.

W. SOMERSET MAUGHAM: "Has it occurred to you that transmigration is at once an explanation and a justification of the evil of the world?" asked the English novelist and dramatist, adding, "If the evils we suffer are the result of sins committed in our past lives, we can bear them with resignation and hope that if in this one we strive toward virtue our future lives will be less afflicted."

STEVIE NICKS: Best known for her work with Fleetwood Mac, the American singer is adamant that this is her last incarnation on earth, having lived before as an Egyptian high priestess, a concert pianist, and a victim of the Holocaust.

GEORGE S. PATTON: American General George "Blood and Guts" Patton's actions made him a hero in the Battle of the Bulge, the largest and bloodiest fought by American troops during World War II. It was, however, just one of the conflicts in which he played a role over many lifetimes. He could remember being at the walls of Tyre with Alexander the Great and was equally certain that he was a member of the Greek phalanx that met Cyrus II, the Persian conqueror who founded the Archaemenid Empire half a century before the birth of Christ. In other lives he fought in the Hundred Years' War on Crécy's field and as a general with Joachim Murat, the brilliant eighteenth-century cavalry leader. The feelings evoked by this string of past-life memories were movingly captured in Patton's 1944 poem, "Through a Glass Darkly."

PACO RABANNE: Concurrent with his career in haute couture, the French fashion designer has been on a spiritual quest, inspired by his own experiences. These include past-life memories, which formed the basis of one of his books, *Journey: From One Life to Another.*[10] He tells us that in the distant past he came to Earth from another part of the universe to help found Atlantis. In ancient Egypt he was a priest who helped assassinate and embalm Tutankhamen and by the eighteenth century he was a prostitute—the only life he recalls in which he was a woman.

HELEN REDDY: Internationally known for her anthem, "I Am Woman," singer Helen Reddy has retired from her musical and acting career that spanned thirty-five years and is now a clinical hypnotherapist in Sydney, Australia. She says she has had flashes of her own past lives, but nothing of any consequence. Some of her patients regress to previous lives, she said in a recent interview,[11] but she also gets many deceased relatives—a parent or grandparent—communicating. "A lot of people can get too embroiled in past lives and the most important life is the one you are living right now," she adds.

DEMIS ROUSSOS: The larger-than-life Greek singer, who was once known as "the love walrus," believes all of his four wives had been with him in past lives.

ALBERT SCHWEITZER: "Reincarnation contains a most comforting explanation of reality by means of which Indian thought surmounts difficulties which baffle the thinkers of Europe"—so said the German theologian, philosopher, and physician.

STEVEN SEAGAL: The well-known star of action movies was declared a reincarnated lama and sacred vessel of Tibetan Buddhism in 1997 by Penor Rinpoche, the Supreme Head of the Myingma School. One critic, however, said that as much as he respected Penor Rinpoche, "recognizing a tulku, especially when it is an American person with lots of fame and fortune, is like buying a stock option."

MARTIN SHEEN: The American actor is a firm believer in reincarnation, arguing that families do not come together by chance. "Our children," he explains, "come to us to make up for indiscretions in past lives. They are hold-overs from lifetimes we have not solved."

JERRY SPRINGER: Those who have watched Springer's TV shows may find it difficult to picture him as an English knight, but that is the life he saw after being regressed on TV by Dr. Bruce Goldberg.[12] He recalled being severely wounded in battle, defending the honor of a noblewoman who later employed him as a butler because he could no longer function as a knight. Today, he realized, that woman is his daughter.

SYLVESTER STALLONE: With a psychic mother, it should be no surprise that Stallone volunteered to be regressed on the same TV show as Jerry Springer. He reported lives during the French Revolution, when he was beheaded by the Jacobins, and as a male American Indian. Asked how he felt about the way he died in France, he replied, "It doesn't hurt. You don't feel anything except your head hits the basket." He also remarked that his North American Indian life appeared to have bled through into this one for he can do Indian dances, such as the eagle dance, and feels a very strong kinship with wolves.

LORETTA SWIT: The actress who played Major "Hot Lips" Houlihan in the long-running TV series *M*A*S*H* is a staunch believer in reincarnation. She says[13] she often senses events from her past lives. Loretta believes in one former life she was a princess in seventeenth-century France in the royal court of Louis XIV and in another she was a powerful, eleventh-century Chinese landowner who ruled over a large estate. That life seems to have spilt over into the present one in which she owns many Chinese rugs, statues, and vases. "Even my housekeeper is Chinese."

B. J. THOMAS: "Raindrops Keep Falling on My Head" and "Hooked on a Feeling" are among the million-selling songs we associate with the singer-songwriter who, along with his wife, Gloria, was regressed by Dick Sutphen.[13] They recalled past lives together, including one in Switzerland in 1742 in which she had been his grandmother, and another where they were an aristocratic French couple. By the 1800s he was a "grand and terribly fat" opera singer. They were back together again in this life, Gloria revealed in her regression, because "we're paying back a lot of karma. Karmically we arranged it so there is no way to run away from ourselves or each other."

MARK TWAIN: In his autobiography, the American author and humorist claimed, "I have been born more times than anybody except Krishna."

REV. CHAD VARAH: Although a Church of England priest, the founder of the Samaritans (whose telephone hotline offers people the opportunity to be listened to in confidence and which has extended globally to become Befrienders Worldwide) was a firm believer in reincarnation. He spoke openly on the subject in TV interviews and in a documentary about his life, and his autobiography was appropriately titled *Before I Die Again*.[14] On one TV show he said we had all been on earth before "as a human being and sometimes you've been a different sex."

RICHARD WAGNER: The German composer declared, "In contrast to reincarnation and karma, all other views seem petty and narrow."

CHARLES, PRINCE OF WALES: The heir to the British throne is known to have an interest in reincarnation. In a piece he wrote about the need for less materialism in celebrating the Millennium,[15] he said the "concept of renewal" was not the monopoly of Christianity but "is central to many of the great faiths." He added: "Socrates taught that the soul reincarnates every thousand years, when it has the opportunity to make a new choice about its destiny."

DIANA, PRINCESS OF WALES: Much of what we read about the late princess is wild rumor and hearsay. But Andrew Morton's *Diana: Her New Life* (1994), published three years before her tragic death, is acknowledged as being close to an official biography because of the subject's secret cooperation. In it he reveals Diana believed she had been a nun in a previous life. Among the thousands who paid tribute to her following her death was Gulu Lalvani, the Asian businessman who found himself at the center of media speculation after taking Diana to a nightclub earlier in the year. He reflected Hindu belief when he said: "She believed in reincarnation. She'll be back."

WALT WHITMAN: The American poet expressed it beautifully when he wrote, in "Song of Myself," "And as to you, Life, I reckon you are the leaving of many deaths, (no doubt I have died myself ten thousand times before)."

MONTEL WILLIAMS: Before being regressed by Dr. Bruce Goldberg, the TV host was hostile to the idea of reincarnation,[16] but that did not prevent him from experiencing a dramatic past life in which he was a slave in the South during the American Civil War. He saw himself surrounded by four or five white farmers who wounded him, then killed him. The lesson learned from that previous life, it was suggested, has influenced his present incarnation in which he is involved with many groups aiding underprivileged black children.

WILLIAM WORDSWORTH: The English poet expressed his belief in reincarnation with these words from "Intimations of Immortality":

> *Our birth is but a sleep and a forgetting:*
> *The Soul that rises with us, our life's Star,*
> *Hath had elsewhere its setting,*
> *And cometh from afar:*

Not in entire forgetfulness,
And not in utter nakedness,
But trailing clouds of glory do we come
From God, who is our home

We tend to think of belief in reincarnation as an "Eastern" philosophy, but as most of the comments and events quoted above indicate very clearly, it is a concept that is embraced by many individuals in the West. What is more, for the most part it does not rest on a particular religious belief but either on personal experiences or by applying logic to the hidden processes behind the evolution of humankind and reaching the conclusion that an indestructible soul is at the core of our being.

Part Three

The Future

Chapter 14

The Feel-Good Factor

For a large number of people—perhaps the majority—their interest in reincarnation is not about finding scientific evidence of past lives but about attempting to understand themselves better or make sense of their current life by putting it into perspective against a possibly rich, adventurous, and historical tapestry of former existences. As well as those who seek to be regressed simply out of curiosity, others undergo regression in the hope that it will reveal past-life reasons for the problems or conditions they are experiencing in this life and offer a degree of resolution.

Why would being regressed to a past life increase satisfaction with the present life?

Surprisingly, it seems that for many individuals the situations they "see" during a regression provide insights that can have a rapid and lasting therapeutic effect. A number of therapists are on record as saying that of all the "tools" available to them in treating patients, past-life therapy is one of the most efficient in terms of producing a "feel-good factor" in those who experience it—which is probably why the number of people working in this field has grown exponentially from the handful who pioneered its use in the 1960s. Interestingly, some of those practitioners—notably Brian Weiss and Robert G. Jarmon—were skeptical of a past-life dimension to their therapy work until they stumbled across it accidentally, usually by not giving a hypnotized patient the correct, or precise, instructions when regressing him or her to an earlier event in the current life and being astonished when the subject began talking about a totally different existence.

Jarmon, for example, had been a physician working at a New Jersey hospital for two decades but had also offered psychiatric counseling for many of those years. In his book *Discovering the Soul*[1] he tells of a patient, whom he calls Anna, who consulted him in 1986 in the hope of altering undesirable habit patterns that were leading to weight gain. She readily agreed to hypnosis but after two months developed abdominal pain and stopped menstruating. Jarmon knew there were a number of possible causes including an ovarian cyst, colitis, diverticulitis, appendicitis, or even an ectopic pregnancy. With her symptoms intensifying, her abdomen becoming more swollen and tender, and all his own tests proving negative, Jarmon insisted she see her gynecologist immediately. He diagnosed an ectopic pregnancy (in which the fetus develops in the fallopian tubes instead of the uterus). An operating room was prepared for exploratory abdominal surgery while she was sent to the sonography lab, which would confirm the presence of either a fetus or something unusual, such as a tumor. It found nothing. The operation was cancelled, and Anna returned to see the psychotherapist to explore the reasons for these physical symptoms.

"Go back now to where your problem started," Jarmon told Anna, once she was relaxed on his couch. "Go back to where it began."

At that point in time, he tells us, he had neither belief nor interest in reincarnation, which he regarded as "the stuff of fiction" with no more relevance "than a belief in leprechauns." For that reason, the hypnotic instruction he gave Anna was meant to apply to her current life, since as far as he was concerned, that was the one and only life she had lived and was capable of exploring. He was about to be disabused of that notion. Deep in trance, Anna began to moan and hold her side. When he asked what was troubling her and where and when this was happening, Anna replied, "Long ago, not now, not here." Then, to his utter astonishment, she said, "My name is Elizabeth," and began speaking of a life in which she was nineteen years old and experiencing great difficulties in the fifth month of pregnancy. A priest and a physician sat at her bedside, discussing her condition. The doctor

The Feel-Good Factor   141

wanted to remove the unborn child from her womb to save her life, but the priest insisted that "we cannot take life even to save a life," adding, "If God wills that the woman die, then she dies." And that, it seems, is precisely what happened, in an unspecified European country, at an unknown time, because it seems Elizabeth felt the answers to these questions were unimportant. Anna then described her after-death experience, floating up and into a tunnel of light.

The sequel was as startling for Robert Jarmon as the regression itself. When she emerged from trance, Anna declared, "My God! You finally did it, Dr. Jarmon. I feel great. The pain is gone." So, too, were the abdominal swelling and tenderness. Anna phoned the awe-struck physician later that day to announce that her period had started again, after an interval of five months. When she returned to his consulting room a few weeks later and was taken back once more to that deathbed experience, she relived it in greater detail. In doing so, Anna, whose parents, husband, and entire family were Jewish, began reciting words that Jarmon, a Roman Catholic, recognized as the Act of Contrition, the prayer a Catholic says at the end of confession or during last rites. Out of trance, it was clear that Anna had no knowledge of this religious ritual. It was at that moment, Jarmon reveals, that he knew he had "begun a journey unlike any we could dream up."

The answer to the question, "Are these therapeutic memories evidence of reincarnation?" has to be that in 99 percent of cases they fail to provide convincingly detailed information about the lives they describe. The evidential nature of memories produced by such regressions is usually far weaker than cases involving children's spontaneous recall, though there are exceptions. This is not to say that regression cases necessarily involve false memories. It could be that the regressed person *is* seeing an actual past life, but the nitty-gritty of that life—names and dates, for example—is of secondary interest. After all, the therapist is not being paid by the client to unearth fascinating facts about a long-forgotten previous existence; his or her remuneration comes from helping the patient deal with or overcome certain issues. Asking for names, addresses, and the other "mundane" data on which reincarnation researchers thrive would just get in the way of the ultimate, therapeutic goal. In fact, some past-life therapists are not even concerned whether their patients are actually experiencing a real past life when regressed or are simply subconsciously fabricating a former existence to help them come to terms with or rationalize their current situation.

In 1994, reincarnation researcher and academic psychiatrist Ian Stevenson cast a very critical eye over the whole subject in a paper titled "A Case of the Psychotherapist's Fallacy."[2] He kindly allowed me to publish it in full, in the same year, in a magazine I edited, resulting in numerous readers' letters from practitioners who strongly disagreed with his views. Stevenson's paper opened with a brief history of modern psychotherapy, from the publication of H. Bernheim's classic *Suggestive Therapeutics* (1884) and psychotherapy's subsequent increasing acceptance by the general public, if not by scientists, through to H. J. Eysenck's paper "The Effects of Psychotherapy: An Evaluation" in the *Journal of Consulting Psychology* (1952), which concluded there was no evidence that it was effective. This was followed by far more research into different modes of psychotherapy—such as psychoanalysis, behavior therapy, and client-centered therapy—which, Stevenson tells us, "failed to show any superiority in outcomes of one type over another." Other studies even showed that having psychotherapy was no better than being on a waiting list or being given an "attention placebo."

That, in turn, led to speculation that if psychotherapy itself was not producing the effective outcomes, perhaps something else was achieving the successful results that some patients were reporting. Maybe it was the therapist's supportive and empathic behavior or the belief on the part of both therapist and patient that psychotherapy would be beneficial—and not the method *per se*. Whatever the explanation, various therapists turned to hypnosis as a way of differentiating their methods from the common ones, and that—particularly after the publication of Morey Bernstein's Bridey Murphy book—opened up the possibility for some of them to use it to explore past lives. Although Stevenson has shown that phobias can apparently have a past-life origin in spontaneous cases suggestive of reincarnation, he argues that looking for phobias in a past life with hypnosis "requires overlooking the considerable evidence that hypnosis, although it may make some memories more accessible than they ordinarily are, can also increase inaccuracies in memory and, in sum, does not enhance memory. Undeterred by such facts, numerous hypnotherapists have promoted hypnotic regression to previous lives until it could fairly be described as a current fad."

Then, rubbing salt into their wounds, Stevenson adds:

> Although many of these hypnotists are obviously uneducated and
> behave little better than circus shills, others have graduated from first-
> rate colleges and universities, as the jackets of their books never failed
> to emphasize. Such hypnotists (with proper education and training)
> should know better, but some of them nevertheless write books that
> sell well in "New Age" bookshops and airports. To my knowledge,
> however, none has ever published a report of claimed beneficial
> results from this kind of therapy in a referred scientific journal.

To support his argument, Stevenson cites five examples of reported past
lives remembered under hypnosis where the facts given are demonstrably
wrong. For example, he cites a patient who claimed to remember a life in
1473 when she had been a boy "living within sight of mountains in the Netherlands"—the flattest country in Europe, if not the world! He spares the
blushes of the therapists in all of these cases by not naming them.

Stevenson goes on to say:

> I particularly disapprove of those therapists who try to have it
> both ways—affecting to be themselves uncommitted and indiffer-
> ent to the question of whether reincarnation occurs or does not,
> they yet entice patients with the hope of a cure from remembering
> a previous life. It is not difficult to induce a hypnotized person to
> imagine himself or herself in a previous life. The scenes are vivid,
> the emotions intense; no wonder the patients become convinced
> that they have relived a real previous life. A thus regressed patient
> may, moreover, seem to remember some traumatic experience in
> the "previous life" that is relevant to present symptoms, and he or
> she may feel better afterward. These events, however, are not evi-
> dence that the patient did remember a real previous life. In only a
> tiny handful of cases has the apparent previous personality stated
> verifiable information. In even fewer is it possible to be confident
> that any accurate details were not normally learned.

Stevenson's criticisms will be viewed as churlish by many of those operating in this field who argue that he is missing the point. It has to be admitted,

though, that the claims made by some of those offering past-life therapy are suspect, and the need for licensing of such therapists is an important issue that still needs addressing in some countries. For one thing, setting themselves up exclusively as past-life therapists *presupposes* that the origin of their patients' problems is in a previous existence. Therapists ought to be casting their net widely, starting with the present life, when looking for the causes of fears, phobias, or other psychological problems in their clients. Similarly, those needing therapy are perhaps not best placed to determine, in advance of a consultation, why, or in which life, their difficulties originate.

Hans TenDam, a Dutch past-life therapist with considerable experience, concedes in his masterly book on the subject *Deep Healing* that little research has been carried out into the efficacy of this method of treatment. The most important, in his view, was conducted by American therapist Winafred Blake Lucas who has shown that during effective past-life regression both patient and therapist exhibit a brain-wave pattern that is simultaneously high on beta and delta and low on alpha and theta. Hazel Denning, who was executive director of the Association for Past-Life Research and Therapies (APRT), which is now known as the International Association for Regression Research & Therapies (IARRT), also published the results[3] achieved by eight therapists with nearly one thousand patients between 1985 and 1992. Of the 450 patients who could still be tracked after five years, Denning found that almost two-thirds reported benefiting from the treatment. In 24 percent of cases, the symptoms had completely gone, and a further 23 percent reported considerable or dramatic improvement, while another 17 percent had experienced noticeable improvement. Just over one-third, 36 percent, said they had not improved.

Ronald Van der Maesen from the Dutch Association of Past-Life Therapy (NVRT) has also conducted several research programs, including a sizeable project in 1994 that investigated the results of regression therapy with 401 clients—many of them difficult cases—of thirty-two therapists. Six months after the end of this therapy, 50 percent reported that their problems had largely or completely been solved. A further quarter of those questioned showed some improvement, while 20 percent experienced no benefit. These results were reached on average with fifteen hours of therapy conducted during a total of six sessions. His doctoral dissertation of 2006 provides information on his other studies, including the past-life therapy outcomes of subjects suffering from Tourette's syndrome and others who heard voices.[4]

Carol Lawson and Miles Austin

I was ambivalent about the benefits of past-life therapy until I met Carol Lawson, a successful British businesswoman who also gave psychic readings. This unusual combination had resulted in the media, in the south of England, calling upon her to express an opinion on a variety of paranormal topics whenever the need arose, and she was usually happy to oblige. So, when Meridian Television needed a volunteer to be hypnotized back to a past life by London psychotherapist Miles Austin, Carol readily agreed. During that recorded regression, Carol wept as she spoke vividly of a life on Atlantis. It made riveting television viewing, and everyone was pleased with the result. Off camera, Carol told Miles about a disfiguring problem that had plagued her for thirteen years and defied medical explanation. At six-monthly intervals, her thumbs would become sore and swollen, resulting in the nails falling off. New nails would then gradually start to grow until, once fully developed, they too would be ejected. Doctors suggested it might be a form of dermatitis, but the creams they prescribed did not alleviate the unsightly problem. So Carol readily accepted Miles's offer to conduct a private regression to see if it would throw any light on her condition.

At a later date, under hypnosis and away from the inquisitive gaze of TV

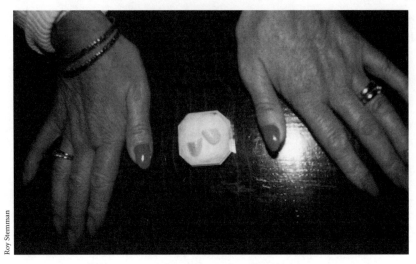

Roy Stemman

Carol Lawson's thumbnails

cameras, Carol recalled three other past lives: a Native American Indian male with a daughter named White Star; a Cockney woman named Mary; and a West Country woman named Melissa who lived over 380 years ago. It was Melissa's life that held the key to Carol's puzzling medical condition. She described an event in that life when curiosity led her to walk to a neighboring village to find out why the men of her own village had climbed onto their horses and followed a carriage that regularly passed through as it transported a grand person—possibly royalty, she thought—to some unknown destination. Reaching this village, she saw the horses tied up outside a building from which dreadful screams emanated. Peering inside, when a soldier's back was turned, she saw a man in a long red and gold robe being horribly tortured. Unfortunately for Melissa, her presence was soon noted and she was taken inside where she, too, was tortured . . . by having dirty iron thumbscrews applied to each hand and slowly and painfully tightened.

"I felt a tingling in my hands and fingers and my arms going numb, as I relived the torture," Carol told me when I interviewed her about the experience.[5] "It was horrible." Then the soldiers took Melissa outside and she was hanged. Such stories are commonplace in the consulting rooms of past-life therapists and are either a tribute to the resilience of the human soul to cope with such extreme experiences, or evidence of the tremendous imagination of the human mind when encouraged to express itself freely. Carol added this observation about her experience: "Up until that time, even though I was involved in spiritual work, I never gave any thought to reincarnation. I don't know whether I believed it or not. It certainly had never occurred to me that my nail condition might have a past-life cause."

The punch line to Carol Lawson's story is that after remembering those cruel events of 1613 under hypnosis, Carol's condition started to improve dramatically. During a two-and-a-half year period she had lost her thumb nails only once. She kept the rejected nails, beautifully painted and sitting on a bed of cotton wool in a small presentation box, as physical evidence of her past-life memory.

Though past-life therapy does not usually produce one iota of tangible, checkable evidence to support reincarnation, perhaps the results are themselves proof positive of the soul's continuation through many lifetimes, carrying with it issues that need to be resolved even centuries after the events that gave rise to them. On the other hand, there is plenty of evidence that, in the wrong hands, some therapies can be damaging rather than beneficial to the client. In a single case in Texas (1997) $5.8 million was awarded to a patient who had been led to "remember" that her family had "practiced murder, cannibalism, sexual abuse, and incest." And two patients of a Minnesota psychiatrist were awarded sums of $2.67 million and $2.5 million because "under hypnosis and sodium amytal, and after being fed misinformation about the workings of memory, they had come to remember horrific abuse by family members." I must stress that these cases all involved feeding false information or leading questions during regressions to periods in their current lives, but the same influences could just as easily apply to past-life regressions, though hopefully without the dreadful consequences of the former.

The following advice to would-be past-life therapists from Trisha Caetano, a former APRT president, is very relevant in this respect, partly because of its common sense but also because it shows that many individuals without proper training or appropriate qualifications were being attracted to psychotherapy:

> One of the greatest offenses in therapy is telling people what their problem is, where it began, and what they need to do to get rid of the problem. Second to that is bludgeoning the person into the area the therapist thinks the problem is in. The basic truth is that

the individual knows exactly what the problem is because he or she experienced the cause. Because the client knows the cause, he or she also knows the solution. It is our responsibility to get the client to this subconscious information so the problem can be resolved. Asking questions and hearing the answers with no value judgments until the "interview" is finished is a cornerstone of this technique. The cardinal rule is: don't evaluate, invalidate, judge, give opinions, hint, tell, or bludgeon. Ask.

Not all psychotherapists believe our past lives are the cause of so many problems in our present existence. Scottish reincarnation researcher Tom Barlow has been regressing people for more than forty years but insists, "I don't see that anything that has occurred in a past life should create a problem in this life. If people have that fixed in their mind, it is a psychosomatic situation and it should be able to be removed fairly quickly. To me, past-life regression therapists are jumping on a bandwagon."

British Jungian psychologist and Oxford University graduate Dr. Roger Woolger, who now lives in the USA, views the subject very differently. He told me in an interview[6] in 1994:

> I think my position is a little unusual. I don't hold a belief for reincarnation. I don't care whether you can prove it or whether you believe in it or not. What is certain is that when the unconscious mind is given the opportunity to play stories as if they are past lives, it comes up with staggering solutions, releases, and spontaneous healings that you don't get in other therapies. So, as a pragmatist, I've been drawn to past-life regression as a much more effective therapy than a lot of others. . . . In comparison, past-life therapy is faster, it works deeper with the emotions, and it gets to the core of certain bodily "stuck" places . . . holding patterns.

Having said all that, Woolger admitted that with time and experience he had learned, "there's a very clear distinction between the fantasy reconstructions and the genuine article: they have a different feel about them." He has been regressed many times during which "remnants" of past lives have come to the surface. His book *Other Lives, Other Selves*,[7] he told me, had received only one bad review. That was from Dr. Ian Stevenson, and a lively exchange between them had ensued because, Woolger explained, "I felt he was basically putting down therapy. As I say in the book, there's a whole difference in approach between parapsychology, which is trying to prove reincarnation, and therapy, which is using stories that may or may not be true. It's important that we do not confuse these two very different approaches."

That's easy for a past-life psychotherapist to say, but for the public at large it must be very difficult to differentiate between the two distinct methodologies involving apparently recovered memories, usually obtained under hypnosis. On the one hand, we have in-depth regression research, such as the Bridey Murphy case and others, which Stevenson and others regarded as providing possible evidence of reincarnation. On the other, we have regression dialogues that are produced with the aim of solving a patient's problem, but make no attempt to verify the statements made. While the former are evidence-based, the latter are judged only on their ability to provide physical or mental benefits for the subjects, and many therapists acknowledge some, at least, to be fabrications constructed by the mind to achieve a therapeutic outcome. Since this is a book on reincarnation rather than about healing or the power of the mind, my focus must be on cases that provide evidence of individual consciousness surviving death and being incarnated in a new body, rather than on the colorful stories that emerge in past-life therapy. Nevertheless, we cannot totally dismiss the latter, as they may offer us insights that are not available from spontaneous cases.

The irony is that while Stevenson's dogged perseverance in collecting a wealth of information about spontaneous cases has given us the most scientifically based data on reincarnation, it is the best-selling books by leading regression therapists, not all of whom are as candid as Woolger about alternative interpretations of their patients' memories, that are shaping public attitudes on and belief in past lives. However much scientists may dismiss their work, we need to recognize that, at the very least, the efforts of past-life therapists, in addition to bringing benefits to many sufferers, may also be opening windows on the enormous potential of the human mind and the evolution of the soul, through which man has not been able to peer . . . until now.

An exciting future of discoveries about human consciousness, its enormous potential, and possibly its ability to exist independently of our bodies awaits those brave enough to explore further.

Chapter 15

Life between Lives

On my first visit to Lebanon to make a TV documentary on the reincarnation beliefs of the Druze community, I was joined by Roland Littlewood, a bearded, pipe-smoking professor of anthropology and psychiatry from London's Royal Free and UCL Medical School, who is a skeptic of things paranormal. Working with him was a very enjoyable experience even though we interpreted many of the cases differently. So it was a great blow when he was taken ill toward the end of filming. At first, it was thought he was suffering from an inner-ear infection, but it soon became clear that it was more serious. As soon as it was realized he had suffered a stroke he was taken to a Druze hospital and then transferred to the American Hospital in Beirut. Thankfully, he survived the experience and after several weeks of medical care was able to fly back to the UK and continue his academic pursuits. The filming had to be abandoned, of course (I returned later with a different skeptic, Chris French,[1] to remake the documentary), which gave me plenty of time to ponder the possible outcomes for Roland. The Druze believe that, at death, the soul *instantly* transfers from one body to another. In the unlikely event that Roland's condition deteriorated and led to his demise, should we go immediately to the hospital's maternity ward in search of his reborn soul? As it happened, we did not need to do so. Besides, it would be a couple of years, at least, before any of those newborn babies would be showing signs of unusual and identifiable behavior—such as wishing to smoke a pipe.

The Druze, as far as I know, are the only people who believe in instantaneous rebirth. Their teachings tell them that "the soul does not lose a breath between one life and the next." While there are some Druze cases where this seems to have been the case, there are others where there is a gap—sometimes months, sometimes years—between a remembered death and the date of birth in the current incarnation. They explain this by saying that in such cases the soul would have incarnated into *another* body during that "missing" period, but for such a short time that it has not brought any memories of that existence into the present life. If that were so, I would expect a far higher infant mortality rate than appears to be recorded among the Druze.

Leaving their unique belief aside, we have to accept that any explanation of the reincarnation process must also include the intermission periods between death and a new life that is a feature of the vast majority of spontaneous and regression cases. Where does the soul go between lives? What does it experience in that spiritual existence? Who decides it should return for another incarnation on earth?

Reincarnation researchers do sometimes get positive responses when they ask spontaneous-recall subjects if they remember what happened to them after they died but before they were reborn. In some cases information about an interlife is volunteered without any prompting by the investigators. It is difficult to draw any meaningful conclusions from the statements that have been recorded, except to observe a significant cultural or even religious influence on what they claimed to have experienced in the spiritual world. In some cases, however, the existence experienced could best be described as unexciting or monotonous. Take, for example, H. Fielding Hall's very early account[2] about the devoted husband and wife in Myanmar who appeared to be reborn as twin boys Maung Gyi and Maung Ngé in 1886 (see chapter 10). As well as telling Hall about their former lives as husband and wife, the boys also spoke of an intermediate stage. "After they died, they said they lived for some time without a body at all, wandering in the air and hiding in the trees. This was for their sins. Then, after some months, they were born again as twin boys."

In Ian Stevenson's extensive Turkish files, we find the case of Celal Kapan,[3] a boy who recalled a life as Saban Sagur, a young man who was killed on a ship at a dockyard in 1951, about a year before Celal's birth, after being accidentally struck by a heavy object. The boy described the scene immediately after his death, watching as an ambulance rushed him to hospital, a doctor pronouncing him dead, and his body being washed. He even described his own burial.

In chapter 8 I discussed cases in which Burmese children were apparently born with memories of being Japanese soldiers who died in that country during World War II. The British also suffered many casualties and fatalities while fighting the Japanese occupation, and among them was a British airman who died when his aircraft crashed and was apparently reborn to a woman in that village. When Ma Par, born in 1946, was able to speak she claimed to have been that airman, describing a previous life in England in which she was married with a wife and three sons. She spoke of the crash and subsequent burial alongside the pilot. When describing herself in that life, Ma Par said she was blond. Unusually, this was mirrored in her present life: Stevenson describes her as an albino. After death, the airman went to England to see his family, but the "King of Death" did not allow him to stay there. He paid a second visit but was again pulled back to Burma and "ordered to be reborn." Throughout his time in the interlife state, he had stayed in an acacia tree, close to where the plane had crashed and its occupants had been buried. One day, he had seen a group of women inspecting the graves. He particularly liked one of them, followed her, and it was to her that he was reborn.

The famous Shanti Devi case (see chapter 5) also includes quite extensive memories of an intermediate stage between lives. She described that experience in response to questions from a number of investigators, including Stevenson. In Sushil Bose's monograph, *A Case of Reincarnation* (1952),[4] when asked how she felt at the time of death, Shanti replied:

"Just before death I felt a profound darkness and after death I saw a dazzling light. Then and there I knew I had come out of my body in a vaporous form and that I was moving upwards. . . . I saw that four men in saffron robes had come to me. . . . All the four seemed to be in their teens and their appearance and dress were very bright. . . . They put me in a cup and carried me. . . ." Shanti Devi said she was taken to "the fourth plane" where there were no dwelling places and even more saints than she had seen on the third plane and they were brighter in appearance. "And in the midst of them, seated on a huge, dazzling throne, was Lord Krishna (one of the most popular Hindu gods). He was showing each person a record of his activities on earth, good and bad, and accordingly what would be his condition in the future."

Compare that with another case involving an Indian girl, Santosh Sukla,[5] born in Uttar Pradesh in 1950, who claimed before the age of two to remember a previous life when she was called Maya in Sitapur. Her parents believed she was referring to a distant cousin, Maya Devi, who had died two years before Santosh's birth, and who had predicted she would be reborn into the Sukla family. During the investigation of this case, Santosh's mother told the researcher about her daughter's description of what had happened to her, after she (as Maya) had died:

> She also said that after dying she was taken by four persons to a river and was immersed. She cried, and then she was taken up to a village where there were many fruit trees and gardens. There was a person there in yellow clothes sitting on a wooden bed. She sat down there, against a pillar, and remained. There were many persons there, and they used to pluck the fruit and eat them; but she just watched these persons. Then she was asked if she would eat; she accepted and they gave her some fruit. She remained there for a year and was then born here.

Let me quote one more of Stevenson's cases, this time of a Thai boy, Chanai Choomalaiwong,[6] born in 1967, who remembered being Bua Kai Lawnak, a schoolteacher who had been shot and killed in 1962. As well as recalling that he had been taken to Ban Khao Sai to be cremated, Chanai gave this description of what happened to him after death:

> They punished me by forcing me to take off all my clothes and took me to a huge lotus pond. They then forced me to walk through the jungle of Lotus. I experienced great pain and discomfort for a long time until I reached the edge of the pond. They gave me my clothes back at that time. Two men accompanied me for a distance and said that they could come only so far and that I was to be reborn now. Then I was unconscious after that.

A five-year period elapsed between the death of Bua Kai and the birth of Chanai, yet his description of an intermediate stage gives no sense of that passage of time. Stevenson comments: "Chanai's apparent memories of events after Bua Kai's death resemble in some respects accounts of other subjects and differ in other respects. For example, Thai subjects more commonly remember being taken in hand by one discarnate person—the 'man-in-white'—not by two."

Dutch researcher Titus Rivas has drawn attention to the memories of Feitze Beimholt[7] who was one of the stars of *Showroom,* a popular TV series in Holland about eccentric individuals with unusual ideas or alternative life styles. Feitze lived with his brother Hendrik somewhere in the countryside in the rural province of Drenthe, following a rather traditional way of life, while everything around them was changing. A self-made philosopher, Feitze wrote a booklet, *De Nieuwe Dag in Gouden Glans* (New Day in a Golden Glow), which includes a spiritual worldview involving concepts such as reincarnation. In it, he claims to have had vivid spontaneous memories of a previous life, also in Drenthe, in the nineteenth century. It ended with a rather sudden and unexpected death, and he recalls seeing his own body lying on the ground. The sunlight he then saw was indescribably beautiful.

Feitze simply wandered about through the fields and enjoyed everything he saw. He did not attend his own funeral, as he was too fascinated by his experiences as a wandering spirit in Drenthe. His adventures continued for about seventy years, then:

> One day, I was walking along a sandy road and I reached a crossing. For the first time, I had to choose whether I would go left or right. I went right and after a while I reached Smilde, near the woods of Jans Popken. On a small lane, there was young woman standing, who had pitch-black hair. She was collecting firewood and I walked around her. Suddenly, I felt a pleasant warmth and I knew that I was safe. The little woman was pregnant.

So, how do these often rather puzzling spontaneous accounts of a spiritual existence between lives compare with what is said by subjects during regression when discussing that waiting period between lives? The celebrated Bridey Murphy case (chapter 6) provides us with an immediate example.

Hypnotist Morey Bernstein was very curious about the interlife stage and repeatedly asked the entranced Virginia Tighe what had happened to her after she had died as Bridey Murphy. She described her death from a fall, watching her own funeral, and seeing the tombstone on her grave. Bridey also spoke of a place where she waited, where there was no sense of time, no day or night, just a constant light. Only the sense of sight and sound remained. There were no rules and no war. Some of the people there had the ability to see into the future, and they told her that there would be a war before she was reborn. Virginia was born in 1923, five years after the end of World War I. Most surprising was the revelation that there is no love in the "other world." Indeed, families did not necessarily meet or stay together. Bridey said she met her younger brother who had died when a baby: He had grown up and could now speak. Immediately after death she stayed with her (living) husband, Brian, for some while, but he would not listen to her when she tried to talk to him. She was aware of day and night because Brian would go to bed and get up. It appears that this place (the spirit world, or another dimension) was confusing to Bridey, either at the time or when trying to recall it. Eventually, a woman came and told her that it was time to go—and then she was born again, as Virginia Tighe.

Many subjects who have explored apparent past lives under hypnosis have brought back insights about the purpose of their present existence and the choices they had to make before being reborn. One of the best examples of this is recounted in psychiatrist Brian Weiss's book *Many Lives, Many Masters*.[8] A patient named Catherine was able to recall several past lives that not only shed light on her fears and phobias in this life but also cured them. What made Catherine so remarkable, however, were her discussions with "the Masters" whom she met in the interlife and who were able to speak to the hypnotist through her. At first, Weiss dismissed what she was saying as mumbo-jumbo, but his attitude rapidly changed when they conveyed personal information about his father and baby son that Catherine could not possibly have known.

"Your father is here, and your son, who is a small child," the voice speaking through the entranced subject announced. "Your father says you will know him because his name is Avrom, and your daughter is named after him. Also, his death was due to his heart. Your son's heart was also important, for it was backward, like a chicken's. He made a great sacrifice for you out of his love. His soul is very advanced . . . His death satisfied his parents' debts. Also, he wanted to show you that medicine could only go so far, that its scope is very limited."

Brian Weiss admits those words made him go numb. His son Adam had died when he was only twenty-three days old, in 1971, from a heart condition exactly as Catherine had described—which occurs in only one out of every ten million births. His father died in 1979, and his daughter is named after him. This experience, he admits, "completely changed the rest of my life." Catherine also discovered from the Master Spirits that she had lived eighty-six times in the physical state so far. Weiss's book has had a tremendous impact on people around the world. When I met him in London in 1996 it had already been translated into many languages and had been at the top of the best-selling list in Taiwan for the past two years. It has also sold as many copies there—a country with a population of twenty-five million—as it has in the USA.

We do know, however, that other therapists were making similar discoveries about the interlife as early as the 1970s. The case files of Canadian Dr. Joel Whitton, for example, whose medical qualifications were obtained at the University of Toronto and who went on to become chief psychiatrist of the Toronto school system, go back to 1973. Within a year he had discovered the interlife (or *bardo,* to use a Buddhist term). His book about those experiments, *Life between Life,* was coauthored with Joe Fisher.[9] He had selected Paula Considine, forty-two, who is described as "the epitome of the North American housewife," as his main research subject because of her ability to be hypnotized to a deep level. Starting early in October 1973, she spent more than one hundred hours in deep trance over a period of a year, giving coherent descriptions of a long succession of incarnations, most of them female. Six months into the experiment, something totally unexpected happened.

Paula was talking in a deep trance about a life as Martha Payne on the farm, when Dr. Whitton decided he needed to learn more about the last days of her previous life as Margaret Campbell. Interrupting the personality that was speaking through Paula, he instructed her: "Go to the life before you were Martha." He then waited for the child-like voice of Martha to be replaced by the French-accented enunciation of the elderly Canadian housekeeper. Instead, after a long period of silence, Paula announced, in a dreamy voice, "I'm in the sky . . . I can see a farmhouse and a barn." When asked what she was doing "up in the air," his subject replied, "I'm waiting . . . to . . . be . . . born. I'm watching . . . watching what my mother does." Her response to another of Dr. Whitton's questions was, "I have no name." Inadvertently, he had stumbled upon a state of disembodied awareness, but he did not begin to explore this mysterious zone until a year later and the publication of Dr. Raymond Moody's groundbreaking study[10] of near-death experiences, *Life after Life,* which reported patients' apparent encounters with the next world. "In time," according to Whitton's coauthor, "he would become the unofficial cartographer of this no-man's-land, a seasoned explorer in the limbo world."

California hypnotherapist Dr. Edith Fiore also reported in *You Have Been Here Before*[11] that some of her subjects ventured into the interim between lives to find "pure energy and light" while others saw "beautiful lakes, beautiful scenes, gleaming cities." There was also mention of encounters with "planners" or a "board of advisers," who assisted in the choice of the next incarnation, which in some cases was preceded by the soul "hovering" over its mother before birth. A year later, San Francisco clinical psychologist Dr. Helen Wambach revealed the results of her mass hypnotic studies in *Reliving Past Lives,*[12] showing that most people chose to be born even though they would rather remain in "the lightness and the love" of the between-life state. Her subjects told of having no gender in the interlife and said they had agreed reluctantly to be reborn after consultation with "advisers," "a board," or "a group of authorities."

Another psychotherapist who has been successfully tapping into the interlife state for some time is Dr. Michael Newton, whose *Journey of Souls: Case Studies of Life between Lives*[13] has helped him gain a reputation as an innovative therapist along similar lines to Brian Weiss. Indeed, he has made a specialty of exploring the spirit world through hypnosis. Exactly when he made this discovery is not known—his first book, which offers twenty-nine case studies, is largely devoid of dates—but it is said to be based on his interlife investigations during more than thirty years with over seven thousand clients.

The concept is simple and plays a significant role in Buddhist teachings, where "bardo" means intermediate or transitional state between two lives on earth. The interlife stage is not just a spiritual waiting room where we kill time between lives. It is our home. We are all spiritual beings who incarnate into the physical world in order to gain experience and learn lessons. We then return "home" where our spirit guides, helpers, and teachers assist us in understanding what was achieved in our last life, or perhaps what we failed to achieve, and advise us in making decisions about our next life. Psychotherapists are starting to refer to it as a "superconscious" or "metaconscious" state, and the discovery that it can apparently be accessed just as easily as a past life is causing a lot of excitement in the world of regression therapists. "Life-Between-Lives" (LBL) is the new buzz-phrase as they look to extend their capabilities—and clientele—in response to a growing demand. So much so that the first European Life-Between-Lives Regression Training took place in the Netherlands in 2004 at the World Congress of Regression and Past-Life Therapy.

We must acknowledge that apparent journeys to the interlife are no more verifiable than most past-life memories recalled under hypnosis. But if what is reported is for real, then it means that we each have an "oversoul" that knows precisely why we are here and what we are supposed to be doing with our lives, even though we are blissfully unaware that this spiritual blueprint exists. If this is so, then exploring a single past life in an altered state of consciousness is like looking at our soul through the wrong end of a telescope. Turn it around, and we could see and understand the full picture and start to reap the benefits.

Chapter 16

Future Lives

Hold tight. If you thought some of the claims about past-life incarnations and interlife memories that I quoted in the preceding chapters were difficult to swallow, the ride is about to get even rougher. So, fasten your seatbelts as we prepare for the inevitable turbulence that accompanies crazy concepts and far-out speculations—together with the possibility that some of them may just be real—as we set off . . . into the future.

Retrieving useful or beneficial information from past lives or the interlife may seem to have pushed back the boundaries of possibility to their limits, but that's not the case. There is, say some researchers, yet another dimension that may yield answers to our questions about life's purpose and to which psychotherapists and regressionists could hold the key. According to these paranormal explorers, individuals entering an altered state of consciousness can be guided to view their *future* lives as easily as their previous existences or the interlife existence. The problem, from an objective, scientific point of view, of course, is that most of us are not going to be around long enough to determine how accurate other people's visions of their next life will be. As for our own future lives, we won't be able to validate them until we have incarnated again, by which time we may well have forgotten the vision we saw in our present life. Such objections, I must add, have not dampened the enthusiasm of the handful of investigators who have made the future their specialty.

Claims of seeing or even traveling into the future raise inevitable questions about the nature of time, free will, and even the ethics of knowing in advance what is going to happen to us and acting on that information. Seers, soothsayers, and fortune-tellers have exerted influence over many of the world's leading decision-makers and continue to do so. Their predictions, right or wrong, invariably relate to events in the immediate future, whereas regressionists or their subjects appear to have extended the mind's precognitive reach into another existence: into lives that have not yet been lived, in bodies that have not yet been created. Let's take a look at what we know about the attempts that have been made to travel forward in time, in this life and the next.

Dr. Helen Wambach, a Berkeley, California, clinical psychologist and researcher, started looking at past-life regressions in the 1960s with a view to debunking them. Instead, she found the evidence compelling, sharing it with the public in *Reliving Past Lives* and *Life before Life*.[1] By then, she was also exploring at her workshops the possibility of "progression" into the future, both in her volunteers' present lives and also their next incarnations, in two distinct time periods: 2100 and 2300 AD. Her technique was to ask her subjects to move forward in time to their birthdays in those specific years, and she would then ask them a series of questions about the conditions surrounding life at that time. The purpose was to offer a "democratic" picture of the future, by gathering and collating the accounts of as many hypnotized individuals as she could and looking for common elements to help collectively predict the future, rather than following the prophecies of a single seer. One of her best regression subjects, Chet Snow, a sociologist and historian, recalled a life in the Crusades as well as being a Knight Templar. He also proved capable of journeying into the future with ease. He was not alone and Dr. Wambach soon had a sizeable database of such cases. However, she died in 1985 before she could complete a book based on this research, and so Snow took over the work as coauthor of *Mass Dreams of the Future*.[2]

While most of Wambach's subjects appeared to encounter an invisible barrier in describing events that had not yet happened in their present lives, Snow had no difficulty. Just as regressions relating to past events in the current life have given rise to false memories in some people, Snow suggests, similar problems seem to arise in moving forward in this life. In their current body, some memories—past and future—proved to be out of reach, or recalled inaccurately. He adds, "I think it has something to do with body-organ consciousness." When retrieving memories from a life in which they inhabited *another* body, they seemed to enjoy greater freedom.

"I was able to look forward in time and see some things that are already coming true," Chet told me when I interviewed him in 1995, "and these were published in the book ten years ago. Already the Yugoslavian situation is where it is, the Russians are looking much less nice—there's a real political difficulty there which could well come to the surface again, as I saw. The weather situation; the increasing volcanic and earthquake activity; all of which is put forward for the mid-90s, with drugs, drought, and floods all coming one on top of the other, as it were, are leading to this period of great change."

If the visions Snow experienced when progressed by Dr. Wambach are correct, much worse is to come, including, Snow added, "the disappearance of California and other parts of the USA." The dates given for most of these happenings were "awesomely close to the present day" when we discussed the Wambach research in the mid-1990s. For example, in one progression Snow found himself in Arizona in July 1998 where "there was this cold black sky, with sort of volcanic ash in the air, and I was coughing. I was not happy about being there, in a kind of survivalist situation in Arizona, but since that time, through a whole series of circumstances connected with my work, I've moved there and recently we bought a house in Northern Arizona."

Like many other predictions of doom over the centuries, the date referred to in Snow's progression (July 1998) has passed without incident in his personal life, and Chet and his wife, Kallista, continue to be prominent presenters of New Age ideas. There will be those who regard Snow's "progression" as a total failure, while others will see it as evidence that he was tuning into the likely scenario of climate change and associated events, but he got the timing wrong. As for the lives he and others foresaw in future centuries, only history will be able to pass judgment. But the statistics of those experiments tell us something rather intriguing. Only a very small percentage were able to progress to a life in 2100 AD, whereas a larger, but still small, number could retrieve information about living in 2300 AD. There may be several reasons for this, including the possibility that the world's population will be far fewer one hundred years from now, then begins to increase once more.

Jenny Cockell is an English chiropodist who wrote a fascinating book, *Yesterday's Children,*[3] about a past life in Ireland as Mary Sutton, which she remembered clearly and which she and independent investigators were able to verify. She followed that with a very different book, *Past Lives, Future Lives,*[4] in which she reveals that she also has "memories" of future lives. Cockell has undergone hypnotic regression to help recall what she has seen with greater clarity. She tells us she is certain she will be reincarnated as a female called Nadia in Nepal in her next life, when the planet's population will be smaller and its animal life will be less evident—possibly as a result of pollution. Her book contains sketches of the place in which she will live as Nadia: a village set against a hillside in a mountainous area characterized by finely textured, reddish-orange soil. Looking at a map of Nepal, Cockell felt drawn to an area to the east of the country, midway between Mount Everest and the border with India, and was able to identify a village named Kokuwa as the nearest to where she will live.

"This experience of looking into the future had a different quality from remembering my past life as Mary Sutton," Cockell explains. "Those had been like any other memories; there was never anything strange about them. With this new experience I felt that we were linked; I was living the feelings not so much as a memory, but as though I was in the past and two-year-old Nadia was remembering me from her life in the future, in the year 2040. Jenny Cockell's "memories" also include two other lives, one in the twenty-second century, when she is living in mainland Europe, possibly Poland, and is impoverished, and the other in the twenty-third century, when she is an American woman working as a technician for Unichem. She warns us that the human population appears to have dropped drastically and man's indiscriminate use of chemicals seems to be the main culprit.

"Whatever visions of the future may show, it is a future that includes each one of us," she writes. "Seeing ourselves and others in the context of time stretching back and forward through history and through many lives can help us to understand our individual roles as interdependent and our responsibilities as universal. Our attitudes today will make a difference to our future, as individuals and as a society. We can all make tomorrow a place for hope."

During my investigation of the subject, well over a decade ago, I was introduced to a group of people in the south of England who had been experimenting very successfully with time travel, and they invited me to give it a try. "We are able to direct you so that you experience only positive and beneficial things—so you will not be traumatized by seeing yourself, for example, being hung, drawn, and quartered," Frances Wade assured me.[5] "You can go anywhere and experience anything perfectly safely. Time is an illusion. Time travel shows that there is only the now: past, present, and future all together in the one." Having said that, the time-travel team told me that although many of their subjects had been able to travel into the future and see what would be happening to them days, months, or even years ahead, no one had yet been able to go so far forward that they entered a new incarnation.

I gave it a try, but was not convinced that what I "saw" and "felt" in my mind's eye was anything more than my imagination, though it did remain with me quite strongly for several days. I have to confess that the experience was decidedly low-key compared with the astonishing stories that are regularly produced by some of psychotherapy's high-profile exponents and their willing subjects.

Take, for example, the long-running experiments of Dolores Cannon, which, if taken at face value, suggest she found the key to a door that not only simultaneously opened on the past and the future, but behind which stood one of history's most famous prophets: Nostradamus. It's a bizarre story that Cannon herself found difficult to accept at times but which she has recorded at length in her trilogy, *Conversations with Nostradamus*,[6] which describes her experiments in detail as well as providing the reader with new interpretations of Nostradamus's puzzling quatrains. This new understanding, the American psychotherapist told me[7] after the final book was published, had come directly from the famous French seer. The spirit of Nostradamus? I asked. No, Nostradamus himself, speaking to us from his life in sixteenth-century France, having broken through the space-time barrier in order to communicate directly with the twentieth century.

This is the stuff of science fiction, of course . . . but what on earth persuaded the Arizona regressionist that these communications were anything more than the product of an overactive imagination? It started, she told me, when she was conducting a normal past-life regression in the mid-1980s with a woman named Elena, an artist and mother of ten children. Elena, it transpired, had been Dionisus, one of Nostradamus's students in the 1500s, and this memory somehow acted as a catalyst enabling the French seer to communicate directly with Dolores Cannon through her hypnotized subject. It was, she added, against all the rules. Elena was speaking of Nostradamus as if he were in the room with them and Dolores Cannon was able to put questions to him through her hypnotized subject. By agreeing to "meet" in a special place in the spiritual world, they started work on interpreting the quatrains. After just a couple of sessions, Elena, who was clearly frightened by the communications that were coming through her, moved to Alaska—which is a pretty drastic way of opting out of a psychic experiment. Before she departed, however, Nostradamus indicated that he would be able to continue his communications through others and gave instructions on how to locate him. He also agreed to a test, whereby he would make his presence known to the psychotherapist by signaling in a way her subject would be unaware of.

He did this successfully, Cannon claims, through two more subjects, enabling her to complete the revisions to his famous work. Brenda, a college music student, gave six months of her time helping Cannon and Nostradamus interpret three hundred quatrains before the demands of her education and job made it impossible to continue. At that point a young astrologer, John Feeley, another past-life subject, became the seer's earthly conduit and brought new insights to the project until he moved to Florida. In all, says the psychotherapist, a dozen individuals were able to establish contact with the living Nostradamus, enabling her to complete the updating. Like many other prophets of doom, according to Cannon, Nostradamus, using a black obsidian mirror to focus his psychic powers, tells us that the Earth will soon shift on its axis. When this happens, extraterrestrials will come to our aid. There will also be a third world war. His quatrains also tell of the birth of the Antichrist, and Dolores Cannon has even been able to find individuals able to produce Identikit drawings of the Antichrist and his horoscope.

In "Celebrity Believers" (chapter 13) I refer to TV host Jerry Springer being hypnotized back to a previous life by Dr. Bruce Goldberg. In the same session, Los Angeles-based Dr. Goldberg also took Springer—a healthy skeptic—into a future life in which he will be a rancher/farmer named Bobby, living in Montana and involved in a government project to raise crops on the moon. A father of four, he will die at the age of sixty in that life, when his craft crashes during a return trip to Earth.

Dr. Goldberg, it transpires, is a firm believer in the value of hypnotic progressions. "Many people consider progression a form of wishful thinking," he tells us in his book *Soul Healing*.[8] But that, he argues, does not account for individuals seeing things over which they could not have any control, such as "the reading of a newspaper headline that exists five years in the future that describes a natural disaster or the election of a president or a war, and having that event occur five years later exactly as it was read in trance." If Goldberg is telling us he has such cases in his files, he fails to substantiate this sensational claim. What he does present, instead, is some equally sensational claims relating to a couple of his patients, which, I warn my readers, require the suspension of all your critical or skeptical faculties.

The first of these involves a clinical psychologist named Pete who consulted Dr. Goldberg in 1984 with a hand-washing compulsion. The cause was found not in a past life but in the future. Moving forward in time to the twenty-first century under Goldberg's guidance, Pete said his name was now Ben Kingsley and he is working in a nuclear research facility in Tulsa, Oklahoma. It is August 2088 AD and his obsessive-compulsive personality, coupled with being a workaholic, result in him having a breakdown and configuring all the computers so that they cause a catastrophic meltdown. The skeleton crew and Ben are killed and the entire Tulsa area is affected by nuclear radiation. Somehow, it seems that in this life Pete was tuning into that future life and the anxiety it was causing, which led to the hand-washing compulsion.

Before real estate prices start tumbling in Tulsa and a mass evacuation begins, I have some good news. "That future was just one of at least five major probabilities," Goldberg tells us. "Pete had perceived a negative frequency or probability, though he had at least four others from which to choose. The solution to his problem was really quite simple. All I had to do was to have him perceive the other four choices and then, after he selected the ideal frequency, program that frequency to be his reality. By doing this I would help Pete to switch frequencies so his future would be quite different than it would have been had we failed to act on the knowledge provided during the progression." So the people of Tulsa can now sleep soundly in their beds, Pete has totally recovered and no longer wastes gallons of water trying to wash away nuclear contamination that will no longer occur, and Dr. Goldberg has found a way of manipulating other people's futures in a way—if it were real—that makes the wonders of genetic engineering pale in comparison.

Another patient, Emily, suffered a gastrointestinal disorder that was traced by Goldberg to a life she would be leading in the thirty-sixth century when she is Sequestra and living on Phonican, a planet in the Andromeda system. I won't spoil your enjoyment by revealing what happens next—it could be the next plot for a *Star Wars* sequel—but suffice it to say that Sequestra not only won the day on Phonican but also has rid herself, as Emily, of colitis and is enjoying a new lease on life. Dr. Goldberg, who has degrees in biochemistry, dentistry, and counseling psychology, clearly believes these progressions to be real. "The fact that each and every one of my patients can control their own destiny is fulfilling to me beyond measure," he writes.

Apparently, Goldberg's predilection for studying future lives has led to rumors on the Internet that he is a time traveler, or chrononaut, who has returned from the future to live on earth at this time in order to open our minds to reincarnation and the existence of the soul. Interviewed about that very topic by Art Bell on the *Coast to Coast AM* show, Goldberg refused to confirm or deny the rumor. A page of his website also asks the question, "Is Dr. Bruce Goldberg a Time Traveler?" and it offers some clues, from which I, for one, conclude that he certainly believes that to be the case. "If I am a time traveler," he tells visitors to his site, "I most definitely would be from the thirty-fifth century when teleportation is developed as a means of time travel. . . . The thirty-fifth century is truly a golden age. More advances will be made technologically and spiritually in that century than in any other in history! The average age is between five hundred and nine hundred years old, due to an energy-charging device called the alphasyncolarium that stimulates our adrenal glands and gonads to increase its production of the hormone DHEA." During the radio interview, Goldberg briefly described the host's past life in Atlantis at about 50,000 BC when he was a geophysicist/quantum physicist named Drako. Goldberg also lived at that time, as a medical TV reporter named Forat—Atlantis had both radio and television, he assures us, adding that he obtained this information from the Akashic Records.

So, to answer the time traveler question, he responds, "I can only say that a true chrononaut takes an oath never to reveal the fact, unless it is an emergency to do so. To do so would be a breach of what is known as timeline international security laws that exist in the future." Well, chrononaut or not, Goldberg would sure make a great writer of science-fiction screenplays if he ever gives up his hypnotherapy day job.

I came across an unexpected reference to a predicted future life in an interview that Kala Ambrose conducted with former singer Helen Reddy. At one point in their discussion, which was serialized in three parts on the Examiner.com website,[9] Kala volunteered: "My mother went through a past-life regression several years ago and . . . [also] saw her future life. She passed away within a couple of years after doing that. It was very interesting, as she was able to describe this future life. . . . She and I were able to talk—where she will be, when it will be, the time and the place—and I am going to have the opportunity in this lifetime to follow up on the information she gave me and perhaps meet her at that time, in that place, as that person. So I'm looking forward to that and seeing how it transpires." I've suggested to Kala that she deposit this information with a research body so that it can be verified—if and when it happens.

Well, I warned you that our journey into the future could be a rough ride. For the time being, however, we're firmly back on planet Earth and you can remove your seatbelts. It's now time to try to make sense of what we've encountered so far, and to sort fact from fantasy.

Chapter 17

Fact or Fantasy?

I have learned, over the years, not to get too excited when I read a newspaper headline about a new reincarnation claim. India's *Deccan Chronicle* demonstrates why. In 2009 it announced,[1] "Boy claims rebirth in same family five times," and its story began promisingly: "When sixteen-year-old Ajay died in a road mishap earlier this week, he left behind a tale of intrigue, wonder, and suspense." Apparently, when Ajay was old enough to talk, he revealed that he had previously been the son of his grandmother Rambeti, explaining exactly how he had died in that life by being poisoned by a neighbor. His next three incarnations were "as a housefly, then as a bee, and then as a snake." It was true that a snake had slithered into their courtyard in 1991 and had been beaten to death by Rambeti's mother-in-law. Ajay said he remembered being that snake before he was reborn as Rambeti's daughter's son, only to die again at the age of two after choking on food, and then returning as Ajay to Rambeti's daughter-in-law in 1993.

With his tragic death in 2009, I suspect the family is now very cautious about how they respond to insects, animals, or reptiles that find their way into the household.

Rebirth as a human or animal—transmigration—is a belief embedded in many cultures, and it results in some very bizarre claims. A sixty-one-year-old

Thai man, for example, was imprisoned on the island of Phuket in 1998 after being caught semi-naked trying to make love to a five-ton elephant.[2] Kim Lee Chong's defense was that he believed the elephant to be the reincarnation of his wife, who had died twenty-eight years earlier. "I recognized her immediately . . . by the naughty glint in her eye," he said in his defense. Unimpressed, the court sentenced him to fifteen years' imprisonment. I assume it was an experience the elephant is also unlikely to forget. Meanwhile, in India, a family in Kathasakar village, Giridih district, is delighted that Dhani Murmu has kept her deathbed promise, made in June 2000, to come back to them in another form. Her husband told the local media that he believes she has returned to him as a pangolin, an animal that eats ants.[3] "We love the mammal as our mother," said Dhani's eldest son. "It is part of our family. Someone from Orissa wanted to take it for a hefty price, but can we sell our mother?"

After he was sentenced to five years in prison in 2007, a forty-six-year-old Buddhist bank robber in West Germany, identified only as Peter K., made an unsuccessful bid to have his pet cat Gisela visit him.[4] His application was based on his belief that Gisela was his reincarnated mother. When he first met the stray cat, she looked at him just as softly as his mother, Gisela, had always done, and they remained inseparable until he was incarcerated. The local court in Werl declined the request for "visitation rights for his mother in the form of a pet cat," because, "the prisoner has provided no evidence to prove the reincarnation."

Even more bizarre is the story of an Indian undergraduate, Abhishek Parikh,[5] who claims to be the reincarnation of snake god Naagraaj's wife and says he is capable of transforming into a snake after midnight and resuming human shape in the morning. Naagraaj is widely worshipped in India. "Even in this life, in my present form, I continue to be his wife," the twenty-eight-year-old told the media in 2006 while on a holy visit to Kedarnath in Guna district. Abhishek, who dresses as a woman, said the "partial transformation" only occurs when he dances at midnight at a particular temple at Khanpur and claims to have shown the police a videotape of this mutation. I'm not sure why the police would be interested: Visitors to YouTube would be a much more appreciative audience. The realization that he was, and still is, the wife of Naagraaj came to him while meditating in worship of Lord

Shiva. "The fact that I am a male by birth is not a hindrance in carrying out my duties as Naagraaj's wife," he insisted.

No such physical change accompanied the claim[6] of an unemployed English man a year later. Steve Cooper, who was thirty-two in 2007, is regarded by many as a reincarnation of the goddess Bachucharaji, the patron of Indian eunuchs, who thousands of Hindus believe can cure infertility. Prior to his move to a remote jungle temple in Gujarat, Steve, who calls himself Pamela, lived in a tiny flat in Tooting, southwest London, where Indian friends told him he looked and moved just like the ancient goddess. That doesn't sound like a compliment to me, but apparently it was and it encouraged him to move to India, where his arrival was welcomed. When he walks through the local village, people flock to greet him, shouting, "The goddess is here."

A very different reaction greeted a stray dog that wandered into the Jerusalem financial court in 2011 and refused to leave. Dogs are considered impure in traditional Judaism. The Israeli website Ynet[7] reported that the incident reminded a judge of a curse that had been passed on a now-deceased secular lawyer, two decades earlier, bidding his spirit to enter the body of a dog. Fearing he had been reincarnated as the dog, the court condemned the stray to death by stoning—the sentence to be carried out by local children. Fortunately, it escaped before the fatal punishment could be inflicted.

Equally surprising claims are to be found in other cultures. Take, for example, the killer whale (orca) named Luna, who was born in Puget Sound in 1999 but separated from his mother at the age of two, preferring the waters of Nootka Sound, hundreds of miles away off the west coast of Vancouver Island. The Canadian Department of Fisheries and Oceans was soon concerned about his unusual behavior, and particularly his inclination to interact with people and boats. Apparently healthy and happy, he delighted tourists with his inquisitiveness, but the authorities decided he must be lonely. After years debating what was best for Luna, it was decided in June 2004 to return him to his family, for his own good and also for the safety of people on board the boats he encountered. "Luna nudged their boat, spun it around like a toy in a bathtub, bounced it up and down by pushing on the hull, and spy-hopped directly in front to keep it from speeding away," according to one book, which added: "It was not the behavior of a wild animal shying away from human contact. As the summer progressed, he became more insistent in his interactions and harder for boaters to escape." The Mowachaht/Muchalaht First Nations people had no difficulty understanding why Luna was behaving in this way and desiring human interaction. He was, they said, the reincarnation of Chief Mike Maquinna's father,[8] who had been their previous chief and, according to his son, had made a deathbed wish for his spirit to inhabit a killer whale. For that reason, they thwarted a plan to reunite the young killer whale with his pod in Puget Sound by luring Luna out to sea in their canoes by singing traditional songs and stamping their paddles on the bottom of the boats to draw him away from the marine scientists who were planning to rescue him. Two years later, in 2006, thanks largely to the intervention of the First Nations people, Luna was still swimming in Nootka Sound when he met his death after playfully interacting with a tugboat whose powerful propeller blades mortally wounded him. Presumably, he chose to reincarnate as a human after that brutal experience.

Equally bizarre is the story of Colorado psychic and animal communicator Ellen Kohn, who not only claims to be able to speak with living animals, but also says she can find the reincarnations of deceased ones.[9] In 2009 she was approached by Christine Horowitz after her thirteen-year-old golden shepherd, Dina, died from cancer. Having previously consulted Kohn when her mother's cat disappeared, she remembered the psychic saying she was able to contact pets in the afterlife. Even so, Horowitz was skeptical that the reincarnation of Dina could be found. "How would we find this puppy? Thousands are born every day," she reasoned. Those doubts dissolved when Kohn began channeling the dead dog and asked Horowitz about Dina placing her paws on her shoulders. That convinced her: She had often danced with Dina's paws on her shoulders, just as Kohn described. The psychic continued talking with Dina's spirit, who led her to a picture of a puppy on a pet website. Horowitz went to visit the dog and nine months later was certain the foxhound mix, named Annie, was Dina's reincarnation. Even her skeptical husband admitted that Annie does things just the way Dina did. Kohn says all her work of finding lost pets or communicating with them in the spirit world is made possible by "tapping into the metaphysical, giant, universal pool of consciousness" that we all have access to, even if we don't use it.

You may think the concept of animals communicating from the next world about their future incarnation is stretching credibility to its limits, but if so you are probably unaware of a Californian psychic, Barbara Bell, who said in the early 1990s she was channeling messages from her daughter's Barbie dolls.[10] More down-to-earth, perhaps, but still strange, is the claim of disgraced Jamaican-born Canadian sprinter Ben Johnson, once described as "the world's fastest human being," to be the reincarnation of an Egyptian Pharaoh who was poisoned.[11] In this life, the sprinter's astonishing performance in the hundred-meters final at the 1988 Summer Olympics in South Korea, when he broke his own world record with a time of 9.79 seconds, won him a gold medal. It was taken away three days later when he was disqualified after a drug test revealed the presence of stanozolol, an anabolic steroid, in his urine. Though he subsequently admitted having used steroids in his running career, he also alleged that the Olympics drug result was caused by a spiked beer given to him in the doping control room. And in his self-published autobiography, *Seoul to Soul,* he not only says that his arch rival, sprinter Carl Lewis, was behind the drug set-up, but that it was also Lewis, in Egyptian times, who had poisoned him when he was Pharaoh Khufu. Lewis, who came in second in the Olympic final, received the gold medal after Johnson's disqualification. These past-life "insights" appear to have come from Johnson's "spiritual adviser," Bryan Farnum.

It is important to realize that in all of these examples, those involved were not hypnotized or otherwise encouraged to recall a past life. They are individuals who, for whatever reason, are convinced that reincarnation offers an acceptable explanation for their own behavior or that of others—animal or human—however implausible it may be to the majority of humanity. Above all, they demonstrate the incredible strength of belief that some people have in certain concepts that allow them to accept without question happenings that the rest of us, rightly or wrongly, would regard as totally irrational. Under hypnosis, however, that rationality appears to be peeled away, allowing our minds or our imagination to roam freely in search of events, stories, scenarios—call them what you will—that either satisfy our own needs or provide responses to what we believe our questioner, the hypnotist or psychotherapist, wants to hear. And buried in amongst all of this verbiage may just be small nuggets of information that provide evidence for reincarnation. That's the challenge that faces researchers looking for proof of past lives recalled by adult subjects in an induced trance or other states of consciousness. There are, however, basic research methods and techniques that can and should be employed to help sort fact from fantasy.

Arnall Bloxham was a respected hypnotherapist in Cardiff, South Wales, who regressed and recorded the revelations of four hundred subjects over a twenty-year period as they described their past lives. When television producer Jeffery Iverson heard them, he was so fascinated by their content that he spent a year conducting his own research to try to determine whether they were strange historical romances or real evidence of reincarnation. "The Bloxham Tapes" became the subject of a book[12] and a BBC documentary, *More Lives than One?*, in which the eighty-year-old hypnotist and some of his subjects were able to recreate their journeys into the past for the TV cameras. A number of these lives came to an end with a powerful and dramatic display of emotion as the hypnotized subjects recalled their agonizing deaths.

One of Bloxham's subjects was an educated Swansea man, Graham Huxtable, who regressed two hundred years and recalled in a coarse West Country accent a life in which he was press-ganged onto a thirty-two-gun frigate in the British Navy, *HMS Aggie.* In his book, Iverson tells us that Lord Louis Mountbatten, former First Lord of the Admiralty, had a copy of this regression tape on permanent loan, adding, "Researchers and the opinions of some of Britain's finest naval historians dropped into my lap as a result of Earl Mountbatten's interest. He had been so fascinated by the tape that he had his nephew, Prince Philip (Duke of Edinburgh), and some other top naval men try to trace the ship in which the "gunner's mate" was serving in an action against the French off the coast of Calais around the year 1800." No ship of that name was discovered.

In the course of his research into Bloxham's subjects' accounts, Iverson was able to weed out some that were clearly not what they seemed. One involved a celebrity: Queen Elizabeth I.

"As I listened to the tape, I noted that the lady did not appear to undergo any real change of voice or personality in the way the others did," Iverson writes. "And she also seemed to think it was she, as 'Queen Elizabeth,' who had caused Sir Walter Raleigh to be beheaded. In fact, it was Elizabeth's successor—James I. Sadly, I abandoned her regression, writing it off as cryptomnesia plus inadequate reading. Sad, because she added spice to history with an account of the Virgin Queen making love to Sir Walter in the cabin of his ship."

The undoubted star of the TV documentary was Jane Evans, an office worker in her thirties who was regressed to six former lives: in the third century as a tutor's wife in the Roman British city of Eboracum (or York); as a twelfth-century Jewess, also in York; as a servant to the French merchant prince Jacques Coeur in the fifteenth century; as a Spanish handmaiden to Catherine of Aragon in the sixteenth century; as a poor sewing girl in the reign of Queen Anne in the early seventeenth century; and as an American nun at the turn of the twentieth century. She may have lived other lives, but after recalling six of them, she became "a bit fed up and frightened by it all," refusing to do any more. Her recall of these lives contained a wealth of potentially verifiable material, of which Rebecca in twelfth-century York, during the 1190 massacre of Jews in that city, proved particularly impressive. There was, however, one claim that appeared to be totally false.

Her regression—indeed, her life—came to an end when soldiers discovered her and her daughter Rachel hiding in the crypt of a church. Professor Barrie Dobson, reader in history at the University of York who had recently written about the Jewish massacre in the city, studied transcripts of the regression at Iverson's request, finding it "impressively accurate." He also concluded that St. Mary's Church in Castlegate was the likely place in which Rebecca and her daughter were killed. But, like all other surviving medieval churches in York, it had no crypt. Then, a chance discovery by a workman during renovation work at the church, just six months after the BBC TV crew filmed Jane Evans's regression, appeared to indicate there had been a crypt at St. Mary's.

In the conclusion to his book, Iverson made his own attempt at assessing the Bloxham material, observing, "Nor can I even guess how Jane Evans was familiar with some of the facts and locations she speaks of with such assurance. She has, after all, never set foot in York nor the Loire Valley of France, and she visited America only after she had recorded her regression as the American nun." He does, however, concede that his search for the truth about the Bloxham Tapes—which every historian and psychologist who heard them confirmed to be real—had left him with no certainties, only new mysteries.

When Melvin Harris, a skeptical paranormal detective, conducted a reinvestigation of the Bloxham past-life cases, he focused on Jane Evans's memories, which Iverson had described as "the most consistently astonishing," and came to a very different verdict. Harris concluded that "the claims made for the tapes were false and the result of misdirected and inadequate research." Jane Evans's account of a life as the maidservant to Catherine of Aragon, for example, "could easily have been based, sequence for sequence, on Jean Plaidy's historical novel *Katherine, The Virgin Widow.*" Her "recall" of life as a teenage servant of Jacques Coeur included a detailed description of the interiors and exterior of his magnificent house, as well as a reference to the carved tomb of Agnes Sorel, the King's mistress, which Iverson claimed had only been rediscovered in 1970. Harris, on the other hand, pointed out that Coeur's house is one of the most photographed and filmed houses in the whole of France, and the "forgotten" tomb had, in fact, been a tourist attraction for the whole of the twentieth century and is described in detail in H. D. Sedgwick's *A Short History of France,* a book published in 1930 that had remained popular for decades and was often found in public and school libraries. And a 1948 novel on Coeur's life, *The Moneyman* by T. B. Costain, could have been the source for all the flourishes that made her account sound so authentic. Above all, Harris tells us, it explains why in that "past life" Jane Evans knew Coeur had an Egyptian bodyslave but was totally unaware that he was married with five children. Every historical account of his life included his family history, whereas the novel did not, because as its author explained in an introduction, "I have made no mention of Jacques Coeur's family for the reason that they played no real parts in the events which brought his career to its climax."

As for Rebecca and Rachel's death in a York church, after pointing out various errors in the detail of Jane Evans's past-life account, Harris quotes Prof. Barrie Dobson against the idea of a crypt being found, adding that Iverson had taken out of context or misinterpreted information given to him by Dobson in informal correspondence that was never intended for publication. The professor gave Harris full permission to quote a statement he supplied, dated January 15, 1986, that "it now seems overwhelmingly most likely that the chamber which workmen reported encountering when renovating St. Mary's Castlegate in 1975 was not an early medieval crypt at all but a postmedieval charnel vault."

Most damning of all from a reincarnation perspective, perhaps, was Jane Evans's account of being Livonia. This "memory," Harris shows, is without a doubt based on a 1947 novel, *The Living Wood* (and as a 1960 paperback, *The Empress Helena*) by Louis de Wohl, in which the author used historical and fictitious characters to tell an exciting story about fourth-century Roman Britain. Although she had no memory of having read this book, Jane Evans clearly had done so, for her "past-life" recall not only included Constantine, Helena, Constantius, Allectus, Carausius, and Osius—all historical figures—but also Hilary, Valerius, and Curio, who had been invented by de Wohl.

It seems, therefore, that in Jane Evans's case, and possibly in many other regressions, the memories originated not in past lives but in the pages of historical novels which she—an avid reader—had long forgotten reading. She then had the subconscious ability to retrieve, edit, and combine them creatively into a story in which she played a leading role. It takes a researcher of Melvin Harris's tenacity to trace such accounts and either eliminate or confirm them as a source of the colorful stories that emerge under hypnosis.

Cryptomnesia is the scientific term for the mental phenomenon of recovering a past memory without recognizing it as something one has previously seen, read, or experienced. Coined by Théodore Flournoy during his investigation of medium Hélène Smith,[13] to explain the origin of her memories, it is a possibility that must seriously be considered as an explanation in every case of alleged reincarnation, particularly those memories recalled by adults under hypnosis. As well as the contents of books, magazines, and newspapers that may, once read, take up permanent residence in our memories, we must also add TV news, documentaries, and dramas as well as blockbuster movies, which are similarly absorbed and stored in the file drawers of our mind. They may well provide the ingredients on which fertile imaginations can build life stories and present them as reality when given the opportunity.

That was certainly the conclusion of Finnish psychiatrist Reima Kampman,[14] at the University of Oulo, who carried out a series of experiments with hypnotized subjects, many of whom recalled past lives in great detail. Out of trance, they remembered nothing of that previous existence. During a second hypnosis session, Kampman took them back to that life, then asked them to recall where they had first heard the story. His subjects then named the books they had once read but since forgotten, which provided them with the past-life storyline. It will occur to my readers that Arnall Bloxham could have saved Melvin Harris and other investigators an awful lot of time by simply asking his subjects the same question. That would, however, have deprived the general public and even British royalty of debating the issues raised by Iverson's fascinating book and enjoying his gripping documentary.

The possibility of cryptomnesia occurring in cases of adult past-life memories serves to underline the greater importance that researchers place on spontaneous cases involving children, particularly those who are just beginning to speak, and who have therefore had limited exposure to the outside world, let alone to works of historical fact or fiction. The sooner investigators can get to them and their families before "contamination" of their memories by outside influences, the greater the likelihood that positive evidence about their past-life memories can be placed on record.

Chapter 18

Where Are Memories Stored?

Some readers will recall the amusing song "I Remember It Well" from the Lerner and Loewe musical *Gigi,* first performed by Maurice Chevalier, playing the aging Honore, and Hermione Gingold in the role of Marmita, who is also getting on in years. Later, Peter Sellers and Sophia Loren had a hit record with their version. Perhaps some of you are too young to have heard it, and others may have heard it but forgotten it. As for me, I remember it well.

What the lyrics tell us—as if we need reminding!—is that memories are notoriously unreliable, and two people experiencing the same event may recall it very differently at a later date. It's a point made by Julian Barnes in his memoir[1] *Nothing to Be Frightened Of* in which he explores how we color memory in with our own cheap paintbox and our favorite hues: "Thus I remember Grandma as 'petite and opinionated.' My brother, when consulted, takes out his paintbrush and counter proposes 'short and bossy.'" Another English writer, Ian McEwan, made a similar point in a discussion with journalist and columnist Nigel Farndale, describing the strangeness of reading memoirs written by friends—in his case Christopher Hitchens, Martin Amis, and Julian Barnes—which feature anecdotes about him with which his own memories always differ considerably.[2] "You realize the story belongs to the person who writes it down," he concludes. Amusingly, Farndale refers to the launch of socialite Sir David Chang's website, ICorrect, which in the words of one commentator "gives the rich, powerful, and influential a platform to respond to online slurs." Cherie Blair, Kate Moss, Michael Caine, Stephen Fry, and Jemima Khan were among those who had been "busily correcting" other people's errors soon after the website's launch, Farndale wrote, adding, "Yet how do we know they are telling the truth? And perhaps more significantly, how do they know?"

Despite its proven unreliability, memory plays a key role in most reincarnation accounts—not only the subject's claim to remember what happened in a past life, but also the memories others have of first hearing that testimony. Who said what, when, and what happened next? The answers to these questions take on a special significance for researchers as they try to unravel claims and counter-claims in cases of apparent past-life recall. They know from experience that once a child's past-life memories start to fade, as they usually do well before puberty, the young subjects' statements are likely to be based on what they remember saying when they were younger, rather than what they still recall of a previous existence. And like most stories that are oft-repeated, they are likely to be exaggerated or to change in other respects during the retelling.

It is important, therefore, in any discussion of reincarnation to understand as much as we can of the mechanics of memory before we place too much reliance on what someone claims to recall. The biggest obstacle in accepting past-life accounts as real memories is that most people believe our memories are stored in the brain, and for very good reason. When the body dies, so does everything associated with it. End of life. End of story. End of memories. Cautious researchers investigating reincarnation cases are well aware of this apparent state of affairs and, for the most part, do not challenge it head on. Their role as scientists is to examine what is, after all, a global phenomenon exhibiting striking similarities, without prejudging how it occurs, even though that must be their ultimate aim. They know, once they eliminate all other possibilities, that if some cases of past-life recall remain unexplained then they have strong scientific evidence for the existence of an indestructible soul—and that would have enormous implications.

Why do we view memories as being inextricably tied to our physical brains? It's a perfectly understandable conclusion on a number of levels.

Some brain injuries, for example, can result in a total loss of memory or a change of personality. Neurosurgeons know exactly which parts of the brain control our behavior or desires and can adjust them with surgical interventions. We also know that we are likely to experience a deterioration in short-term memory as we advance in years, though our long-term memories are less affected by the aging process unless dementia or Alzheimer's takes its toll. There are mental exercises that are supposed to slow down our mental decline but there would seem to be little doubt, faced with such evidence, that our ability to store and retrieve information is highly dependent on the condition and age of our brain.

Before we dismiss our brain as just another physical organ that is as susceptible to wear and tear as any other part of our body as we get older, let us reflect on aspects of its capabilities that are truly astonishing. These hint at its tremendous potential and perhaps offer a glimpse of something far more significant than neurons and cellular networks animating the brain. It challenges us to find an answer to the question: Is our brain doing all the work, producing works of art and making exciting scientific discoveries, as well as storing and retrieving our memories, or is it just a piece of clever hardware that enables the spiritual software of our soul to operate in a physical environment? In considering that question, the extraordinary talents of autistic savants, particularly their phenomenal feats of memory, must be taken into account. Dustin Hoffman memorably portrayed such an individual in the movie *Rain Man,* which won four Oscars in 1989. It was based in part on the life of Kim Peek, who was regarded as a "megasavant" because of his incredible photographic memory. It is believed he could recall the content of at least twelve thousand books from memory. Peek was born with brain damage, including the absence of the bundle of nerves that connect the brain's two hemispheres. Neurons in his brain are thought to have found a way of compensating for this by making unusual connections that increased his memory's capacity. The downside for Peek, and many other savants, is the social difficulties they experience to varying degrees.

Despite being blind and severely disabled, Derek Paravicini[3] is an extraordinarily talented pianist. Born prematurely, the English autistic savant has severe learning disabilities but also absolute pitch and the ability to play a piece of music after hearing it just once—a skill he first demonstrated at the age of two. By the age of nine he gave his first major public concert in London. Yet Derek cannot count to ten nor tell left from right and needs 'round-the-clock supervision. He is one of only twenty-three autistic savants in the world. Math and syntax are the special skills of another English autistic savant, Daniel Tammet,[4] who holds the European record for reciting the mathematical constant pi (π) to 22,514 decimal points, which he achieved in five hours and four minutes in a 2004 sponsored-charity challenge. Daniel also mastered the Icelandic language in a week. His numerical wizardry is based on an ability to see numbers as colors. In his mind, each positive integer up to 10,000 has its own unique shape, color, texture, and feel, so that the results of calculations appear as visual landscapes in his mind without conscious effort. Savantism expert Darold Treffert says that the one thing almost all savants have in common is a prodigious memory that is "very deep, but exceedingly narrow."

In recent years, it has been discovered that other people—individuals who appear to be perfectly normal in every way and are not socially inept in the way many savants are—also have astonishing memories. What began as research by scientists in the Department of Neurology at the University of California, Irvine,[5] focused on the abilities of a single subject, "AJ"—"the woman who cannot forget"—has since been broadened to investigate similar savant abilities in five others, including actress Marilu Henner,[6] who played the role of Elaine O'Connor Nardo on the hit TV sitcom *Taxi* between 1978 and 1983. Their ability to recall even trivial things that have happened to them or which occurred on any date in their adult life has been given the name hyperthymesia or "superior autobiographical memory." After the researchers published a report on their five-year investigation of AJ in *Neurocase* in 2006, she was identified as American Sinfonietta violinist Louise Owen. She explains her memory skills in these words: "When I hear the date, it's like my brain immediately goes to a position on a calendar, and once I locate it, I see what happened instantly. I usually describe it as time travel. As soon as you say that date, I'm instantly there. I know how I felt, I know what happened that day. It's as if it happened five minutes ago, as opposed to twenty-two years ago." The scientists involved are still exploring how it is possible. Assuming this is purely a biological phenomenon, it suggests that our brains are databases with the limitless ability and capacity to record and store our every experience. For the majority of people, however, the memory compartments remain largely closed, allowing only fleeting glimpses of tiny portions of this huge storehouse of information. Just a handful of people appear to have universal access to the contents of their personal memory bank, opening it up and retrieving what they require in seconds.

Hypnosis, as I have already discussed at length, seems to have the key to unlocking past memories for some people, and I offer the following example to demonstrate not only the incredible latent talent to memorize material we are exposed to, but also to personalize it as if we were involved. In the previous chapter I referred to the experiments of Finnish researcher Reima Kampman.[7] In one hypnosis session, a nineteen-year-old student was regressed to a life she apparently recalled as Dorothy, a thirteenth-century innkeeper's daughter. While talking about that existence, she surprised those present by singing "The Summer Song," not in her native tongue but in an old form of English. Once out of trance, the student had no knowledge of the song. Then, in a subsequent session, she was asked to go back to the time when she had seen the words and music of the song. She remained in her current lifetime, going back to the age of thirteen when she recalled taking a book called *Musiikin Vaiheet,* a Finnish version of Benjamin Britten and Imogen Holst's *The History of Music,* from a library shelf. It was found that it included the song "Sumer is icumen in" and the words just happened to be in medieval English.

But however incredible our memories, they may not be confined to our brains. With the introduction of organ transplants, a new phenomenon has been observed that suggests that every part of our bodies may "know" about us. Take, for example, the case of a boy who liked to write poetry, compose songs, and play music, whose life was tragically cut short at the age of eighteen in an automobile accident.

A year after his death, his parents found an audiotape of a song he had written, entitled, "Danny, My Heart Is Yours," which told how he felt destined to die and give his heart to someone. His parents had agreed for his organs to be transplanted, and the recipient of his heart was an eighteen-year-old girl named Danielle. When she met the donor's parents they played her some of his music, and though she had never heard the song before, she was able to complete the phrases. There are now a considerable number of cases in which the behavior or preferences of organ recipients seem to change and align with those of the donor after the transplant. So, what do you think happened to a twenty-nine-year-old lesbian and fast-food junkie when she received the heart of a nineteen-year-old "man crazy" female vegetarian? After the operation, the recipient—who at that stage knew nothing about the identity of the donor—reported that meat now made her sick and she was no longer attracted to women. In fact, she became engaged to a man.

Theories abound to try to explain what is going on here, and some form of "cellular memory" is among the most popular. At the very least, it suggests that memory may not be confined to the brain, after all. The examples I have just quoted come from a study conducted by Paul Pearsall, Gary Schwartz, and Linda Russek, titled "Changes in Heart Transplant Recipients that Parallel the Personalities of Their Donors."[8] They studied ten heart and heart-and-lung transplant cases, finding "striking parallels" in each one. Pearsall, a psychoneuroimmunologist and author of *The Heart's Code,* has independently interviewed 150 organ recipients, leading him to the conclusion that cells of living tissue have the capacity to remember. Schwartz and Russek, coauthors of *The Living Energy Universe,*[9] have offered a universal living-memory hypothesis in which they suggest all systems store energy dynamically, and this information continues "as a living, evolving system after the physical structure had deconstructed." Such theories may well point us toward a better understanding of where our memories are stored, but it is individual case studies, I find, that have the greatest impact. I particularly enjoyed Paul Pearsall's account[10] of a young man who, when he came out of transplant surgery, said to his mother, "Everything is copacetic" (in excellent order). His mother was puzzled, as it was a word she had never heard him use before. He continued to use it regularly, as he recovered. Only later was it discovered to be a word used between the donor and his wife as a signal, particularly after an argument, so that when they made up they knew everything was in order. They had argued just before the donor's fatal accident and had never made up.

Reincarnation researcher Ian Stevenson has pointed out that observations of paranormal phenomena, including reincarnation cases, "require a radical revision in present concepts of the relation between mind and body." He goes on to suggest that our minds could "consist of some nonphysical substance" and conjectures that "minds are not brains but users of brains."

His reincarnation research successor at the University of Virginia, Dr. Jim Tucker, puts it this way in *Life before Life:*[11] "Even though our everyday experience may tell us that our consciousness begins with our birth and ends with our death, a reasonable alternative is that our brains serve as vehicles for consciousness during our lifetimes, and that consciousness existed before our births and can continue after our deaths until it finds another vehicle in a new body." Talking only of memories is to lose sight of a much bigger picture, for as Tucker reminds us, "some physicists now consider consciousness to be an entity separate from the brain and one with important functions in the universe." He explains: "Conscious observation, at least, appears capable of affecting the future and even the past on the level of the microscopic quantum world." Stanford physicist Andrei Linde, for example, says that a consistent theory of everything that ignores consciousness is unimaginable. "We may assume," Tucker adds, "that a fundamental component of the universe, if that is what consciousness is, exists separately from our little brains here on Earth."

I am going to give the last word on the subject, for the time being, to Michael Levin of the Forsyth Institute at the Harvard School of Dental Medicine. In a review of Jim Tucker's book,[12] he makes an interesting observation, after commenting that the work of both Stevenson and Tucker was making an important contribution to biology. Referring to the "Future Research" section of Tucker's book, he suggests a potential area of experimental research.

> It turns out that there is a type of worm that can regenerate (regrow) its head (including brain, etc.) if it is cut off. These worms can also be trained to perform simple tasks—they have memories and remember. Some truly astounding work in the 1970s (which is now being pursued in our lab) has shown that if trained worms are cut up, and the tails are allowed to form a new worm (with a new brain), the resulting worm remembers the original training (McConnell, 1965). This work demonstrates that (assuming the memory is in the body at all) knowledge and information can be stored outside the brain.

Chapter 19

Alternative Explanations

Researchers investigating past-life claims only entertain the possibility that they provide evidence for reincarnation after they have eliminated all other possibilities that might offer another source for the "memories" that are being recalled. There are, in fact, more possible alternatives for such cases than we might expect. Having said that, reincarnation remains the most likely explanation for the very best cases. Here are some of the alternatives:

Spirit Possession

This is an explanation that will appeal only to those who are willing to accept the duality concept that man consists of body and soul as separate entities. Those offering this as a realistic alternative argue that in *every* single case of apparent reincarnation, what is actually happening is that an earthbound spirit has attached itself to a person and it is that spirit's memories that are being recalled, not a past life. As a blanket explanation for *all* reincarnation cases it has its shortcomings. Why, for example, does a child's memories fade after a few years? If a spirit possesses them in infancy, why does it not continue to do so as the child matures? Does the spirit tire of its attachment after just a few years, or does the child's developing spirit reject it? The theory seems to raise as many questions as those relating to the reincarnation hypothesis.

Having said that, there are a few rare but well-documented cases that suggest spirit possession can occur, in which case it could be argued that the same phenomenon could be happening with children who appear to remember a past life. There are, however, important differences.

One of the earliest cases,[1] which occurred in the USA in 1877, involved Mary Lurancy Vennum, who at the age of thirteen appeared to be possessed by two different entities. The first was described as a sullen old hag, whereas the next was a young man who had run away from home. At this point, it sounds very much like a case of multiple personality disorder. Her parents were introduced to a hypnotist who induced a trance and spoke to Mary's "sane and happy" mind, which told him that "an angel" named Mary Roff wanted to replace the other two. Sure enough, Roff not only appeared but took over Mary's body completely. The possessing spirit was easily identified: She was the daughter of the people who had recommended the hypnotist and had died when she was just one year old. This possession was so total that Mary Lurancy Vennum went to live with the Roffs, until, three months and ten days after she appeared, Mary Roff suddenly disappeared and the teenager returned to her natural parents.

This case is not unique. Two similar cases, but with different outcomes, have been investigated in the twentieth century—both in India.

The first involved a young married woman, Sumitra Singh,[2] who in 1982, soon after the birth of a son, had suffered fits and then began speaking as if she were three other people, two of them women (one a goddess, the other a woman who had drowned) and the third an unidentified man. It was the goddess, Santoshi Ma, who announced in 1985 that Sumitra would die in three days' time. That is precisely what appeared to happen and her family testified that her body had no pulse for three-quarters of an hour. Then, as preparations began for her funeral, she suddenly revived . . . not as Sumitra, but as Shiva, who claimed to have been the mother of two children and who was murdered by her in-laws. Shiva remained for the rest of her life in Sumitra's body, writing letters to her natural father complaining that "God has dumped me here" in Sumitra's body and in a dirty home, which she compared unfavorably to her previous existence. Shiva's spirit has since died a second time, following the death of Sumitra, whose body she had taken over. This fascinating case was recently re-investigated by Antonia Mills and is the subject of a lengthy report in the Society for Psychical Research's Proceedings.³

A very similar and remarkable transformation, but without a death apparently occurring, was experienced in 1974 by a thirty-two-year-old unmarried woman, Uttara Huddar, who awoke one day in her home in Nagpur, in west-central India, and instead of speaking Marathi, her native tongue, began speaking a language her parents could not understand. Her personality had also changed and she called herself Sharada. Others recognized the language she spoke as Bengali, which Uttara had never learned. This was extremely disturbing for the family, naturally, and also for Sharada, who could not understand why she was suddenly in a different place. However, it was not a permanent change. The Sharada personality "appears" for different periods, from one day to six weeks, and then Uttara repossesses her body again. Each personality, when it takes control of the body, is oblivious to the existence of the other. This may sound like a form of multiple personality disorder, but it seems Sharada did once enjoy a totally separate existence, living between 1810 and 1830 and dying from a snake bite on her toe. Also, she provided investigators with details of her Bengal family and they were able to trace its genealogical records and confirm information she gave. Lastly, her ability to speak Bengali—a phenomenon known as xenoglossy—would also appear to rule out the possibility that the "intruder" is just an aspect of Uttara's personality. Sharada, incidentally, said she had no idea where she had been since her death.

If the Sumitra/Shiva and Uttara/Sharada cases are as reported—and both have been investigated by seasoned reincarnation researchers—they would seem to offer unusual, even unique, variations on a reincarnation theme in which, for whatever reason, a soul either replaces another in an adult body, or takes on a shared "tenancy" with the original owner. Both cases are discussed in detail by researcher Satwant Pasricha in her book *Claims of Reincarnation*.⁴

Extrasensory Perception

Another possibility that has to be seriously considered in interpreting the evidence provided by cases of apparent reincarnation is that the minds of those making the claim—usually children—are somehow able to acquire, or tune into, information about the life of a person who has died. Sometimes referred to as "super-psi," the theory presupposes the existence of such super psychic abilities, which, it has to be acknowledged, are *not* recognized by scientists in general, any more than reincarnation. In other words, it merely "explains" one paranormal conundrum with another. Besides, in nearly all spontaneous cases the subjects show no psychic abilities, such as telepathy, so why would it manifest only in respect to one individual (the past-life personality) who is unknown to the subject and his or her family? This hypothesis requires the child to gather information about the deceased from various living people, by telepathy, clairvoyance, or some other form of psychic sensing, and assemble it into a coherent "memory" of key moments in that "remembered" person's life. Alternatively, he could acquire that information, by the same means, directly from the deceased person, in which case he or she would be acting like a medium in contact with a spirit. Some commentators find this theory attractive, but they offer no reason to explain why this extraordinary ability is focused on just one person who was previously unknown to the subject's family. Why can the child not use super-psi abilities to read the minds of close relatives or friends and see into their pasts?

Announcing Dreams

An unusual element in a small number of cases involves dreams in which a deceased person, almost always known to the dreamer, forecasts his or her return. Sometimes, the dream person specifies where and to whom he will be reborn, saying something along the lines of, "I am coming back to be your son." Researchers who encounter this element in cases need to be certain that the dreamer has not helped make the dream come true by encouraging the child to believe he is the reincarnation of the person seen in the dream, either by asking him leading questions or unwittingly feeding him information about the deceased. In that way, the apparent rebirth would be simply a wish fulfillment, and it is understandably difficult for researchers to speak with certainty about what information may or may not have been conveyed by the dreamer (usually a parent) to the child. Investigators always draw attention to this shortcoming, but they also point to items of evidence where the child appears to remember something about the former life of which family members, including the dreamer, were unaware. Even without such dreams, in cases where reincarnation is reported within a family, researchers need to satisfy themselves that the beliefs of those involved have not been influenced by grief and the desire to have the dead person back in their family.

Maternal Impressions

The development of an embryo may be affected by something the mother sees or experiences during pregnancy. This is particularly relevant in cases where birthmarks and birth defects are an important element.

Cryptomnesia

The chapters dealing with regression cases have already explored this alternative explanation, which suggests that our mind has the ability to absorb and retain an enormous amount of information, very little of which we can recall in detail in a normal waking state. Indeed, cryptomnesia could explain a very large number of cases that emerge under hypnosis. In spontaneous cases it is a less viable alternative explanation since, usually, the subjects and their families appear not to have been exposed, in any form, to the events or details that are recalled. It has to be recognized, of course, that the advent of mass communication methods—radio, television, and computers—which are reaching into every corner of the globe and exposing new generations to a wealth of information, may require cryptomnesia to be considered in far more cases in the future.

Akashic Records

This is another theory, like super-psi, which offers an explanation based on something for which there is, as yet, no scientific proof. The Akashic Records are supposed to be an etheric database containing every thought and deed of the planet's entire population. Furthermore, in theory these records are mentally accessible by anyone with the ability to "tune in" to them. It's an interesting and widely accepted concept, but even if it were true, the same objections to the super-psi hypothesis must also be raised for the Akashic Records with respect to spontaneous cases. Why would a child recalling a past life have access to "records" relating to only one deceased person? And how did the subject choose that previously unknown individual? These are questions that are seldom addressed by supporters of the Akashic Records hypothesis.

Multiple Universe

Also described as either the multiverse, parallel universes, or quantum universes, depending on who proposed a particular theory, these are conjectured to be other dimensions beyond our observable universe, whose existence can be interpolated from quantum mechanics. These very complex ideas appear to allow the possibility that we also exist simultaneously in different dimensions, and since they are devoid of time and space as we experience them on earth, we could in theory interact in some way with one of those dimensions and acquire the information that manifests as past-life "memories." Not only is this a theory that is beyond the comprehension of most people (and my summary may well have oversimplified it), but it is also far less meaningful as an explanation than the simple and direct reincarnation interpretation.

Fraud

Last, but certainly not least, is the very real possibility that, in some of the reported cases of rebirth, fraud is the most likely explanation. A poor family that receives the soul of an individual whose past life was affluent might have much to gain by making contact with that previous family. Gifts would be given and perhaps the child's education would be paid for. There are undoubtedly genuine cases that reflect this situation. It has, however, been noted that the number of cases in which a soul appears to be demoted, from one life to the next, appear to be greater than those involving promotion—particularly in India's caste system—and that has raised suspicions among skeptics. An unscrupulous, needy family could, theoretically, learn about a recently deceased individual, gather data about that person, and then when another child is born into the family, that son or daughter is drilled to recite the information. However, despite the possible temptations, this does seem to be a rare occurrence: Indian researcher Satwant Pasricha offers only one possible case and makes a reference to another in her book.[5] On the other hand, in some cultures, far from encouraging children to speak about past lives, parents actively dissuade their offspring from doing so, even to the point of beating them.

All these possible alternative explanations need to be borne in mind, as we start to examine the very best cases of reincarnation that have been investigated.

Part Four

Implications

Chapter 20

Best Evidence for Rebirth

There is no shortage of impressive case studies that suggest reincarnation is a fact but to present the evidence of just one case in its entirety and evaluate it properly would require many more pages than I have at my disposal. Besides, such cases are already written up in great detail and published in lengthy reports in a variety of academic journals, many available online, as well as in the investigators' own books. For that reason, the following collection of some of the cases that particularly impress me contains only brief accounts, with the exception of the first two, which are from my own notes and interviews conducted during the making of a TV documentary. The footnotes for each of the others will lead those with a desire to read more about them to sources that go into far greater detail.

I have grouped them under headings that highlight common characteristics or themes, while acknowledging that some cases are so rich in content that they could comfortably occupy two or more categories. Finally, before opening up the casebook, I need to make the observation that no reincarnation researcher has yet discovered a case that provides 100 percent proof that a subject has been reborn. Perhaps they never will. But some researchers, as you will see, appear to get very close, to the point where scientific rigor requires them to remain firmly on the fence, but privately they are convinced that reincarnation is the *only* explanation that makes sense of the data collected.

Casualties of Conflict

Violent deaths feature prominently in reincarnation cases. The overall figure is 51 percent, ranging from the lowest rate of 29 percent among the Haida people of northwestern North America to an astonishing 74 percent in Turkey (Stevenson, 1997a, Vol. 2). These incidences far exceed those of violent death in the general populations of those countries. Is this because the trauma of a violent death causes it to be remembered in a future life? Or is it because the life was cut short that the soul has had to be reborn?

Haneen al-Arum with her past-life husband, Ajaj Eid

During my visits to Lebanon it was inevitable that I would encounter cases that had their past-life roots in the various bloody conflicts that have afflicted that country over the past four decades. Two particularly impressed me. The first is encapsulated in a photograph I took of an elderly man, wearing a white Druze tarbush (fez) and sporting a long white beard, with a pretty young girl seated on the arm of his chair, her hand resting affectionately on his arm. Ask someone to write a caption for this image and they are most likely to suggest that it shows a granddaughter visiting her grandfather. The truth is startlingly different. My picture, both families believe, shows Ajaj Eid and his wife Safa (now reborn as **Haneen Al-Arum**, a bus driver's daughter). Safa's life had come to an abrupt end on January 17, 1984, when the sixteen-inch guns of the US battleship *New Jersey* began shelling the Druze positions in the Chouf mountains above Beirut. The much-loved mother of five, a schoolteacher who taught Arabic, followed her husband out of their home to warn him to be careful, after he went to help a neighbor whose curtains had caught fire after an explosion. Still able to recall that day, Haneen—who was eleven years old when I met her at the spot where Safa's life ended—told me what happened next. "There was more shelling and a piece of shell hit my neck and I died."

| Safa Eid and her son Riad (standing) with husband (seated) | Haneen Al-Arum with her present-day mother (right) and past-life daughter |

Hareen Al-Arum with her past-life son and daughter, Riad and Shahira, and the author, Roy Stemman

As soon as she could speak after her rebirth as Haneen three years later, she began calling for her son, Riad. She told her parents, "I am Safa," adding that she was from Bchamoun and the Eid family. In a culture that accepts reincarnation, many go in search of family members that might have been reborn, and Shahira, one of Safa Eid's daughters, was no exception. She learned of three young girls who might be her mother's reincarnation, one of whom was Haneen. When they met and she asked the young girl, "Do you recognize me?" Haneen replied "You are Shahira, my daughter," and they hugged and kissed. I saw for myself how very close Haneen was to all the family members when I accompanied her to the Eid home. When first taken there by car, I learned, Haneen had pointed immediately to the house where the curtains had caught fire, as she stepped from the car. Shahira, still testing Haneen to be sure she was her mother's reincarnation, started to walk up some stairs as if heading for the family home, but the young girl corrected her, pointing down the hill, instead. Shahira changed direction and entered the first gate. "This is not our house," Haneen protested. When they reached the right house, she remarked that the front had changed. This was absolutely right because in the same shelling that had taken her life, the house was damaged, and her son Riad had decided to reposition the steps when it was rebuilt. At the front door, Shahira rang the bell and a woman answered. "This is Layla, Riad's wife," Haneen announced. Correct, again, as was her identification of Riad, who was sitting inside with a friend, and her observation that her husband, Ajaj, now had a beard—he had not grown one when she was Safa. Riad asked Haneen to describe the layout of the home, which she did to his satisfaction, and then when he took her around she

Roy Stemman

stopped at a display cabinet and remarked that she had hidden money in the lower compartment for Layla. She was clearly disappointed to see it had now gone. In fact, Layla confirmed to Riad that she had found it and removed it. Layla also had a test question for Haneen: "Is that where you kept your

Druze sheikhs listening to their spiritual leader

gold?" she asked, referring to the compartment. "I never had gold," Haneen responded. Safa and Ajaj were Druze sheikhs and, as religious people, did not have jewelry.[1]

◇

There was something about the appearance of the young boy who is the subject of my next Lebanese case that fully justified the description "old soul in a young body."

We met twelve-year-old **Rabih Abu Dyab** at his school where he talked about his memories of having been a famous Lebanese footballer and pop singer, Saad Halawi. He had died when he went into a building in Beirut that was also an ammunitions dump and an explosion had occurred. Rabih began speaking of his former life at the age of three-and-a-half but, because his past-life personality was someone famous, skeptics will suggest that he learned about Saad by normal means. When I visited his home and met his parents they assured me their son had not been

The author with Rabih Abu Dyab

exposed to magazine stories or TV reports about Halawi before he started talking about his previous life, because at that time they were living in Saudi Arabia and did not receive Lebanese magazines. On the other hand, his mother, Raabi'i, assured me she was very familiar with the footballer and his singing career. "Yes, of course, all the Lebanese, a long time ago, knew him. We used to hear him a lot. Before Rabih was born he had a nice song, 'My mother how could I forget you?' which was very famous." There was, however, much more to Saad Halawi than football and singing. Rabih told me

Rabih Abu Dyab with a poster of his past life personality: Saad Halawi

that about six months before he (as Halawi) had been killed, he had become a Druze sheikh and had withdrawn all his records from the shops.

According to Raabi'i Abu Dyab, her son was only four years old when he first met a member of Saad Halawi's family. "We had gone to the house of Hassan Hamad Halawi [Saad's cousin] but we didn't find him. He heard we had visited and he came here to our home with a friend. Rabih recognized him and agreed to go for a walk with them. They were gone for two hours during which time he asked Rabih many questions. When he came back to the house he was convinced 100 percent that Rabih was Saad, because he was remembering everything. And then Rabih said something to Hassan; he asked, 'Where is Abu Randour?' It was a name Saad Halawi used for his brother Suhare when they went to play football—not everybody knows it. When he heard that, Hassan started crying and said, 'OK, there's no doubt.'" It would have been better to have heard the testimony directly from Hassan, but he was not available during our visit for reasons relating to his work, we were told. However, I did meet Suhare ("Abu Randour") who came to my hotel in Beirut, bringing with him an album of photographs and newspaper cuttings about his brother. He was clearly still grieving over his loss. Suhare told me he had met Rabih and was satisfied he was the reincarnation of Saad, but he had trouble coming to terms with the fact that his brother was now in a different body . . . that of

Rabih Abu Dyab
at the football club

a young boy. Saad's best friend, Ghassan Abu Dyab, who in 1997 was the Lebanese football team's coach, was similarly convinced, though he had decided not to let a relationship develop between him and Rabih because it affected him so much. "When I first saw Rabih and invited him to my home, I felt this was Saad Halawi," he testified on camera, his voice breaking with emotion, "because he had depth of vision and in his looks, for his age, I felt it was him. Especially after he made me listen to some of the poems he was writing and a song he had written for the Safa football team."

The TV documentary I was making in Lebanon ended with a first-ever meeting between Rabih and Saad Halawi's sister, Samar Nassereddin, about whom the boy had often spoken. He was not told whom he would be meeting as he stepped into the school library, but it would not have been difficult for him to work out the identity of the stranger he was being introduced to, as the camera filmed the encounter. Samar fed him enough clues and Rabih eventually observed, "There's an incredibly strong resemblance between you and my sister." She responded affectionately and the camera crew was then asked to leave so that they could have a private conversation. Afterward, she confirmed on camera that she accepted Rabih as her famous brother, reborn, before walking off arm-in-arm with him.[2]

Rabih Abu Dyab and his past life sister, Samar

Digging Up the Past

It was another TV company that flew numismatist **Jim Bethe** over from the USA to be filmed in a Welsh park looking for the treasure he said he had buried there in a previous life. The company had read a report I had published of Bethe's past-life memories and decided to take it further. It even got permission from the local authority to do some digging. Jim had been speaking about a past life since the age of four and particularly of a buried chest of jewels. Under hypnosis in 1988 he claimed to have been a British soldier, Jonathan Seaman, born in the late 1700s, who had been a cartographer in the King's Army. While stationed in India, he had acquired a small casket of jewels that he brought back to England and hid, along with two other boxes of valuables, in a pigsty in Swansea, southwest Wales, which led down to a cave. He also mentioned the treasure being in water. Finding the actual spot was going to be difficult, so the TV producer arranged for dowser Elizabeth Sullivan to assist. Between them, Bethe and Sullivan identified a spot and digging commenced on a cold winter's day in late 1994 as a small group of us watched. I wasn't expecting anything to be found as the team dug down between the roots of trees with spades, in a copse alongside an open field. But, to everyone's astonishment, a concrete "floor"was uncovered, though clearly of modern origin. It required a mechanical digger to excavate farther, revealing much older brickwork and, below that, a tunnel and water. The search had to be abandoned for safety reasons, though the TV company announced its intention of involving other experts and digging even deeper. Since then, nothing more has been heard. Perhaps they found the jewels![3]

A graphic description of a civil war battle that raged around a castle on the banks of Loch Martenham in Scotland was given by **Peter Hulme** during a hypnotic regression conducted by his brother Bob. Historians knew nothing of a battle in that vicinity and locals were even unaware there had been a castle until Peter and Bob, together with another brother, Carl, did their own research and found a seventeenth-century map showing a castle, the ruins of which they were able to locate and uncover. Metal detectors also produced strong signals for objects in the loch's shallow waters, which they suspected were cannon balls, but did not have the right equipment to retrieve them. Peter's past-life memories, when he was John Rafael serving under a Captain Leverett, also led the brothers to a "dried up ravine" in Scotland that he said had been a campsite for five hundred men in 1646. Despite no records existing to confirm the site had ever been used for such a purpose, metal detectors recovered a haul that included musket balls and relics typical of a civil war encampment. Though they had not been able to confirm Rafael's existence, they *were* successful with his commanding officer, Captain Leverett, whom he remembered as being tall, blond, and speaking with an American accent. Research at the London War Records show him to have been based in Nottingham but to have originated in Massachusetts. He eventually returned to the USA and became that state's governor.[4]

Ram Dayal Sharma, a rather unsavory character and petty thief, accidentally shot himself dead while cleaning a gun in northern India, but was apparently reborn as Naripender Singh in the same village just two hundred yards from where he had once lived. The two families knew each other but were not friends. When he was old enough to speak, Naripender is said to have recognized Ram's widow, Javitri; his uncle Niranjan Lal; and a friend, Chhajju Singh, who had been an accomplice in his crimes. They accepted Naripender as Ram reborn because of knowledge of a personal nature that he conveyed to them, and he visited them often. He even told Ram Dayal's widow about treasure he had buried in the house and discussed with Chhajju the booty they had taken in a robbery forty years earlier. Naripender was born within a few days of Ram Dayal's death and had birthmarks that appeared to coincide with a wound inflicted earlier in that life, as well as the gunshot wound to his chest. This was one of ten cases (out of a total of forty-five, all of which featured birthmarks or birth defects) in four states of northern India, investigated by clinical psychologist Dr. Satwant Pasricha, under the auspices of the National Institute of Mental Health and Neurosciences in Bangalore, mostly in collaboration with the University of Virginia, USA.[5]

In a lecture to the Society for Psychical Research in London, its former honorary secretary and a member of its hypnosis committee, Dr. Hugh Pincott, told of a regression session in which he was involved. A young female subject apparently recalled a life four centuries earlier in a house that she described in detail, saying that one of the rooms had been converted into a chapel. He was able to locate it in the county of Hampshire. Together with a colleague, Pincott visited the house, where its present owner told them he knew that its present conservatory had once been a chapel. "What he was not aware of," Pincott added, "which we were able to point out, was the presence of a hidden cupboard behind a panel. Knowing where it could be opened, we did so in the owner's presence. It contained the deeds of the house, kept there for nearly four hundred years, and which the girl had told us about on tape."[6]

Helen Pickering was one of four Sydney housewives seemingly regressed to past lives by Australian psychologist Peter Ramster for a very evidential 1983 TV documentary. None of the women had ever left Australia yet they recalled lives in Western Europe in the eighteenth and nineteenth centuries. Pickering, for example, remembered a life in Aberdeen, Scotland, where she was a man, James Archibald Burns, born in 1807. She even produced a drawing, while in trance, of the city's Marshall College of Medicine as it was in Burns's day, when he was a teacher there. It has changed significantly since then. Pickering was flown to Scotland and was filmed visiting the college, where the accuracy of her drawing was confirmed by local historian David Gordon, the only man who had that information, having collected every plan and drawing from the college's earliest times. He expressed doubt about just one detail: the former existence of a door, shown on Pickering's drawing, where now there was only a wall. After her visit, however, additional plans of the college were located and "Burns" was proved right. There *had* once been a door exactly as shown.[7]

Those who had life readings from **Edgar Cayce,** Virginia Beach's famous "Sleeping Prophet," invariably wanted to know who they had been in a past life. The entranced Cayce usually obliged with a name and enough other material to make it possible to confirm the existence, or otherwise, of the past-life person identified. Few, it seems, recorded the results. So, in the late 1990s, the Edgar Cayce Foundation sponsored a major research project, headed by anthropologist Dr. Rosalie Horstman Haines, to look for confirmation of historical data in the two thousand life readings he gave. When I visited the Cayce headquarters and met Dr. Haines in 1999, she revealed that they had so far confirmed the existence of one past life. A musician who consulted Cayce was told he had been B. A. Seay, indicating that records of this person might be found "among those of a Masonic order in the western portions of Kentucky." Asked to be specific about the place and number of the Masonic Lodge, the entranced Cayce responded by saying they were "at the Beverley Masonic Lodge. The last of the secretaries of these, as we find, was

John T. Stigger. The present, N. A. Booker, on a rural route between Hopkins-ville and Clarksville." Asked where records of B. A. Seay could be found in Virginia, Cayce replied, "In the records of Henrico County." The foundation's researchers have since established that Bernard A. Seay, with a membership at the Masonic Lodge in Kentucky as indicated, did exist and was captured while carrying the 14th Virginia colors at Gettysburg.[8]

Although written as a novel, past-life therapist **Linda Tarazi**'s captivating *Under the Inquisition* makes its readers very aware of the fact that it is based entirely on transcripts of regression sessions with a woman subject who pro-vided an astonishing wealth of fascinating but often obscure information. In fact, Tarazi wrote an account of the case for the *Journal of the American Society for Psychical Research* (October 1990), seven years before it was pub-lished as a book. It took Tarazi three years to research the evidence produced under hypnosis, including a year spent in Spain combing through archives, to establish the accuracy of what her subject, a Chicago housewife who is given the pseudonym Laurel Dilmen, recalled about her supposed sixteenth-century life as Antonia Michaela Maria Ruiz de Prado. That life began in 1555 on the island of Hispaniola but was spent mostly in the south-central Spanish town of Cuenca and ended with drowning off an unnamed Carib-bean island. What emerged under hypnosis was "an exciting, romantic life filled with erotic adventures as thrilling as any historical romance of movies, television, or novels," Tarazi wrote. "At first, in fact, her tale led me to believe that it was the fictitious creation of an active imagination."

Well aware of the possibility of cryptomnesia, Tarazi asked Dilmen while she was under hypnosis, but not in the "Antonia" life, to search her memory and tell her the names of all history books she had read outside of school. The hypnotist checked them all out, confirming that none provided the pertinent, obscure facts that emerged in Antonia's past-life recall. Her subsequent three-year quest to either corroborate or disprove well over one hundred facts took Tarazi to two dozen libraries and universities, traveling to Spain, North Africa, and the Caribbean, as well as correspondence with historians and archivists in order to verify the information. She also checked American and British movies as well as TV specials to see if any of these could have been a source for the extraordinary details provided by "Antonia." She drew a blank.

In that past life, Antonia spoke Spanish, Latin, and German but was unable to converse in those languages under hypnosis. However, "she pronounced names very well, recited the prayers required by the Inquisition in Latin, referred to special methods of making the sign of the cross—the *signo* and *santiguado*—unknown to most Spanish-speaking priests today, and composed words and music to a song in Latin and music for the Latin Pater Noster, both of which she is recorded singing." Also, several vital pieces of information were to be found only in old Spanish books, and some only in the Municipal, others in the diocesan archives of Cuenca. Yet Dilmen "has no Spanish ancestry, has never been to Spain, and has no familiarity with the language." One by one, Tarazi was able to confirm the existence of every person named by Dilmen, including her sixteenth-century lover, Dr. Francisco de Arganda. Yet so far, there is no proof that the main character, the novel's heroine Antonia Michaela Maria Ruiz de Prado, who has apparently reincarnated as Laurel Dilmen, ever existed.[9]

I've Been Here Before

Memories of a huge building hewn out of pink and black stone haunted the young **James Arthur Flowerdew,** starting with a vivid dream at the age of twelve. But when he asked his father where it was—assuming it was a place to which he had been taken when much younger—he was scolded for fantasizing. Unusually, these dreams of a large city surrounded by desert, along with spontaneous flashes of memory, grew stronger in adulthood, particularly when he saw similar structures. Eventually, he recognized it when watching a BBC TV documentary about Petra, the Jordanian capital city of the Nabataeans, whose treasury building is a majestic example of rock cut architecture. By then a successful businessman, running a garage in Norfolk, England, Flowerdew was certain that he was seeing glimpses of a former life in which he was a soldier who was killed by a spear near the temple. He contacted the BBC about his strange memories and was invited to talk about it on television. News of this eventually reached the Jordanian government, who invited Flowerdew and a BBC film crew to visit Petra, which dates back to the sixth century BC and existed until taken over by the Romans in 105 AD. Before making the journey, he was introduced to a world-renowned archeologist, who was amazed at Flowerdew's descriptions of aspects of the city that would be unknown to most people. He even explained the purpose of a curious structure that puzzled the experts: It was a guardroom where he had been a soldier two thousand years earlier. When he flew to Petra in August 1978 with, among others, Prof. Iain Browning, one of the world's leading authorities on the city, he was asked how he would find the city. "Looking to the east of the rocky area about 180 miles from Amman and well into the desert," he replied, "we must look for a large rock which looks like a volcano with the top cut off. Petra lies just beyond." Which was absolutely right. And he led the group into the city through the narrow entrance to the Siq without difficulty, showing an intimate knowledge of the city's buildings and their purpose, with just one exception. "I don't remember that at all," he said, pointing to the magnificent amphitheater. "You wouldn't," he was told. "It was built by the Romans long after you had died." The archeologists were puzzled by row upon row of scooped out pigeon holes in the exterior wall of his old guardhouse. It was, Flowerdew explained, "The Office of the Duty Roster" and the holes were arranged in three perpendicular sections representing "On duty in the City," "Off duty," and "On duty outside the City." Each of the sixty to seventy officers had a different-shaped stone tablet that was placed in the appropriate cavity, enabling the commanding officer to keep track of his men. "He filled in details, and a lot of it is very consistent with known archaeological and historical facts," the expert told BBC TV viewers, "and it would require a mind very different from his to be able to sustain a fabric of deception on the scale of his memories—at least those which he's reported to me."[10]

Another Englishman, **Peter Avery,** who was a renowned Persian scholar and translator of *Omar Khayyam,* twice experienced the phenomenon of *déjà vu*, earning him a chapter in Ian Stevenson's book on European cases suggestive of reincarnation. Avery recounted how, when he made his first visit to the central Iranian city of Isfahan in 1950, he found he knew his way around by some instinct. He had never seen a map of the city nor read a guidebook. In the medieval Madresseh he felt a strong sense of "knowing the place intimately; of returning, as it were, home to where I had once been 'at home.'" He was open to the possibility that these memories were either of a past life or were inherited, as one of his direct ancestors had been the celebrated seventeenth-century pirate, Captain Henry Avery, who preyed on shipping in the Indian Ocean.[11]

Unfinished Business

Among those who feel they have been reborn in order to complete a task, or make amends for things left undone in a previous life, the case of **Jenny Cockell** is unforgettable. From early days, she recalled a life in the Irish Republic as Mary Sutton, in a place she was able to identify on a map:

Malahide. Her final memory of that life was lying in bed in a large room that was not in her home, knowing she was about to die and fearing for the welfare of the children she was leaving behind. Slowly, from memories that continued to seep through, she pieced together a coherent story of a woman whose husband, John, had a fondness for alcohol that led to him being violent against her. She had given birth to eight children, dying just one

Jenny Cockell and her past-life son with Roy Stemman

month after her last child, Elizabeth, was born. With so many offspring, it was clear that John Sutton was not capable of bringing them up himself, hence Mary's dying concerns that had spilled over into this lifetime as Jenny Cockell. Indeed, after she died, her husband arranged for the children to be fostered by others, with the exception of Sonny, the eldest boy, whom he kept—and Sonny soon left of his own accord. The exciting culmination of Jenny's dogged research to confirm the accuracy of her own past-life memories, assisted by independent investigations, was when she was also able to bring her past-life family back together again. Most of them had not been in touch with each other since childhood. A reunion was filmed by a TV crew, in Malahide, coinciding with Cockell's book about her two lives, *Yesterday's Children* (1993). I appeared on a number of TV chat shows with both Jenny and Sonny, at that time, and it was decidedly odd to hear an elderly man referred to by a middle-aged woman as "my son," and for him to look at her affectionately and describe her as "my mother."[12]

Special Knowledge

If children can carry memories across from one life to another, how about aptitudes and special talents? There are many examples where this seems to be the case, though we have to acknowledge that such innate skills may also be due to genetic memory or other normal causes. The case of **Purnima Ekanayake** is not so easily dismissed. Between the ages of three and six, the Sri Lankan girl spoke often about a life in which she had been a man whose family made Ambiga and Geta Pichcha incense. He had been married to a sister-in-law, Kusumi, and his mother's name was Simona. Purnima even knew her past-life school: Rahula. That life came to an end in a traffic accident when the man was selling incense from a bicycle. Her parents—he the principal of a secondary school and she a teacher—rationalized their daughter's claims after they were unable to find the brands of incense she mentioned on sale in their town of Bakamuna. They decided she had heard the name Ambiga in a TV jewelry advertisement, and Geta Pichcha was a variety of jasmine grown in their own garden. Their attitude began to change, however, when they took Purnima (who was not then old enough to go to school) with them and a group of pupils to the famous Kelaniya temple near Colombo, 145 miles from their hometown. On arrival, she told her parents she had lived on the other side of the Kelaniya River. Since a new teacher at her father's school, W. G. Sumanasiri, was a recent graduate of Kelaniya University, he agreed to research the case. He discovered three families making incense in the area, and one of them, named Wijisiri, produced brands named Ambiga and Geta Pichcha.

It was time to call in an expert. Most of Erlendur Haraldsson's past-life research has been conducted in Sri Lanka, and between September 1996 and March 1999 he made five visits to investigate the case further. The present owner of the incense-making company was L. A. Wijisiri, whose brother-in-law and associate, Jinadasa Perera, had died in an accident with a bus in September 1985 as he was taking incense to the market. Among the statements made by Purnima was that in that past life she (as Jinadasa) had two wives, which proved correct, and also the name of the place where she/he had died. She also recognized various people from that life when she and her family visited her former home and even knew how incense was made (knowledge even her parents did not have), correctly stating which of the two possible methods the Wijisiri family used. Purnima also had birthmarks on her body which, when she met the Wijisiri family, she attributed to the injuries she suffered in the accident that took her life.[13]

Violent Deaths

Like many youngsters who have strong memories of a previous life, **Nazih Al-Danaf** was insistent from a very early age that his parents take him to his former family. They and his six sisters and one brother were used to him talking about a life in which he carried guns and hand grenades and owned a red car. He wanted to go there to see his children and fetch his weapons. They resisted his pleas until early 1998, when he was six, and then drove him to Qaberchamoun, where he said he had lived in his previous existence. Arriving at an intersection where six roads converged, Nazih told his father which one to take, explaining that they would soon come to a road that forks off upward, adding, "My house is there." They parked at the first forked road, and while Nazih and his father walked up its steep incline in search of his former home, his mother, brother, and two sisters stayed with the car. They decided to talk to a man who was cleaning his car nearby, and in response to his question, Nazih's mother explained that her son seemed to remember a past-life in the vicinity. Kamal Khaddage takes up the story: "They asked if I knew someone who had been shot; they did not know his name, but he had carried handguns, hand grenades, and had owned a red car." He was surprised, as the boy appeared to be describing his father, Fuad Khaddage, who had died some years earlier. He called his mother, Najdiyah, who was working in a field, and as she arrived, Nazih and his father returned from their search. Kamal told his mother that Nazih claimed to be her husband reincarnated. When asked by his father whether Najdiyah had been his wife, the six-year-old just looked her up and down, then smiled. So Najdiyah decided to test him. "Who built the foundation of this gate at the entrance to this house?" she asked. "A man from the Faraj family," Nazih answered correctly. Inside the house he went by himself to a room and pointed to a cupboard, indicating first the right side, saying, "Here I used to put my pistol," and then, on the left side, "Here I used to put my weapons," using an Arabic word that means unspecified weapons. This was absolutely right. He demanded to know where they were and Najdiyah told him they had been stolen. Nazih recalled his former wife slipping and dislocating her shoulder, requiring her to wear a cast for some time. Asked if he remembered how their young daughter got sick, he said, "She was poisoned from my medication and I took her to hospital." This was true, as was the statement that he had come home drunk one night and Najdiyah had locked the door, so he went to sleep outside on a rocking sofa. Nazih reminded her that he had taught her to shoot, using a barrel in the garden as the target. "This is it," he said when they went to look at it. Their son Kamal had wanted to throw it away but Najdiyah had said to him, "Maybe my husband comes back reincarnated and recognizes the barrel," so it was left there.

Reincarnation researcher Erlendur Haraldsson was able to meet the subject when Nazih was eight and still had some recall of his past life. He made three trips to Lebanon, starting in May 2000, during which he spoke to and collected testimonies from numerous witnesses to Nazih's statements made before the two families met, as well as accompanying him and family members to the Kaddadge home, where he observed affectionate embraces between Nazih and his past-life family as they said farewell. Among those who testified to Nazih's astonishing memories was Fuad's brother, Adeep, a Druze sheikh, who is a senior employee of an airline in Beirut. The six-year-old was taken to his home after the first meeting with the Kaddadge family. He told Haraldsson that he saw a boy running toward him, saying, "Here comes my brother Adeep." Nazih declared: "I am your brother Fuad." When asked for proof, Nazih replied that he had once given Adeep a handgun as a gift. What kind of gun? "I gave you a Checki 16" (a gun from Czechoslovakia) the boy responded, asking if he still had it. "Then I hugged him and was 100 percent sure that he was my brother."

Haraldsson regards this as one of the strongest cases he has investigated, which is appropriate since it also has strong links to the Druze religion, for which, I explained in an earlier section, reincarnation is fundamental to their teachings. Fuad was employed for thirty years at the Druze Center (Dar El

Taifeh) in Beirut, where he worked for Sheikh Al Aql, the spiritual leader of the Druze. As well as being the center's manager, Fuad was also the companion/bodyguard of Sheikh Al Aql. Described as fearless and brave with a liking for weapons, Fuad was assassinated, along with two guards at the gate, when three men broke into the Druze center on July 22, 1982, trying unsuccessfully to set the building on fire.[14]

World War II Deaths

It is hardly surprising that the deadliest military conflict in history, World War II, with over sixty million people killed, has produced some startling and impressive reincarnation cases. In modern times, none has caught the American public's imagination more than **James Leininger's** story.

The Louisiana boy had nightmares as a child, then began speaking of his final moments in a previous life: "Airplane crash, plane on fire, little man can't get out." Over time, he was able to tell his parents, Bruce and Andrea, that his aircraft had operated from the boat Natoma (aircraft carrier *USS Natoma Bay*) and been shot down by the Japanese. Flicking through a book that his father had received from a book club, the two-year old pointed at a picture of Iwo Jima, an island with three operational airfields that the United States captured from the Japanese in a battle that lasted more than a month in 1945. "Daddy, that is where my plane was shot down," said James. Bruce Leininger decided to investigate further, discovering that only one American pilot died during the battle: twenty-one-year-old Lt. James McCready Huston, Jr., flying his fiftieth mission. His son also remembered the name Jack Larsen, who proved to be a fellow airman who had flown alongside him on that final mission. The Leiningers have video footage of James, aged three, apparently carrying out pre-flight checks on an aircraft. And when his mother bought him a toy plane, drawing attention to a bomb on its underside, her young son corrected her, saying it was a drop tank—a term she had never heard. The story of their four years of research and gradual acceptance that their son is the reincarnation of James Huston is told in his father's book, *Soul Survivor.* Huston's sister Anne Barron and cousin Bob Huston are among those who are now convinced that the World War II fighter pilot has been reborn. James Leininger no longer has memories of that previous life, but he is as fascinated as others about those statements he made as a young child. Now a teenager, he is also seen to have a striking facial resemblance to the World War II fighter pilot.[15]

The story of **Carl Edon,** an English boy, is remarkably similar to that of James Leininger, with one notable exception.

Born in Middlesbrough in 1972, he also remembered being a bomber pilot whose aircraft crashed "through the windows of a building" after being hit by enemy fire. The enemy, however, was British, for in that past life Carl was a German airman, whose aircraft was apparently shot down over northeast England, where the Edons lived. Carl's memories began at a young age. Once he could draw, he produced Nazi symbols. He recognized a picture of Hitler, gave it a stiff-arm salute, and began to goose-step. He drew the cockpit of the plane and said it was a Messerschmidt. Among his recollections was the fact that he lost his leg when the plane plunged to earth. A chapter was devoted to him in *The Children that Time Forgot.*[16] Carl and his family were visited by Ian Stevenson and the case is included in his book of European cases. All the evidence led Carl's parents to believe that in his past life their son was Heinrich Richter, a crewmember of a Dornier E217-4 that crashed on January 15, 1942, and from which three bodies were recovered. In 1997, building workers clearing land at the spot discovered a buried German Dornier bomber and in it the body of the fourth crew member, Heinrich Richter, whose right leg had been severed by the impact. He was buried with full military honors and a local historian tracked down his relatives in Cologne. When Carl's parents saw a picture of the German gunner they were stunned by the remarkable similarity in appearance between him and Carl.[17]

Much of the evidence, collected by different people, is confusing. Despite the similarity in appearance and the severed leg, we have to acknowledge that Carl claimed to be a pilot, but Richter was a turret gunner. He said he had crashed through the windows of a building but the Dornier plunged to earth on a railway siding at South Bank, Cleveland. He said he had a younger brother who was a pilot, but both of Richter's brothers served in the German Army. Local historian Bill Norman wrote a book about the event,[18] which refers not only to the crew of the aircraft and his contact with their families but also to Carl Edon's memories. Though he does not accept reincarnation as the explanation for Carl's memories, he kindly contacted Sylvia Schubert, a relative of the Richters, to ask the first name of Heinrich's father—which Carl Edon said was Fritz. She replied: "I have contacted Werner and first he told me that Heinrich's father was called Heinrich, too. But as a precaution he wanted to look in old documents and what a surprise—in an old register of the Richter family is written that Heinrich's father had *three* first names. His complete name was: Friedrich Wilhelm Heinrich Richter." Fritz is the common German short form of Friedrich. So, it's another strange coincidence in the Carl Edon story. Though it doesn't satisfy me that he was remembering the life of Heinrich Richter, his memories and behavior suggest that he may have been remembering the life of another German airman. Tragically, Carl was brutally murdered just a few hundred yards from the crash site in 1995.

No such doubt exists for an equally remarkable World War II story, with a very similar theme to the preceding cases. It concerns Scottish-born **Ken Llewelyn,** who, when I met him in 1994, was a senior public relations officer with the Royal Australian Air Force. In the 1960s, before moving to Australia, Llewelyn had been a pilot in Britain's Royal Air Force, but although good at his job, he had to leave because of a fear of flying at high altitude.

An explanation for this seemed to be offered by a Canberra medium who told him that in his previous life he had been in the German Luftwaffe and been shot down over England. While all the information given did not seem to be accurate, it offered Llewelyn an explanation for his phobia. Then, on a visit to England, he consulted other mediums who told him he had been decapitated in his former life, with one assuring him that he would receive information from a relative that would be helpful. When Llewelyn visited his brother in Wales, he received surprising news. "He told me that while on patrol duty in the marshes of Norfolk around 1942, he had actually picked up the headless body of a Dornier pilot still wearing all the Luftwaffe badges and insignias." He decided to investigate further, discovering that the plane had crashed at Sheringham and the pilot's name was Friedrich Wilhelm Dorflinger. A hypnotic regression soon afterward enabled Llewelyn to recall his last moments in the stricken Dornier, with its controls jammed and an engine on fire. He told the crew to bail out. This case has an astonishing climax. Llewelyn tracked down his Luftwaffe co-pilot, Helmut Scrypezak, the only member of the crew to survive, and they met, with a local teacher acting as translator. Scrypezak confirmed all the details of the Dornier's technical difficulties that Llewelyn had experienced during regression and which required him and the others to bail out. "When the time came to go, we both threw our arms around each other with tears in our eyes," said the man who had apparently been both a Luftwaffe and a Royal Air Force pilot in the same century.[19]

There are a number of similarities between the last two cases, of course, and those involving Japanese air crew shot down over Burma. Strangely, in all these instances, the souls of the victims have seemingly reincarnated in the countries in which they died, rather than returning to the nation for which they were fighting.

The cases I have quoted are but a selection of some of those that have impressed me over the years, based on the evidence provided, most of which has been exhaustively researched by independent investigators who confirmed the accuracy of the claims presented. As I pointed out at the outset, they all have flaws of one kind or another, and the quest for "the perfect case" continues. We come closer to that goal, it seems, in cases that involve not only memories of a past life but a corresponding physical element in the form of birthmarks or birth defects. Fortunately, as we are about to see, there is an abundance of such cases.

Chapter 21

Birthmarks
A Lasting Impression

As he and other reincarnation researchers collected cases over the years, it became obvious to Ian Stevenson that birthmarks and birth defects often provided powerful, contributory evidence of a claimed past life. Time and again, the subjects of these cases or their families drew attention to birthmarks and birth defects that seemed to coincide with wounds, scars, or marks on the body of the person the subject claimed to have been in a past life. Often these were related to fatal injuries that brought that previous existence to a sudden end. Statistics held by Stevenson's department at the University of Virginia indicate that around one-third of cases feature physical marks or abnormalities of this kind. In one group of 895 cases studied,[1] out of more than two thousand on file, 35 percent involved birthmarks or birth defects. Then, isolating forty-nine cases where it was possible to obtain adequate data to compare these with the position of wounds on the past-life person, it was found that the location coincided in forty-three of them—an impressive 88 percent. Critics of reincarnation cases may argue that the evidence provided by children's memories alone is not enough to persuade us they have been reborn. If, however, a child not only talks about a previous life in enough detail for its family to identify a possible past-life personality, but also is born with birthmarks or birth defects that are highly relevant to that previous life, then a new, *physical* dimension is added to that of the mental evidence.

Having made this discovery, Stevenson began holding back many of the birthmark cases he had investigated in order to publish them all together, on the basis that they would have greater impact if used in that way. The result is his monumental *Reincarnation and Biology: A Contribution to the Etiology of Birthmarks and Birth Defects*,[2] which consists of two illustrated volumes, each of more than one thousand pages, the first dealing specifically with birthmarks and the second devoted to "birth defects and other anomalies." As well as representing the most extensive and detailed investigation of reincarnation, they are a testament to one scientist's dedication to his chosen field of study: survival of death, paranormal phenomena, and in particular, reincarnation. It is the longest-running parapsychological research program ever conducted. As well as providing a new perspective on rebirth, Stevenson and his fellow researchers have also uncovered dramatic and exciting human stories that would not be out of place in a novel.

Take, for example, his investigation of a Turkish boy who was given the name Dahham at birth but insisted on being called Cemil as soon as he could speak. In time, his family decided to change his name officially and he became known as Cemil Fahrici.[3] The reason for his insistence was that he claimed to remember the life of a distant relative, Cemil Hayik, a celebrated bandit. Hayik's troubles began, Stevenson tells us, when he killed two men who had raped two of his sisters. He was charged with the murders but managed to escape and spent two years living in a mountainous area between two cities, robbing travelers in the isolated region to provide whatever he needed. This was in the early 1930s when France occupied the province of Hatay, and the French gendarmes responsible for policing the area received very little assistance from local people in their hunt for the fugitive, who had been joined by his brother. Eventually, police surrounded Hayik's house and a shoot-out occurred, during which the gendarmes managed to pour gasoline on the building and set fire to it. Rather than be captured, Cemil shot his brother and then committed suicide by placing the muzzle of his gun under his chin and moving the trigger with his toe.

When Cemil Fahrici was born a few days after the death of the Hayik brothers, in 1935, it was noticed immediately that he had a prominent birthmark under his right chin: "a scar-like area that bled for some days after his birth" requiring his parents to take him to a hospital, where the wound was stitched. As he grew up, Cemil suffered nightmares about fighting the French police and gave a graphic account of his death in his previous life and enough other details to convince the Hayik family that he was Cemil reborn. So much so, that they tried to persuade the Fahricis to part with their son. Although Stevenson did not begin researching this case until more than thirty years after the birth of Cemil, he was as thorough as always, interviewing the subject, his mother and stepbrother, other family members, and even the platoon of gendarmes involved in the shootout. In the course of that research he met Cemil Hayik's sister, Rüzane, who testified that she had seen her brothers' bodies after the shooting and was able to give a vivid description of how the bullet that killed Cemil had exited at the top of his skull and lifted out a part of its bone. Until that moment, Stevenson had believed that Cemil Fahrici had only one birthmark: the bleeding wound under his chin.

Having heard Rüzane's description of her brothers' injuries, Stevenson realized that Cemil ought to have a second birthmark coinciding with the point at which the bullet had passed out of his brain. This assumption was based on other cases in his file in which birthmarks coinciding with bullet wounds matched in size and location those on the deceased body, depending on whether they were points of entry (small) or exit (larger). He went back to Cemil and asked him, without explanation, if he had another birthmark. "Without hesitating, he pointed to the top of his head. With little difficulty, I found a substantial linear area of alopecia in the left parietal area of the scalp. It was about two centimeters long and two millimeters wide." Interestingly, Stevenson adds that most informants of Cemil's chin birthmark could not recall a birthmark on his head and it was never discussed. Stevenson points out that Cemil Hayak's exploits were so well-known that it would be difficult for anyone—even his reincarnation—to provide information about his life that was not already known by many people. The strength of the case, therefore, rests almost entirely on the correspondence between the wounds of the deceased and Cemil Fahrici's birthmarks.

A similar discovery was made by Canadian researcher Antonia Mills in 1987 when she was conducting her third investigation of past-life cases in northern India, at the request of Ian Stevenson.[4] They were not cases he had previously investigated. Because the implications of his research are far-reaching, he had sought to have his methods and findings replicated by others, hence the reason for asking Mills to do the research. There have been a number of similar replications by different investigators in various countries, incidentally, and their results have been remarkably consistent with Stevenson's. One of the ten children investigated by Mills was Titu (Toran) Singh, who was featured in chapter 8 because of his strong identification with his past-life personality.

He recalled many details of a previous life, including the fact that he was the owner of Suresh Radio shop. Suresh Verme, as well as being the owner of a shop with that name in Sadar Bazaar in Agra, was also a noted smuggler on the black market. He was shot dead on August 28, 1983, though Titu did not volunteer a description of his murder until asked by a relative of Suresh. By the time Mills paid her visit to Singh, the two families had met and a number of the past-life family had accepted Titu as the reincarnation of Suresh. She was told that when the relatives met Titu at Suresh's father's house for the first time, they had noticed a small round birthmark that looked like a bullet entry wound, at the right temple, where Suresh was shot. They conjectured that several small birthmarks on the back of Titu's skull might be the bullet exit site. Suresh had also been born with a birthmark on the crown of his head and the same mark was visible on Titu's head.

Titu Singh holding a newspaper account of his death in a past life
and the birthmarks on his head that correlate
with the bullet wounds that killed him in that life.

Antonia Mills explains what happened next in her fifty-two-page report on the three Indian cases she investigated: "According to Suresh Verme's postmortem report, which we examined at the hospital where he was declared dead, the bullet that took his life entered on the right temple at the site corresponding to Titu's circular birthmark. The postmortem report said that the bullet exited behind Suresh's right ear. After noting this, I returned to Titu and examined behind his right ear and found that Titu's skull is pushed out at the site indicated as the bullet exit site. Titu's parents had noted this deformity of the skull, but had not associated it with Suresh's death. Titu had not mentioned the mode of death of Suresh until asked by Rajvir Babu Verme [one of Suresh's brothers] at their first meeting."

As well as the evidence from the birthmarks, Titu's behavior was seen as strikingly similar to that of his past-life personality. Suresh was not afraid to fight, according to his father, quoting as an example the fact that in 1975 eight "hit men" grabbed Suresh and put him in their car. He kicked one and jumped through the window into the river, swimming across to the other side to escape. A year before his murder, Suresh had also gone to recover two cars that had apparently been stolen by the same man who had previously stolen his car—the same man later accused of Suresh's murder. Despite being fired at, Suresh jumped from the car and grabbed one of the gunmen by the neck.

Let me quote a final comment from Mills about Titu's unusual behavior for a five-year-old: "On my return trips in 1988 and 1989, Titu was still intensely identifying himself as Suresh. For example, two days before I returned to Agra in July 1988, Titu had insisted that his parents take him to the home of Chanda Babu Singh Bharity, Suresh's father. When they arrived, Titu discovered that [Chanda] was sick, and gave orders for a doctor to be fetched and medicine administered."

There is, however, one discrepancy in this case that it is not possible to resolve because of the absence of confirmatory documentation. According to Titu's father, his son was born in December 1983, which was four months after Suresh's death. However, other members of his family suggested he had been born in the preceding year, before Suresh was murdered. There are cases in which a soul seems to have incarnated into a new body *before* leaving the previous body, but it is difficult to understand—even if it were possible—

how a reincarnated child could be born with birthmarks that coincide with wounds that have not yet been inflicted on the "other" body he is cohabiting.

I should mention at this point that Stevenson regards the eighteen cases in his collection that relate to bullet wounds to the head as the most important cases because they not only display *two* marks (corresponding to the entry and exit points of a bullet) in the corresponding positions shown on autopsy reports, but in fourteen of the cases one is larger than the other and in nine the evidence shows the smaller mark coincides with the point of entry of the bullet.[5] Exit wounds are larger because the bullet's speed reduces as it passes through the head, creating more damage when it leaves. I suspect that in the eighteen cases that Stevenson refers to, no two are identical because the victim could have been fired at from any angle on a 360 degree plane, as well as from different heights, and with weapons of varying caliber and velocity, all of which will determine how much damage is done and where a bullet will enter and leave the head. In one of these cases,[6] a Thai boy named Chanai Choomalaiwong recalled the life of a teacher, Bua Kai, who had been shot and killed by a bullet through the back of his head. Chanai's parents took him to Khao Phra at his request, and he was able to direct them to a house where they found an elderly couple who were the parents of Bua Kai Lawnak, a teacher and small-time gangster. Although there was no autopsy report available to confirm the exact position of bullet wounds to his head, witnesses confirmed that the birthmarks on Chanai's head were in a similar position to those they had seen on the teacher's body.

Intriguingly, I came across a case that raises similar time issues as the Titu Singh case during a visit to India in 1993, when I had the opportunity of meeting two researchers, clinical psychiatrist Dr. Satwant Pasricha and biology teacher Gaj Raj Singh Gaur, both of whom have spent a considerable amount of time investigating reincarnation cases, mostly in the north of the country. They have also worked with Ian Stevenson on some of his visits to India. Gaur, who has researched more than one hundred past-life cases, drove through the night from his home in Jaithra, Etah, Uttar Pradesh, to meet me in Delhi and discuss recent cases in which he had been involved.

One of these involved a child, Gulson Kumar Sakena,[7] born in November 1991 in the same town as Gaur. He brought with him a photograph of the young boy and his parents, which showed his complexion to be much paler than theirs. He had been born with two birthmarks, which were not considered important until Gulson, who had been playing outside the tailor shop of his father, Nand Kishore, became frightened when he saw two men he recognized. He came running into the house, telling his mother, "Those persons killed me. Please hide me, otherwise they will kill me again." Gaur provided me with the names of the men, who came from the Barna district to collect clothes from Gulson's father. Later, Nand Kishore asked his son, who was then just over two years old and had difficulty talking properly, about his memories. He pointed at two places on his body—one on his right cheek and the other on the left side of his abdomen, where the birthmarks were clearly visible.

The story that emerged from Gaur's investigation was that Kanhkumar Pandey—whose life Gulson remembered—was traveling to Etah by bus early one morning when two young men caught hold of him and shot him. There were several eyewitnesses to the crime. This information was given to Gaur by the victim's brother, Gyan Singh Pandey. Investigation showed that the birthmarks on Gulson's body coincided with the bullet wounds that killed Kanhkumar. Curiously, Gulson's father had actually seen those wounds on the murdered man's body, as the attack had happened just one kilometer away from his home and he had passed the scene of the shooting. Furthermore, his son, Gulson, was born just twelve hours later that same day. There has been speculation that a phenomenon known as "maternal impression" might be the cause of some birthmarks in which the mother's feelings—either from seeing a wounded corpse or hearing the details of somebody's murder—are transferred to the embryo, affecting its development. How that mechanism might work in terms of paternal impression (perhaps he described the scene to his wife soon after witnessing it?) is difficult to comprehend, as is the fact that Gulson's pale complexion matches that of the victim.

An even more marked contrast in skin pigmentation and facial features, compared with other people of the same race, is shown in another of Stevenson's Burmese cases—a blond boy, Maung Zaw Win Aung.[8] This case is reminiscent of James Leininger's past-life recall, for he claims to be the reincarnation of an American aviator John Steven, who was shot down over the country now known as Myanmar. Stevenson includes a photograph of Zaw Win Aung, who could easily pass for a Caucasian, but does not indicate whether an airman named John Steven died in the Burma conflict.

Another of the cases Gaj Raj Singh Gaur discussed with me in Delhi was that of Ranbir Singh,[9] a Hindu boy born in north India on December 23, 1990, with most of his right arm missing from just below the elbow. His parents attributed this deformity to "God's will," and it was not until Ranbir began naming people and a place related to a Muslim man, Idrish, who had lost his

fingers and most of the palm of his right hand after an accident with a fodder-cutting machine, that they considered a past-life association. I should mention also that I was told that Ranbir's father had attended

Ranbir Singh with researcher Gaj Raj Singh Gaur

Idrish's funeral five years before the birth of his son, though we can only speculate on whether this has any relevance to his apparent reincarnation into the Singh family.

Soon after my meeting with Gaur in Delhi, I travelled to Bangalore where I had an informal meeting with Dr. Satwant Pasricha, with whom Gaur had worked on the research for the Ranbir Singh case and others, the results of which were published in the *Journal of Scientific Exploration* in 1998.[10] On my way to meet her, at the National Institute of Mental Health and Neurosciences, I passed Whitefields, the second ashram of Sathya Sai Baba, in the north-east of Bangalore. It amused me that while Pasricha spent many weeks each year traveling to the north of India in search of scientific evidence for reincarnation, a world-renowned "godman" and reincarnation was regularly giving audiences and blessings to his followers, virtually on her doorstep.

It is important, at this juncture, to make a general observation about birthmarks and birth defects. As the thalidomide tragedy demonstrated, deformities can be the result of drugs taken during pregnancy. Birthmarks often take the form of "port wine" blemishes on the skin, such as that prominently visible on the head of Russia's former president, Mikhail Gorbachev. But, as Stevenson points out, almost nothing is known about why pigmented birthmarks—moles or nevi—occur in certain places on the skin. In fact, the average adult has between fifteen and eighteen moles on his or her body, the causes and location of which are little understood, except for those associated with a genetic disease, neurofibromatosis. Similarly, attempts by researchers to explain a large series of birth defects as being caused either by chemical teratogens (like thalidomide), viral infections, or genetic factors have failed. Between 43 percent and 65–70 percent of these cases were classified as of "unknown causes." With so much uncertainty about what processes are involved in all manner of bodily and skin defects, it could be highly significant that one in three children who claimed to remember past lives also have birthmarks or birth defects that they or adult informants attribute to wounds on the person whose life is remembered. Stevenson included 210 such cases in his two-volume book. The birthmarks were usually areas of hairless, puckered, scar-like skin—sometimes depressed below the surrounding skin—though others were areas of little or no pigmentation (hypopigmented macules) or of increased pigmentation (hyperpigmented nevi). As far as the birth defects were concerned, these were nearly always of rare types. Where a child's description of a previous life could be matched unmistakably with the deceased person identified, Stevenson notes, a close correspondence was nearly always found between birthmarks and birth defects and wounds on the past-life personality's body. In order to "score" the correspondence between the birthmark and a wound, it was regarded as a satisfactory match if they were within ten square centimeters of the same anatomical location. "In fact," Stevenson observes, "many of the birthmarks and wounds were much closer to the same location than this," adding, "In forty-three of forty-nine cases in which a medical document (usually a post-mortem report) was obtained, it confirmed the correspondence between wounds and birthmarks (or birth defects)." That's a concordance of 88 percent. In nine out of fourteen cases of death by bullet, the two wounds displayed coincided precisely in size and location with the entry and exit wounds on the deceased person's body. Stevenson calculated the odds against the chance of two birthmarks corresponding to two wounds at one in 25,600. Birthmarks are not always the result of maliciously inflicted wounds. A Burmese girl who remembered the life of her deceased aunt, for example, displayed a long, vertical linear hypopigmented birthmark close to the midline of the lower chest and upper abdomen. It had been inflicted by a sharp instrument, but in an operating theater. It coincided with the surgical incision the aunt experienced during surgery for congenital heart disease, from which she died. Referring to cases where a child is born with almost no fingers on one hand (unilateral brachydactyly), usually coinciding with memories of fodder-cutting accidents in a previous life, Stevenson describes the condition as exceedingly rare, adding, "I have not found a published report of a case, although a plastic surgeon has shown me a photograph of one case that came under his care." Stevenson found a number of such cases, including that in India of Lekh Pal Jatav[11] whose name, incidentally, means "tax collector." He became known by that name after someone suggested, soon after his birth, that he must have been a tax collector in his past life and had his fingers chopped off by a disgruntled taxpayer.

Anticipating the argument that some of these previous-life "memories" are a parental fiction to account for the birthmarks, Stevenson remarks that there are important objections to this explanation. He points out that since most parents of the children involved in the study believe in reincarnation, it would be sufficient for them to attribute a lesion or a defect to some incident in a previous life without them needing to find a particular life to fit the case. Also, the lives of the deceased persons in such cases are of varying quality, and while some were models of heroism, others were poor or otherwise unexceptional. Stevenson concludes, with typical impartiality, that it is not his purpose "to impose any interpretation of these cases on the readers of this article" but to stimulate them to examine the detailed reports of the many cases he is in the process of publishing. Some of the most unusual birth defects appear to be caused by particularly gruesome murders or unfortunate accidents. Three of Stevenson's cases demonstrate this rather well, two of which come from Myanmar (Burma).

The mother of Ma Khin Mar Htoo[12] earned money by selling water and food to passengers at Taken railway station in Upper Burma. Before her daughter's conception, she twice dreamed of Ma Thein Nwe, nicknamed "Kalamagyi," a girl who had been killed in August 1966 when a train ran over her. She was the daughter of a woman who also sold water at the railway station. When she was born, Ma Khin Mar Htoo had no right leg from a point about 10 cm below the right knee. She also had birth defects of the fingers on both hands. At the age of three, she began to say she was Kalamagyi and

to describe the accident. She had picked roses and hoped to sell them to passengers on a mail train due in that morning. The points jammed, accidentally
diverting it onto a central track where Kalamagyi was walking with her back
to the train. The cow-catcher on the front struck her, knocking her down,
and the train promptly ran over her. Kalamagyi died instantly and her body
parts were collected together and taken to the general hospital before being
handed in a sack to her family for burial. She had been sliced through diago-
nally across the trunk by the train, and the majority of witnesses who viewed
her remains after the accident recalled that one of the two legs had been
severed below the knee. Only one person thought they could remember her
hands being cut off or mutilated. Ma Khin Mar Htoo was able to identify a
number of people who had been known to Kalamagyi, including her mother.

At the birth of Ma Khin Hsann Oo,[13] in October 1974, she was seen to be
covered extensively by large hyperpigmented nevi, but no one conjectured
about their cause until she started speaking, at the age of eighteen months,
about a previous life. By the age of three she had given her name in that life,
saying she was Ahmar Yee and had died in a car that overturned and she was
burned in the flames. "Shik-koe's car overturned," she told her parents, but
did not give the circumstances of the accident. Though she gave only a few
details, they were sufficient for her family to decide she was talking about
the life of Ma Ahmar Yee, who had died of burns when a truck in which she
and many others had been riding overturned and caught fire, claiming ten
lives. The truck was owned by an Indian Muslim called Shik-koe. Stevenson
tells us that two of the children appear to remember being killed in the
same accident.

Another accidental death report concerns a Turkish boy, Semih (Taci)
Tutusmus,[14] who was born in the Hatay province of Turkey in 1958 with a
severe defect of the right ear. Before he was two years old he began talking
about a previous life when he was Selim Fesli, and a man named Isa Dirbekli
had shot him in the right side of the head. At the age of four, Semih found his
own way to the home in which he had lived in that life—about two kilometers away—and introduced himself to members of the household. He continued to visit the family, but whenever he saw the man who had shot him, he
became angry and threw stones at him. Isa had been arrested for the shooting,
which he at first denied. He then confessed he had been out shooting birds

when he thought Selim, asleep on the ground, was a rabbit and shot him. Realizing his mistake, he fled from the scene rather than face the vengeance of Selim's sons. Selim had died in the hospital six days after the shooting and soon afterward, Isa was imprisoned for two years. At the age of twelve, Semih threatened to kill Isa Dirbekli in revenge for his own past-life death, which he regarded as deliberate. Fortunately, those thoughts eventually subsided, and with the gradual loss of his memories and plastic surgery that gave him an excellent replacement for a real ear, plus the fashion for men in Turkey to wear long hair helping him to cover the birth defect, Semih's life became normal and the last Stevenson heard he had become engaged to be married.

Some cases illustrate rather too well the results of human stupidity under the influence of alcohol. Such is the case of Semir Taci[15] who remembered being called Sekip in his previous life. He had died, he told his parents, after a poisonous snake bit his thumb, which had small scars. His description of events and people in that life reminded his parents of a man called Sekip Karsanbas, who had been raised and befriended by Semir's father, but was something of a loser. He worked in a café, earning a little money but spending too much of it on alcohol. One day, after a quarrel with his wife, he went off to a bakery shop where he learned that a snake had slithered into an adjoining store. "Probably intoxicated," Stevenson tells us, "Sekip went to the shop and rashly picked up the snake, which bit him. The snake was almost certainly an Ottoman viper." He ran home to his wife with his hand bleeding and was then admitted to the government hospital, where he died the following day. When Stevenson and a colleague studied the record of Sekip's admission to the hospital in Antakya, it was recorded that he had been "bitten by a snake on the fingers of the right hand and on those of the left hand." No one had mentioned birthmarks on Semir's left hand so the researchers returned and examined it to see if it also showed birthmarks similar to those on the other hand. It did. "These marks had a distinctive scarlike appearance; they resembled small keloids, a type of indurated scar with a smooth surface that is raised above the surrounding tissues. All the marks had an identical appearance, and I believe that they were all birthmarks," Stevenson confirms.

For me, the most extraordinary case involves another family from upper Burma. In May 1973, Ma Htwe Win[16] was born with several unusual, disfiguring birth defects as well as birthmarks. It is worth mentioning that her mother,

Ma Ohn Tin, had a dream early in her pregnancy that a man who appeared to be walking on his knees, or perhaps on amputated stumps of legs, was following her. She tried to avoid him but he continued to approach her. She did not recognize him. When Ma Htwe Win was born she was seen to have birthmarks on her lower left chest in the region of the heart and on her head. The fifth finger of her left hand was missing. She also had constriction rings around the lower parts of the legs above the ankles and another, particularly deep, constriction ring around the middle of her left thigh. It was only when Ma Htwe Win could speak that an explanation for these defects and markings was offered. She said she had been a man, Nga Than, in her previous life and been attacked by three others. He had tried to fight back but they had stabbed him in the left breast, cut his fingers, and hit him over the head, leaving him for dead. He appears to have been conscious for a while after the vicious attacks and heard his murderers discuss how they would dispose of his body. Ma Htwe Win said they decided to compress it into as small a space as possible by tying the legs back on the thighs. The body would then be short enough to put in a gunny sack and drop into a nearby dried up well. She appeared to be referring to the life of U Nga Than, whose wife had let it be known that he had left her and moved to the south. She then married one of the murderers. One day, while drinking and quarrelling with her new husband, U Nga Than's murder was mentioned, and a neighbor who overheard their heated dispute went to the police. Their investigations led them to the dried-up well from which they pulled her former husband's body, still tied up with the ropes that had been used to make it compact. Stevenson tells us that Ma Htwe Win's mother had actually passed the well just as the police were bringing the body out and untying it. She glanced at the scene and then went on her way. At that time, she was about two-and-a-half months pregnant with Ma Htwe Win, and the dream of a man following her on his knees occurred the very next night.

Another Burmese case with birth defects looking very much like rope constrictions involved a girl, Ma Win Tar,[17] who remembered being a Japanese soldier, captured by Burmese villagers, who tied him to a tree and burned him alive. She gave no name for herself in that life and so her account cannot be verified.

While the widespread incidence of birthmarks and birthmarks among cases suggestive of reincarnation is an exciting discovery in parapsychological research, it seems to have long been accepted by many cultures. An Indian case involving a black thumbnail is a good example of this.[18] The nail on Savitri Devi Pathak's left hand was seen to be black at birth, an oddity to which her parents attached no importance. When their daughter could speak, however, she offered an explanation. In her former life, she told them, a heavy weight used for weighing grain had dropped on her thumb, leaving a permanent bruise. She gave two names, providing enough information about that life for her uncle to find a family whose daughter, Munni, had suffered a blackened thumbnail, caused exactly as Savitri Devi had described. When Munni's parents learned of Savitri's claim to be the reincarnation of their daughter, they said, "If she has a mark on her left thumb, then she is our child." This injury, incidentally, reminds me of Englishwoman Carol Lawson's thumbnails, which kept falling off—apparently due to a past-life experience when thumbscrews were used to torture her—but which ceased to be shed after she relived the event under hypnosis. Savitri's blackened thumbnail was still very much in evidence in her late twenties.

No birthmarks were visible on the body of Juggi Lal Agarwal[19] when he was born in northern India in 1955, and yet one that had gone undetected convinced Girivar Singh that the boy was his reborn son, Puttu Lal, who had died after a violent boundary dispute with neighbors. He had been struck on the head and an infection from the wound had spread along and under his scalp, coming close to his right ear. At that point, an abscess either burst spontaneously or was lanced by a doctor who put in a few stitches. The father went to see Juggi Lal Agarwal, who appeared to be remembering the life of his son, and as soon as they met, he asked to see behind the child's right ear, convinced that if he were the reincarnation of Puttu Lal he would carry a birthmark relating to that injury. Sure enough, he found what he was looking for. Stevenson, when he examined him some years later, testified that the birthmark "consisted of a line somewhat resembling the scar of a small incision; and there seemed to be several tiny punctate scars adjoining it, which might have corresponded to surgical stitch marks."

As well as looking for birthmarks to confirm the authenticity of reincarnations, some cultures even use them, or create them, to convey certainty about rebirth. Stevenson refers to these as "experimental birthmarks" and a good example of this is the Tlingit fisherman, William George (referred to briefly in chapter 10), who told his son, Reginald, "If there is anything to this rebirth business, I will come back as your son." He gave him a gold watch that had belonged to his mother and said, "Keep this for me." It was placed in a jewelry box. And to his daughter-in-law, Reginald's wife, he showed two prominent moles on his left shoulder and forearm, telling her that when he was reborn he would have two similar moles as proof he had returned. When William George Jr. was born, he was seen to have two moles in the same location as his grandfather. At around the age of five, he saw objects his mother had taken from the jewelry box and placed on her bed. One of the items clearly had special significance for the young boy. "That's my watch," he declared.

Ma Lai Lai Way, born in Rangoon, Myanmar, in 1976, suffered with congenital heart disease and failed to survive open-heart surgery. Three of her schoolmates prepared her body for burial and, having heard that placing a mark on a body might produce an identifiable birthmark when the person reincarnated, they decided to put a lipstick mark on the back of her neck. The girls told no members of Ma Lai Lai Way's family what they had done and it was not visible to others who saw her body. A little over a year after her death, her sister gave birth to a daughter, Ma Choe Hnin Htet, who was found to have a prominent red birthmark on the back of her neck, in the same place that the schoolmates had marked Ma Lai Lai Way's body with lipstick, as well as a long, thin faint line from her lower chest to upper abdomen, which corresponded to the cardiac surgery incision. When she could speak, she displayed knowledge of her aunt's former life. Stevenson's observation of this and similar cases is the closest he gets to introducing a little humor into his very serious studies: "It happens that many children—perhaps one-third of all children—are born with areas of redness at the back of the neck. In Western folklore this is often called a 'stork's bite.' The cause of these areas of redness is unknown. Most of them fade away as the child grows older, but the site is obviously not the best one for making experimental birthmarks."

Let me conclude this rapid overview of some of the best evidence for a link between reincarnation, birthmarks, and birth defects with an example in which an unexpected physical mark or defect can even mirror a change in the religious beliefs of subjects' families, from one existence to another. Stevenson's files contain a handful of cases in which male children have been born fully or partially circumcised. In a couple of cases, this was a physical reflection of the fact that in the previous life, for religious reasons, their foreskins had been removed. In one case, in which a Turkish boy, Faris Yuyucuer, had a micropenis, his past-life memories were of a life as Hasan Derin in which the surgeon performing the required circumcision on him at the age of five found a urinary calculus (stone) lodged in the penis near its base. He presumably hoped it would pass down the urethra spontaneously, but it failed to do so and Hasan was unable to urinate. The boy was admitted to the hospital where the penis was incised to the urethra and the stone removed. Hasan made a full recovery but drowned a year later in a lake. The acceptance of Faris as Hasan's reincarnation was based on information he was able to provide and his behavior, not on the fact that his penis was smaller than others at birth. In the case of Giriraj Soni, investigated by Dr. Satwant Pasricha, he talked about his life as Subhan Khan, a Muslim life in which he was a thief and a bully. Not only was he born with various birthmarks that coincided with the wounds suffered when he and his eldest son were set upon by a group of villagers who could not tolerate his behavior any more, but he was also born without a foreskin. Another child, born into a Hindu family, not only remembered being a previous Muslim but also described how he had been circumcised in that life.

Congenital absence of the foreskin is rare, but one commentator has stated that for Morocco's Muslims, being born circumcised is considered a blessing. "Among Muslims (as among Jews) male circumcision has a special importance," Stevenson tells us. "It was widely practiced among the peoples of the Middle East before Islam. The Prophet Muhammad himself was born circumcised and this occurrence contributed to the significance Muslims attach to male circumcision. On the Shi'ite side of Islam, we are told that each of the twelve imams was born without a foreskin."

Which raises an interesting question: Is this because they were all Muslims in their previous lives, carrying into their present existence a physical as well as ideological identification with that religion, or does it indicate the involvement of rebirth as one of the mechanisms, perhaps at a subtle level, in the evolutionary processes of human development?

Chapter 22

Satisfying the Skeptics

Healthy skepticism in all scientific endeavors is essential, and nowhere more so than in the field of parapsychology, for which some skeptics prefer the label "pseudoscience." It does, after all, lend itself to claims of special powers by people whose real talent is deception, either of themselves or others. Those involved in reincarnation research accept that their investigations and tentative conclusions will be closely scrutinized and criticized by a wide range of nonbelievers, from religious extremists and atheists to scientists and magicians, all of whom are unprepared to accept the possibility of a spiritual dimension to life. Indeed, for many people, skepticism has become a new religion whose followers are encouraged by their high priests to worship at the altar of materialism. They deride a wide range of reported phenomena, such as ESP, telepathy, and remote viewing with the zeal one normally associates with brainwashed groups who are incapable of thinking for themselves. Yet many of the scientists who belong to skeptics' organizations are happy to accept the mind-boggling realities of quantum physics—rightly so—while closing their minds to equally challenging possibilities in other fields.

While I do not intend examining the skeptics' arguments in any depth, since some have already been covered in my review of alternative explanations (chapter 19), I believe it's worthwhile looking at what critics regard as

weaknesses in the evidence for reincarnation so far collected, as well as suggesting ways in which it can be strengthened.

Hypnotic regression can be a satisfying, even entertaining, method of
exploring past lives, but I am not convinced that in the majority of cases
it delivers what it says on the packet. Just how much of the content of such
"memories" is based on genuine past-life recall and how much of the ingredients are drawn from other more prosaic sources is very difficult to assess. The
three-year investigation by Linda Tarazi (chapter 20), for example, yielded
fascinating insights from obscure sources in different languages, but the skeptic will rightly point out that this extensive search failed to provide proof that
the subject's past-life personality ever existed. The best regression cases are
usually replete with names, places, and dates that can be checked, though all
too often accounts are published that contain various howlers, much to the
delight of skeptics. Ian Wilson, for example, cites some examples that would
probably not be obvious to a casual reader but that jump off the page when
scrutinized by a seasoned researcher. One hypnotized subject spoke of a person living in the reign of Egyptian pharaoh Ramses III. But the Egyptians
did not use numerals to identify their rulers; that was a system introduced
by Victorian Egyptologists during the nineteenth century. Another regressed
subject spoke of Vikings landing in North America in the eleventh century,
giving a colorful description of them wearing helmets with horns. Again, it
may have reflected the popular conception of invading Vikings, but it is now
known that only individuals of high rank wore such helmets, and they did so
not on the battlefield but in religious ceremonies.

For these and other reasons, spontaneous cases of reincarnation hold
out a far better promise of providing a better source of evidence capable
of producing proof—if such is possible—that reincarnation occurs. Ian Stevenson doubtless hoped that his huge body of evidence based on birthmarks
and birth defects would go a long way towards achieving that goal, but it
got a lukewarm response from the scientific community as a whole. When I
read some of the criticisms that are leveled at reincarnation investigations, I
have to conclude that they are made by individuals who have never taken the
trouble to study his and other researchers' findings. Stevenson did nothing
to encourage popular interest in his work, almost to the end. He published
his findings only in peer-reviewed scientific journals and was reticent about

cooperating with the media. In those few interviews that he gave, he was as vocally cautious as he was in the papers he wrote, refusing to draw premature conclusions about his findings. The cases, he would say, are *suggestive* of reincarnation—no more. Towards the end of his life, however, he agreed to be accompanied for the first time by a skeptical, award-winning journalist on extensive field research. That writer was Tom Shroder, the respected *Washington Post* editor whose book *Old Souls*[1] tells the story of that adventure, accompanying the eighty-year-old parapsychologist on evidence-gathering trips to Lebanon, India, and the American South.

Those, like Shroder, who have seen the care with which Stevenson collects evidence from every possible witness, then checks it against available records, will appreciate how much effort goes into the endeavor. But skeptics who were not present to witness the researcher's encounters with past and present family members in reincarnation cases raise a number of objections. Some argue that leading questions may have been asked of the subjects or that translators with a bias towards reincarnation may have colored their English interpretations of witness statements to give them a more positive spin. One of those who has complained of "inadequacies of interviewing procedures" is Leonard Angel, an instructor in the Philosophy and Humanities Department of Douglas College, Newfoundland, Canada. In the pages of *Skeptical Inquirer*,[2] and also in the pages of a book,[3] he focused his criticism on a single Lebanese case, that of Imad Elawar,[4] in which he claimed Stevenson's conduct "fails on six fundamental points." Stevenson broke the habit of a lifetime by providing the magazine with a reply,[5] even though it was not a scientific journal. Then, when the publication failed to provide him with enough space to do so adequately, he made a longer version available to those readers who requested it. I will not spend time going over this ground again, but it is appropriate to point out that modern methods of information gathering should make such criticisms unnecessary in future. I believe most reincarnation researchers already make video recordings of their investigations, and I see this as essential if we are to view the fuller picture and not be sidetracked by important but easily overcome obstacles. If skeptics challenge the accuracy of witness statements in the future, video and audio recording ought to be available to verify the accuracy of the reports or transcripts on which they are based, as well as the interpretations that are made by the researchers involved.

I would go further in suggesting that, as well as recording statements made by the subject, or remembered by witnesses, researchers could also attempt to gain a fuller picture of the past-life personality from the child recalling that life—after the crucial, volunteered data has been gathered—by asking a series of questions that concern more mundane matters: Can you remember what your favorite meal was? What kind of music did you enjoy? Did you like school? Who were your friends? What work did you do? These are topics that often occur spontaneously in reincarnation accounts, but asking such questions could prompt the subject to remember things that are not uppermost in his or her mind. It is possible that probing questions of this nature are already used by those investigating reincarnation cases, but if so their reports do not say so.

American philosopher Paul Edwards, editor of the eight-volume *Encyclopedia of Philosophy,* made an interesting contribution to the debate with his book *Reincarnation: A Critical Examination,*[6] though its carefully considered arguments and logic are marred by sarcasm and needless jibes. Among those who have addressed some of his criticisms, John Beloff, past president of the Society for Psychical Research, pointed out[7] in reviewing the book for its *Journal* that "given the author's philosophical stance, not only reincarnation, but survival in any shape or form, is an absurdity, no matter how voluminous the alleged evidence . . ." He adds that Edwards's objection to birthmark evidence "is that there is no conceivable way in which scars of the deceased personality could be transferred to the embryo of the person who will claim to be his or her reincarnation."

James Matlock of the Department of Anthropology, Southern Illinois University, was equally unimpressed[8] with Edwards's dismissal of the evidence for reincarnation, saying that the author's reference to the "smug dogmatism and . . . colossal arrogance" of believers in rebirth and karma could just as easily refer "to himself and others of skeptical inclination." Robert Almeder of the Department of Philosophy, Georgia State University, went further[9] in his "A Critique of Arguments Offered against Reincarnation." He points out that in Edwards's view "no reasonable human being could take belief in reincarnation seriously," and that "any argument for any form of personal post-mortem survival is indefensible." Almeder concludes that "the author fails to notice that while pointing to those who believe in reincarnation as religious fanatics or mental incompetents, there are three fingers pointing backwards towards him."

Skeptics, or nonbelievers, it becomes clear, are just as rigid in their mind-set as those who have a strong belief in something or someone. Paul Edwards demonstrated that very well. No amount of evidence, it seems, would ever convince him that consciousness could survive death and on that basis any data that indicated otherwise was clearly at fault. My suspicion is that if the evidence for reincarnation that has already been collected, analyzed meticulously, and published extensively does not persuade skeptics that it is, at the very least, a phenomenon worthy of further intensive study, then no amount of new research material will change their minds.

Xenoglossy

Perhaps a well-substantiated case of xenoglossy (speaking a language unknown to the subject) will make a difference. Psychotherapist Dr. Morris Netherton reports a case of a blond, blue-eyed eleven-year-old boy who, under hypnosis, was taped for eleven minutes as he spoke in an ancient Chinese dialect.[10] When the tape recording was played to an elderly Chinese professor at the Department of Oriental Studies, University of California, it turned out to be a recitation from a forbidden religion of Ancient China. Fascinating stuff, though we must treat this claim as anecdotal unless Netherton can provide tangible confirmation from the professor, or better still, the original recording for analysis by others. Even then, skeptics will argue that this *could* have been learned somehow—such as in the Reima Kampman case in which a Finnish student sang a song in an old form of English (chapter 18). What is needed, therefore, is *responsive* xenoglossy in which a dialogue takes place. If Morris Netherton had been able to hypnotize the boy in the presence of the professor he consulted, and that expert had then conversed with the subject in ancient Chinese, the result would have been a stupendous piece of evidence.

Ian Stevenson has reported two cases[11] in which one subject appeared to be able to speak Swedish (under hypnosis) and the other German, in a normal waking state. He has also discussed at length the Uttara/Sharada case of possession (chapter 19) in which the subject could speak Bengali. Another xenoglossy case was reported in 1953, when Professor P. Pal from the University of Itachuna in East Bengal discovered Swarnlata Mishra, a four-year-old Hindu girl who could dance in a Bengali style and sing in that language, without having had any previous contact with that culture. This case was also researched by Stevenson.[12] Hollywood actor Glenn Ford is also reported to have displayed musical talent at a piano and a knowledge of French during a hypnotic regression conducted by Dr. Maurice Benjamin. In his normal state, Ford could neither play the piano nor speak French. Transcripts of five of his past life regressions are provided in the book *Americans Who Have Been Reincarnated*.[13] Future research along similar lines will depend very much on finding new subjects with similar abilities. It has been suggested that child prodigies may be demonstrating skills carried over from one life to the next, though I believe that argument does not do justice to the creative potential of each human being—unless of course the individual also has past-life memories that coincide with those striking abilities.

Handwriting

In the same way that xenoglossy may demonstrate the carryover of knowledge (language) acquired in a previous life, a forensic expert in India has suggested that comparison of handwriting produced by the past-life and present-life personalities may provide additional evidence for reincarnation, and has produced his first case to demonstrate this. Dr. Vikram Raj Sing Chauhan, president of the All India Forensic Science Association, revealed the case in a presentation at the association's National Conference of Forensic Scientists at Bundelkand University, Jhansi, in 2002. The Patiala-based expert told of Taranjit Singh, who claims to remember the life of a young man, Satnam Singh, who died in a road accident. Taranjit insisted on being taken to his former village, and his father succeeded in locating a family whose details matched those described by his son. When Dr. Chauhan read this story in a newspaper, he did not believe it but decided to investigate it out of curiosity. He was able to take samples of the writings of Taranjit Singh and Satnam Singh, the latter found in the boy's notebooks kept by his family. The *Tribune*, in reporting the conference presentation, explained: "A basic theory of forensic science, that the handwritings of two different individuals cannot be the same, was the basis of his investigation. If Taranjit Singh and Satnam Singh were the same person, then their handwritings also had to be the same." To Dr. Chauhan's amazement, Taranjit's handwriting "corresponded almost exactly" with that of the person he claimed to be in his past life. The only difference "lay in the muscular coordination of the two writers, as Taranjit Singh was not accustomed to writing." Other experts at the conference, according to its minutes, examined the writing specimens and came to the same conclusion. The *Tribune*'s account did not publish a comparison of the boys' handwriting. I must emphasize that this is not about graphology, or the interpretation of a person's psychology based on his or her handwriting. It is purely a forensic examination of two specimens to compare similarities—a scientific assessment that is accepted by American courts in evidence, for example, relating to the authenticity of changes to a will or of the signature on a legal document.

A similar case in which the handwriting *has* been published involves Herminio Miranda, a Brazilian Spiritist who was also a senior executive of Brazilian National Steel Company until his retirement at the age of sixty in 1980. Progressive promotion had taken him to the position of chief executive officer responsible for accounting and finances during almost forty years with the company. Throughout that time, he was also a writer on Spiritism, for which reincarnation plays an important role, producing a total of forty books. Miranda had somehow learned that he was the reincarnation of Robert Browning Sr., an employee of the Bank of England, who was the father of the famous English poet and playwright. The idea of comparing their handwriting came out of an extensive correspondence between Miranda and Joseph Myers in America, whose own reincarnation memory led to him create a website about other cases. The Bank of England responded to Miranda's request for Browning's handwriting by providing a photocopy of his 1863 letter of resignation. Miranda passed the letter, unopened, to his secretary and asked her to type whatever handwritten words had been provided. She then handed the typescript to her boss, who sat down and wrote it in his own handwriting before looking at the Browning letter. They appear to be almost identical. Critics will argue that this experiment was conducted by the subject, so we have to take it on trust. It is worth remembering, however, that this test took place in the 1960s when Miranda was still chief comptroller of

Brazilian National Steel Company, and that Miranda's stature in Brazil was such that he was that country's envoy to deliver their land-lease payments to the USA after World War II. It is difficult to imagine what he might achieve by faking such a claim.

DNA

A further forensic dimension to reincarnation research might also be possible, in the future, by comparing DNA analysis of blood or tissue samples from one lifetime to another. This possibility has been suggested by researcher Walter Semkiw, though it is too early to know whether we should expect to find similarities, or "genetic marking." The fact that facial appearance, birthmarks, and birth defects, as well as psychological factors such as behavior, appear to be carried over from one life to the next suggests that DNA may have a role to play. It may be significant to this line of enquiry that Semkiw's book of case studies[14] includes Dr. Kary Mullis, who received a Nobel Prize in chemistry in 1993 for his invention of the polymerase chain reaction (PCR), which has been hailed as one of the monumental scientific techniques of the twentieth century. PCR multiplies a single, microscopic strand of genetic material billions of times within hours. It is a technique that can be used for DNA fingerprinting and is also used to extract DNA from fossils, so it *may* be a useful tool for future reincarnation researchers. Semkiw suggests that in his past lives, Dr. Mullis was Benjamin Rush, an eminent eighteenth-century physician and patriot, and before that, Martin Luther, the German priest and professor of theology whose translation of the Bible (from Latin) made it accessible to the people for the first time. Dr. Mullis gave Semkiw permission to publish that speculation though he maintains a neutral stance regarding his case.

Twins

It is the similarity in the appearance and behavior of twins that fascinates most people, leading to a widespread belief that they are more likely to experience and report telepathic communication than individuals in a family. Reincarnation researchers, on the other hand, are fascinated by the *differences* between twins and have started to explore the possibility that these dissimilarities may provide strong evidence of rebirth. Monozygotic twins ought to be identical because they originate from the same ovum fertilized by a single sperm, but separate into two zygotes during the first thirteen days, whereas fraternal (dizygotic) twins are formed when two eggs are fertilized by two sperm. Since monozygotic twins share the same DNA, they ought to be identical, and yet in some cases, they are different in appearance or character. For example, Dr. Paul Gringas of Queen Charlotte's Hospital in London reported in the famous medical journal, the *Lancet,* in 1999 that he has studied monozygotic male twins whose hair color—brown and blond— ear shapes, and teeth are different; their facial appearance is no more similar than ordinary brothers; and one is regarded as mentally more advanced than the other. He could offer no medical explanation for these anomalies. Other specialists have also noted the marked differences in character between some conjoined twins. Dr. Gringas's account prompted a response from Dr. Ian Stevenson, who, together with colleagues, has researched more than forty sets of twins where either one or both exhibited past-life memories. He commented on monozygotic twins in Sri Lanka, with very different stature, facial appearance, and behaviors from an early age. More data needs to be collected about such cases, but Stevenson believed there was a strong possibility that these differences in twins who ought to be identical might be explained by physical or psychological influences from a previous life. Recent medical advances have made it possible to examine the genetic makeup of twins, with the discovery that one in ten pairs of monozygotic twins are, in fact, physically nonidentical.

There may be other avenues of research that can be explored by applying new scientific techniques to cases suggestive of reincarnation in the future. For the time being, the evidence that has already been produced is considered by many to be overwhelming—though skeptics are still of a different mind.

Chapter 23

Karma and Destiny

Having problems with your job, your finances, your partner, your in-laws, your taxes, your health, or any one of a thousand other things that ensure your journey through life does not always go as smoothly as you would like? There was a time when you would have blamed yourself or someone else for these woes. Today, it seems, a growing number of people prefer to blame it on their karma. When life sucks, they say it's because of something they did in a past life. This makes perfect sense to some people, but I confess, I am not one of them.

When someone asks me if I believe in karma, my immediate response is to ask them which kind? Usually, this is met by a puzzled silence, so I go on to explain that the earliest ideas about reincarnation did not involve a belief that rebirth was influenced by one's moral behavior in a former life. The concept of karma gradually evolved, but has been interpreted differently by each religion that embraces it, including Buddhism, Hinduism, and Jainism. Belief in karma can be seen as a way of introducing an element of fairness into lives that otherwise might be regarded as impoverished or unjust. Perhaps you have little material wealth in this life because you had plenty in a previous one; maybe you are sick in the current existence because you enjoyed good health previously. It's a balancing act. Some see karma as a system of spiritual justice that metes out punishment and retribution for past-life sins, or rewards for a life of goodness. But who decides? That responsibility is usually bestowed upon a Supreme Being, notably within Hinduism. Even Islam, without mentioning karma, refers to the good or bad that its followers experience as being Allah's reaction to man's own actions. Others, among whom are Buddhists and Jains, interpret karma very differently, seeing it as a simple, natural, universal law of cause and effect whose consequences are automatic, without requiring the intervention of an all-seeing, all-knowing God to dispense justice. Christian teachings do not embrace reincarnation, yet some notable churchmen have openly declared their belief in karma, including Rev. Dr. Leslie Weatherhead, a Methodist minister; Bishop Hugh Montefiore, an Anglican theologian; the Rev. Edward Chad Varah, an Anglican priest; and the Rev. Martin Israel, who was born into a Jewish family but eventually broke from Judaism and became an Anglican priest. The concept of karma, therefore, seems to have permeated the thinking and influenced the attitudes of millions of people around the world, who tailor it to their own needs or beliefs, regardless of the particular doctrine to which they subscribe.

Accepting that a law of cause and effect operates in our lives—whether or not we call it karma—raises many questions that, I suspect, go largely unasked and certainly unanswered by its casual believers. If actions in a previous life have determined who you are in this life and what reward or punishment you can expect for deeds in that former existence, it suggests an element of predestiny. Supposing, for example, you develop a serious and debilitating illness halfway through this life, does that mean you were directed to a body in which to be born that would be susceptible to the development of that condition, allowing karma to take effect and, somehow, balance a karmic debt from a previous life? Does that mean we have no free will; that everything is predestined? If so, why are we bothering? Just let it happen (except, of course, our predestiny probably requires us to make the effort). Or maybe you *chose* to reincarnate into a body that would develop a serious medical condition in order to learn a lesson or voluntarily accrue some good karma. The magical thing about the law of karma is that it can be used to explain, justify, or rationalize almost any event, depending on which variety you pay lip service to. When a tsunami kills hundreds of thousands of people, does it wash away their past-life sins, as well as their homes and their bodies?

This is not only a philosophical challenge for those who believe in karma, of course. Others, whose religion regards God as the supreme orchestrator of all events on our planet, and for whom the concept of rebirth is rejected, still have to face up to the implications of natural disasters and other tragedies and the impact these inevitably have on their beliefs. Such events, with a massive loss of life, suggest to some the existence of group karma, in which large numbers of people are somehow linked to the same destiny and therefore suffer an identical fate. That scenario suggests that earthquakes and tsunamis, rather than being the unfortunate result of natural events on a changing planet, are purposeful occurrences generated by some unseen force to administer cosmic justice. According to Dr. Hiroshi Motoyama, a Japanese scientist, parapsychologist, Shinto priest, healer, and author of over fifty books on mysticism and consciousness, we also share marital and family karma on a personal level, and national, racial, and geographic karma on a group level. Pauli A. Moss,[1] daughter of medical psychologist and parapsychologist Thelma Moss, is among those who claim they can "read" a person's karma. She is said to be an expert in Hindu predictive astrology, which enables her to interpret natal charts in order to determine an individual's "karmic bank balance"—debts and credits held over in specific areas from previous lives.

Assuming there is a law of karma, or cause and effect, operating over many lifetimes, to ensure that the good prosper and the bad suffer or are given the opportunity to make amends, I concluded long ago that it was impossible for us mere mortals to comprehend its mysterious workings. How karma may work is not as important, to my mind, as the acceptance of the fact that we all have personal responsibility for our actions and should live our lives accordingly. That being the case, I make it a point never to waste time wondering whether or not other people's good fortune or bad luck has anything to do with reincarnation. Indeed, those who do make such judgments sometimes regret having done so.

Rabbi Yonassan Gershom, who follows the mystical Hasidic tradition of Judaism, has documented many cases[2] of people who believe they died in the Holocaust—just a few of the six million who perished in horrifying circumstances at the hands of the Nazis. In the early days of his research, two-thirds of those he interviewed had been reborn as non-Jews, leading to what he describes as "wild media speculation" about the reasons. He has since stated that his first sample was too limited, and having discovered hundreds more Jews who were holocaust victims but have returned as Jews, the ratio is now more balanced. Interestingly, he makes a very valid observation about factors that may override the natural desire of a soul to be reborn in the same ethnic or cultural group—a belief that is common to American Indians, African tribes, Indian castes, the Druze, and many others. "But what happens when you have a war and large numbers of people are killed all at once, before what I would say is their normal lifespan?" Gershom asks. "They die as children, they die in bombings, they die on the battlefield. When that happens, I think things get a little mixed up. When you have an atomic bomb dropped on Nagasaki everyone dies at once: it does not distinguish between the innocent and the guilty. It's hard to say it was ordained for an entire city to die because of karma. I don't believe that."

The spiritual implications of the Holocaust have, over the years, proved to be a minefield for those who have offered reasons to explain it in terms of reincarnation. One of its first victims was Air Chief Marshal Lord Dowding, whose leadership in the Battle of Britain made a major contribution to the defeat of Germany in World War II. He told a London audience, soon after the war's end: "I have some reason to suppose that those who sowed the seeds of abominable cruelty at the time of the [Spanish] Inquisition reaped their own harvest at Belsen and Buchenwald." Whatever his source, it is difficult to find the logic in such reasoning. If Spain's fifteenth- and sixteenth-century inquisitors had been reborn as Jews, in order to be put to death in concentration camps, then who were the Nazis who imposed that karmic debt on them? Who are the victims and who are the perpetrators? Such twisted logic might not only be seen to be anti-Semitic but also puts Hitler and his henchmen on a pedestal for wreaking revenge, as the good guys (the victims) become the bad guys, and vice versa.

Surprisingly, there is even an Israeli rabbi who expresses similar beliefs. Rabbi Ovadia Yosef, who heads the Shas party and gives a weekly Saturday night radio sermon, faced fierce controversy in 2000 for declaring that the Holocaust's six million victims were "reincarnations of the souls of sinners, people who transgressed and did all sorts of things which should not be done. They had been reincarnated in order to atone." Though he described the Nazis as "evil" and their victims "poor people," the fact that he attributed past sins as the reason for their deaths caused understandable outrage in Israel and around the world. The then Israeli prime minister, Ehud Barak, told a meeting of his cabinet that the statement was unworthy of a rabbi of Yosef's status—he is leader of the country's largest ultra-Orthodox political party—and Legislator Yosef Lapid, head of the secularist Shinui party and himself a Holocaust survivor, dismissed the rabbi as an "old fool" who had done a service to those who are trying to rehabilitate Hitler's reputation. Despite the criticism heaped upon him, Rabbi Yosef repeated the claim almost a decade later, explaining in another of his weekly broadcasts in 2009 that the Holocaust's victims, "righteous people among them," were punished because of the "sins of past generations."

When Glenn Hoddle lost his job as England's football manager in 1999, he might well have wondered what past-life misdemeanor was to blame. But the cause was in this lifetime. As he prepared his team in the run-up to the World Cup, he made the mistake of discussing karma in an interview with a journalist from the *Times* newspaper.[3] Hoddle had already made headlines when it was revealed he was using a Spiritualist healer and medium, Eileen Drewery, to successfully treat injured players. His comments on karma, however, took him into uncharted waters and the stormy reception they invoked soon led to his dismissal. "You and I have been physically given two hands and two legs and half decent brains," he said in an unguarded moment. "Some people have been born like that for a reason. The karma is working from another lifetime. I have nothing to hide about that. It is not only people with disabilities. What you sow you have to reap." The *Times* spoke to a number of disabled people who found his views offensive and soon it became a major news story around the world, culminating in the Football Association's decision to sack him. Those who took issue with his views, I must add, offered no alternative explanation for why people were disabled or suffered in other ways, and the Dalai Lama supported him. Hoddle, whose mother worked at a school for disabled children, gave just one further interview on the subject, this time to a reporter who was more sympathetic—Harry Harris of the *Mirror*—explaining, "For years I have wrestled over why many people suffer such sadness and tragedy. It is something I really care about. I get very upset when I meet disabled people, or see terrible poverty, or hear of people being abused . . . I have looked into this in detail and have heard a number of theories. Some make more sense than others. Certainly, I do not believe disabled people deserve what they get. But I am seeking some reason for their suffering, as I am sure many disabled people do for themselves."

Similarly, many of those whose reincarnation cases I have discussed must also have asked themselves why, in their past life, they were murdered or afflicted in some way, and why they have brought birthmarks and birth defects into their new life. What karmic law, for example, allows a child to accidentally chop off its fingers in a fodder-cutting machine in one life and then fails to restore them in his new body? Each will doubtless come to his or her own conclusions, assuming they give it any thought at all. Rani Saxena, an Indian girl investigated by Ian Stevenson,[4] certainly did. She had vivid memories of a past life in which she was a prosperous lawyer in the city of Benares and identified so strongly with that past life, despite having married and had children, that she still used masculine verb forms when speaking. So why did she now find herself living as a female in abject poverty? Rani believes it was because she had exploited women in that previous male existence and believed she was now paying the price. It was, she told Ian Stevenson, "God's judgment."

My own view on this thorny subject is that there must be rhyme and reason in the mechanics of rebirth, but they elude me. I also have problems reconciling some of the extraordinary and conflicting accounts thrown up by therapists and reincarnation researchers alike. The former tell us of subjects who, having been regressed to an interlife state, describe planning their next lives with teams of spiritual consultants. The latter often provide us with perplexing hit-and-miss accounts from spontaneous cases, in which certain souls, including airmen who have crashed in foreign lands, appear to seek instant rebirth and gravitate to the nearest pregnant female who happens to be passing. On the other hand, others prefer to wait until a "vacancy" occurs within their previous family.

So my verdict has to be: I just don't know. Perhaps we're not meant to know. Even so, that does not undermine or invalidate the important research that continues to be conducted into claims of past lives.

Chapter 24

Who Are We?

Who do you think you are? That may sound like a rhetorical question, but it's at the very nub of the reincarnation argument. With few exceptions, we all know exactly who we are, both in terms of our exterior appearance and also our inner self. We perceive everything in the world around us in a way that is personal and unique. Our loves, hates, morals, secrets, ambitions, and compassion fuse together with a multitude of other virtues and faults that are all packaged into the soul-entity that is us: the unmistakable creation to which we happily apply the pronoun "I."

All of this points very positively to the fact that planet Earth today is home to seven billion individuals, each living, as it were, in their own world and possessing their own unique identity. All they require to manifest consciously as human beings in a physical environment are bodies of flesh and bones that are fed and watered and animated by a brain for as long as blood is pumped to it from their hearts. When that ceases to happen, parapsychological evidence—particularly that from reincarnation studies—suggests that something containing what we consciously perceive as "us" detaches and continues to exist independently, either permanently in a spiritual dimension or temporarily until reborn again into the physical world. For that to occur, our consciousness needs to be a truly independent entity, rather than, as most scientists would claim, a by-product of the brain, which would therefore die when the body ceases to function. If parapsychologists and the major religions are right and a nonphysical element—soul, spirit, consciousness—survives physical death, scientific proof of this will have enormous implications and will change our perception of humanity's place within the cosmos. While reincarnation studies, along with others such as near-death studies, are pushing back the boundaries, there needs to be a scientific consensus that accepts the existence of a spiritual dimenson interacting with the physical. That, in turn, should shed light on the potential of human consciousness to operate beyond the physical limitations in which we currently assume it functions.

Before examining recent consciousness research, we need to understand that there are aspects of a few reincarnation cases that throw a spanner in the works of a simple chronological theory of soul tranfer. Stevenson, for example, investigated the case of a Thai monk, Chaokhun Rajsuthajarn, who had clear memories of the life of his own maternal uncle, Nai Leng. Chaokhun said he attended Nai Leng's funeral and felt he was greeting the mourners, though they could not see him. At that time, however, he was *already* reincarnated as his nephew, having been born a day *before* his uncle's passing. "I studied this case with much care but couldn't find an explanation for the disrepancy," Stevenson observed in a 1988 interview.[1] Critics, of course, would regard overlapping lives as impossible, but Stevenson's role is to report the facts, not to use them to reinforce a particular viewpoint. Besides, it is not a unique case.

When Alex Shoumatoff, writing for *Vanity Fair* about the conflict between China and Tibet,[2] asked the Dalai Lama if it were possible for a person to reincarnate by taking over the body of someone who already exists, the Dalai Lama replied:

> No, but two separate emanations from the same source can coexist. There are several kinds of reincarnation: One, the previous self takes a new body. Two, the ultimate source of the reincarnation can multiply simultaneously, so in that case rebirth may not necessarily come after a previous death. Two reincarnations can happen. For instance, there are two of [the tulka] Taklun Tsetul, one in central Tibet, the other in eastern Tibet.

Ngawang Zangro, who translated and wrote an introduction to a modern English version of Jamgon Kongtrul Lodrö Tayé's nineteenth-century *Enthronement*[3] about the recognition of reincarnate masters in Tibet and the Himalayas, reveals that "some masters appear earlier or later during the same lifetime." Indeed, the book's author, we are told, died at the end of 1899 and "reincarnated not as one child but as five, each claimed by a monastery with which he had been closely related." Among those whom writer Alexandra David-Néel quoted in her *Immortality and Reincarnation*[4] and met on her travels was a Tibetan contemplative hermit, who spoke to her at a cave in a mountainous valley which had become his home:

> Those wishing to convince themselves of their own immortality by basing it on reincarnations and the memories they have—or claim to have—of their past lives are off course.
>
> They believe that their I is a homogenous block, whereas it is, as taught in Buddhism, an aggregation [the five physical and mental aggregations are the body, sensations, perceptions, mental constructions (ideas and volition), and consciousness or knowledge] whose constituent elements are essentially transitory in nature and have only a momentary existence that is dependent on multiple causes.

Even accounts from hypnotized subjects make much the same point. In his life-between-life research, for example, regressionist Michael Newton was informed[5] by various persons in trance that discarnate entities could choose what percentage of their total energy to incarnate at any one time, depending on the spirit's development (though a minimum of 10 or 15 percent of the energy always remained in the spirit realms). That concept could allow multiple concurrent incarnations to take place, or even for a discarnate entity to communicate from the spirit realms, through a medium, while part of his/her "energy packet" was experiencing a reincarnation.

What these claims or beliefs suggest is that the separateness of our self that we treasure, individually, because it makes us feel special and unique, could be, to borrow a Hindu observation, "a vulgar fallacy, an illusion." The reality is much more complex. Instead of being single souls, it seems we are multileveled or multidimensional. That's a view that is finding support in unlikely places. While scientists like Dr. Ian Stevenson have been beavering away collecting numerous case studies that provide strong evidence for the survival of consciousness from one lifetime to another, scientists working in other disciplines have been coming to similar conclusions, based on hypotheses that examine consciousness from other perspectives. Michael Graziano, Professor of Neuroscience at Princeton University Neuroscience Institute, for example, has developed a theory that consciousness is a perception produced by the brain, a concept he concedes "is decidedly materialistic and atheistic." Yet, surprisingly, he adds in a blog at the *Huffington Post*[6] that "according to the theory, spirits exist—deities, ghosts, souls, the consciousness of other people, one's own consciousness—as rich perceptual simulations run on the hardware of the brain. That perceptual world has psychological reality and genuine importance to human existence." However, if I have understood his theory correctly, they are not real and cannot therefore accommodate the evidence for reincarnation. On the other hand, I believe theories based on quantum mechanics, and particularly entanglement—what Einstein referred to as "spooky action at a distance"—can embrace reincarnation evidence.

One way of looking at how our conscious minds might fit into the grand scheme of things is to view ourselves as being like water molecules in a sea of conciousness: capable of being isolated and examined individually, as a miniscule part of that whole, but totally dependent on and interacting with other molecules to create the ocean. It's not a new idea: similar concepts are to be found in early Hindu teachings, for example, as well as in the writings of philosophers such as William James. But laboratory research coupled with theoretical speculation is giving us a greater insight into the true nature of consciousness and its remarkable capabilities. "The nature of consciousness, its occurrence in the brain, and its ultimate place in the universe are unknown," say Sir Roger Penrose, the eminent English mathematical physicist and professor at Wadham College, Oxford, and Stuart Hameroff, an American anesthesiologist, consciousness researcher, and professor at the University of Arizona. But in a joint paper, published in 2011,[7] they conclude that "consciousness plays an intrinsic role in the universe." They base that opinion on their belief that "consciousness has always been in the universe," and that biology has evolved a mechanism that "orchestrates" quantum computations within our brains to produce consciousness. They call this process "Orchestrated Objective Reduction" or Orch-OR. Their proposal has implications for biology, neuroscience, physics, and cosmology, for it "places the phenomenon of consciousness at a very central place in the physical nature of our universe . . . [and] has a role in the operation of the laws of the universe."

Even if consciousness, in its broadest sense, is universal, there's still a need to understand how it manages to pass from one human life to another, taking with it memories and behaviors. Brazilian parapsychologist Hernani Guimarães Andrade suggested the *biological organizing model* (BOM) more than half a century ago. I am condensing Guy Lyon Playfair's English translation of Andrade's theory[8] to explain it. BOM involves a nonphysical body consisting of two components: the astral, which is the repository of the mind, and the vital, which contains a record of the organic development of our species. The vital is also responsible for "the growth of the body from the initial cell-division stage up to adulthood. It is a historical continuum, a record of our evolution that has served as a blueprint for our current incarnation, and exists in at least five dimensions, four of space and one of time." Andrade, who investigated many reincarnation cases, suggested further that the decision to be reborn may not be a conscious one, but an automatic process of attraction governed by random selection. A mature BOM could have a means of choosing its future mother, while a less mature one may simply attach itself to the first available fertilized egg.

The Conscious Universe[9] and *Entangled Minds*[10] by leading American parapsychologist Dean Radin, senior scientist at the Institute of Noetic Sciences, have done much to open minds to the possibility of what he describes as "a fundamental interconnectedness among all things." For example, he points to experiments conducted at Princeton University and replicated elsewhere, showing that when "a person directs his or her attention toward a remote, physical object, the behavior of an object changes in interesting ways: Tossed dice no longer fall at random, electronic circuits behave strangely, and the human nervous system responds to unseen influences that demonstrate the mind's ability to affect physical objects." He also discusses studies of "field consciousness" in his own laboratory that looked for—and found—correlates in readings from numerous random-number generators and major events on which people's minds were focused, such as the televised annual Academy Awards in 1995. These findings suggest the existence of a "global consciousness": many minds working in unison. The implications of this are enormous. "The idea of the world as an organism has been called the Gaia hypothesis, named after the mythical Greek goddess of the Earth," Radin writes. "Do field-consciousness effects suggest that there may be a mind of Gaia? Just as the individual neurons in the brain would find it hard to believe that they are participating in the complex dance we call the 'conscious mind,' perhaps the individuals of both are participating in the dance of Gaia's mind, and our experiments detected this dance."

Dr. Ian Stevenson, as the researcher who has done more than any other to give the evidence for reincarnation a credible, scientific basis, clearly gave a lot of thought to its *modus operandi.* He calls this intermediate vehicle, which is home to the soul before its next incarnation, a *psychophore,* which means mind-carrying. In conjecturing how the psychophore operates and how it achieves the rebirth it desires, Stevenson makes a number of observations that are important. It needs to be able to influence the outcome of a pregnancy in some way, perhaps by imprinting the embryo or fetus with "some kind of template" that carries memories of past events. Birthmarks and birth defects, he argues, "might be considered mental scars of such wounds that affect another physical body." He also suggests that the psychophore's desire to be either male or female in the next life might be capable of "modifying the vaginal secretions of a woman to give more or less advantage to Y chromosome-carrying sperms (from which males derive) compared with X chromosome-carrying ones."

Paul Von Ward, who runs the Reincarnation Experiment project,[11] claims to have identified and evaluated five factors that appear to be at work in what he calls the *psychoplasm,* a reincarnation mechanism with more capabilities than those known to be involved in DNA transfer and that is "capable of activating genetic off/on switches beyond or different from those normally identified with inherited traits. They are: genotype/phenotype, which determine physical characteristics; cognitive cerebrotypes, relating to mental style and capacities; emotional egotypes, governing how each person copes with the environment; social personatypes, controlling social interactions; and behavioral performatypes, reflecting the individual's creative traits."

These theories share much in common in offering an explanation of how an individual soul might make the journey from one physical body to another, with perhaps a vacation of days, months, or years in between, spent in a spiritual dimension. But there is also growing evidence that while reincarnations occur individually, they may also be linked, resulting in what appears to be a group soul influence that determines when and where those rebirths take place. An English senior consultant psychiatrist, Dr. Arthur Guirdham, wrote a series of books on reincarnation, based largely on his personal experience, claiming that he and many of his patients had all lived before, in the thirteenth century, as Cathars, whose belief in dualism was treated as heresy and cost many of them their lives. The title of one of his books,[12] *We Are One Another,* neatly sums up the interconnectedness of the individuals caught up in his dramatic group reincarnation, as well as reflecting, perhaps, a greater truth that is now emerging in new consciousness studies. There are other parallels to the Guirdham story, such as the discovery that fifty residents of Lake Elsinore, California, could recall during hypnotic regression having all lived during the American Civil War in Millboro, a small town in the state of Virginia.[13]

Smaller groupings, which would include twin souls and soulmates, as well as families, are another possibility. Perhaps we should also be viewing ourselves not as a single, solitary soul but as a facet of something far greater. Each incarnation would be one facet of our soul's existence, while other facets could be simultaneously existing on different planes of existence, or even on Earth—which might explain those cases where reincarnation appears to have occurred before the previous life ended. New concepts of consciousness could also offer us an answer to the perennial question about the Earth's rapidly expanding population. Where do all these souls come from? An ocean of consciousness, if it exists, would have no difficulty in satisfying the demand. Furthermore, advances in technology make it easier to accept such concepts. After all, anyone watching me working at my computer would assume that all the data that appears on my screen exists within its electronics. They would argue that this must be so because there are no wires or attachments that could be feeding it with the mass of information I am viewing. But they would be wrong, of course. Wireless technology gives me and my computer access to an incredible range of information, and I can even store what I want in a virtual memory bank, independent of my computer but accessible by it at any time. Welcome to the world of cloud computing. Perhaps humankind has, without realizing it, been benefitting from *cloud consciousness* since it evolved on Earth.

However fascinating the bigger picture—a universe not only filled with consciousness but animated by it, and groups of souls reincarnating in order to fulfill a shared destiny—the fact remains that the vast majority of us see and experience life through one pair of eyes for several decades, if we are lucky. We are oblivious to a greater reality, what the real purpose of our existence might be, or what fate has in store for us—assuming fate already knows the answer to that. Which brings us to the inevitable question: "How do I find out about my own past lives?" It's a good question, and one that I have deliberately left until last. When I am asked that question, I usually surprise people by asking *why* they want to know. Some have a purpose: Perhaps they are looking for reasons that will explain their fears or phobias. Others are just plain curious. Which is fine. I would direct them to any one of the reputable organizations whose members are past-life therapists with suitable qualifications and high standards, or perhaps to a parapsychological research organization. The purpose of the former, of course, is to help people resolve problems in their life, and many of their members will probably be unwilling to spend time assisting people who are just curious about previous existences. It may take you longer to find a regressionist willing to hypnotize you and record your answers to a host of mundane questions about a former life, as a research project. That previous existence, when recovered, may well turn out to be far less interesting than the one you are now enjoying. It could, on the other hand, contain some surprises. What if your subconscious reveals that you were a murderer in a previous existence? Could you live with that guilt? And what if your hypnotized mind was only concocting a story from information it had collected in the past, perhaps from books or television programs, just to keep you amused? Your guilt about those fictitious events could therefore be totally misplaced. Ian Stevenson has warned that past-life regression can be dangerous,[14] but I know people who have undoubtedly benefited from learning about a previous existence and getting closure on issues that they have brought with them into their present life. Every case, of course, is different.

So, while I do not give advice one way or the other—apart from saying I would have more confidence in the reality of lifetimes I recalled during regression, rather than being told about them by a "past life reader"—I do warn them to tread with caution. There is a purpose in my asking the question, "Why do you want to know who you were in a previous life?" Whoever you were and whatever you did in previous existences, it's what you do in *this* life that really matters. And while the fascinating cases of reincarnation I have described in this book provide very strong evidence for the fact that we are all *spiritual* beings, I also believe that there has to be a reason why the vast majority of us have *no* memories of former lives. It seems that, by and large, we are not meant to remember them. Yet, deep down inside, we will never forget the lessons we have learned during those previous existences and that are firmly embedded in our souls. So perhaps there's no need to gain a forced entry to that hidden chamber of memories. Your present life may well be chosen on the basis of how well you coped with your previous incarnations, and what lessons you still need to learn.

The challenge is to make the very best of your present life, for your own good as well as for others.

Appendix 1

Meet the Researchers
Past and Present

Investigating, collating, and publishing case studies relating to claims of reincarnation is the academic specialty of a small number of scientists and others with a serious interest in the subject. My list begins with the undoubted giant in the field, followed by others alphabetically.

Ian Stevenson, MD

The publication of the Canadian-born researcher's first paper on reincarnation more than half a century ago[1] lifted the curtain on what was to become a lifelong quest. His prize-winning essay, written in honor of William James, an early president of the American Society for Psychical Research, was a review of forty-four cases reported in various publications. He concluded it was a phenomenon worth pursuing and did so with determination for the next forty or more years. Stevenson was already chairman of the Department of Psychiatry and Neurology at the University of Virginia, having been appointed in 1957, and his paranormal research soon caught the eye of influential people. One of these was Eileen Garrett, a famous medium who was also head of the Parapsychology Foundation in New York, who offered to finance Stevenson's first field trip to India and Sri Lanka (formerly Ceylon). He set off to research six cases but uncovered thirty-two during a five-week investigation. He also received encouragement and financial support to study new cases from Chester Carlson, inventor of the Xerox copying process. This resulted in grants and a bequest that enabled Stevenson to create essentially a new field of parapsychological research, becoming Carlson Professor of Psychiatry and Director of the Division of Personality (now Perceptual) Studies at the university, through to his retirement. His numerous scientific papers and books, based on the research he and others have conducted into over 2,500 cases, are now on file at Virginia and being digitized. They present a huge body of evidence, of which his monumental work on birthmarks and birth defects stands head and shoulders above the rest.[2]

Stevenson discovered early on that claims of reincarnation were far more common than generally realized. In September 1962, during his second field trip to Alaska—on the recommendation of Louisa Rhine, whose husband was a pioneer ESP researcher—Stevenson was assured by one of the subjects he interviewed that if he went to Hoonah he would find other cases in its fishing villages, inhabited entirely by Tlingits, the indigenous people of America's Pacific Northwest coast. Stevenson took a seaplane, and upon reaching the harbor, he walked up and down on the dock for a few minutes wondering what to do next. He had no names or contacts, and the seaplane would return in just a few hours. "I decided to ask the first person I met, and this turned out to be Henry Elkin, who came walking along the dock just as I had made up my mind to do this. I accosted him and briefly explained my reason for being in Hoonah. To my surprise and pleasure he opened the front of his shirt and showed me a birthmark on his left chest. He told me he believed he had been shot in the chest during a previous life."[3] Similarly, while investigating cases south of Bangkok, Thailand, with Prof. Kloom Vajropala, Stevenson remarked that there could be a case worth investigating in *every* village. Vajropala disagreed, thinking it a wild idea, so Stevenson suggested they put it to the test, visiting the nearest village and asking if there were any local reincarnation cases. "We went to the village, entered its first boutique (a sort of café), ordered something from the owner, and took our seats," Stevenson recalls.[4] "Then we asked the proprietor whether he knew of any children who claimed to remember previous lives. A boy standing around heard us and immediately said his younger brother was such a person. Thus we came to the case of Anurak Sithipan."

In May 1977, Stevenson wrote the first article on reincarnation to appear in a serious scientific publication,[5] *The Journal of Nervous and Mental Disease.* In that same journal, a colleague, Dr. Harold Lief, wrote, "either he is making a colossal mistake . . . or he will be known as the Galileo of the twentieth century." A modest man, Stevenson would have resisted such comparisons. But it is a measure of his stature, in the eyes of many fellow scientists, that following his death on February 8, 2007, the *Journal of Scientific Exploration*[6] devoted an entire issue to his achievements, with numerous tributes from those who had been privileged to work with him.

Tom Barlow

The Scottish investigator uses hypnosis as a research tool. He has worked with a number of television companies to regress their chosen subjects to a previous life. On one notable occasion, when he and a film crew visited the home of TV presenter Caron Keating, it was her husband—Russell Lindsay— who was regressed at the last moment because Caron could not recall a past life under hypnosis. Researchers subsequently confirmed many of the details of Russell's apparent former life as William Boyd in nineteenth-century Bristol. Barlow also researched the King James IV case and drew attention to the facial similarity between a portrait of the monarch and A. J. Stewart, the woman who recalled that life (see chapter 11). He is skeptical of much that is done in the name of hypnotherapy and has also expressed concern at some hypnotists' lack of "defense mechanisms" when putting their subjects into a trance state. These would ensure they are in total control and can extricate their subjects quickly from a traumatic memory, if necessary.

Gaj Raj Singh Gaur

A biology teacher, Gaur has investigated over one hundred cases of purported reincarnation in northern India. He has also assisted in some of the investigations carried out by Stevenson and Pasricha. He believes "psychic energy" carries over from one life to the next and has a greater influence on the current existence, compared to hereditary factors, if it attaches to a developing embryo at an early stage.

Erlendur Haraldsson

Professor Emeritus at the Faculty of Social Science, University of Iceland, Dr. Haraldsson has been investigating a wide range of paranormal phenomena for over four decades, with a particular focus on reincarnation. His numerous parapsychology papers include field studies undertaken in Sri Lanka and Lebanon. As a psychologist, he has shown particular interest in the psychology of children claiming to recall past lives and how it compares with those without such memories. Haraldsson was working on a project at the University of Virginia in 2007 when Ian Stevenson's health deteriorated and was at his bedside when he passed on.

Jürgen Keil, PhD

An honorary research associate in the Psychology Department at the University of Tasmania, Australia, Dr. Keil has been involved in a number of replication studies of Stevenson's work and has investigated hundreds of cases in Turkey, Thailand, and Myanmar, as well as a few in Syria and Nepal. His research has satisfied him that a "normal" means of communication of past-life facts cannot explain some children's memories, but he appears to be open to the possibility of some form of paranormal transfer of data as an alternative to reincarnation.

Barbara Lane, PhD

Why would thousands of modern Americans choose to spend their weekends sleeping on the hard ground, wearing heavy uniforms, eating stale hardtack, and reenacting battles from 130 years ago? It was a question that fascinated the former reporter turned clinical hypnotherapist, and she embarked on a study to see if memories of former lives might offer an explanation for their passion for the past. She found twelve reenactors—one of whom was a woman—who agreed to be regressed. Despite their skepticism, all recalled a Civil War existence. The sessions were conducted in 1993 and

1994 as part of Lane's dissertation for a PhD in metaphysical sciences from Westbrook University in New Mexico, which was subsequently expanded into a popular book, *Echoes from the Battlefield*.[7]

Antonia Mills, PhD

Currently Professor in First Nations Studies at the University of Northern British Columbia, Canada, the anthropologist began her reincarnation research after Ian Stevenson called at the Vancouver university in the mid-1980s, on his way back from studying rebirth cases among the Gitksan Indians of northwest British Columbia. He asked if there were any graduates or faculty members who might be interested in continuing with the research he had been doing and was given two names. One was Antonia Mills, whose PhD thesis at Harvard University had included an observation about the importance of belief in reincarnation among the Beaver Indians. She accepted Stevenson's challenge and has also gone on to do valuable research in India, including a replication study of Stevenson's findings.[8] Such field trips are not without their difficulties. Mills tells of one subject whose past-life claims included the identity of his murderer. "The alleged murderer and his family identified me and my assistants as undercover agents seeking information for the murder trial, and they threatened the child, his relatives, and the villagers with dire consequences if they should talk about the case."

Satwant Pasricha, MD

Head of the Department of Clinical Psychology at the National Institute of Mental Health and Neurosciences at Bangalore, India, where she is associate professor and additional professor of child psychology, Dr. Pasricha has been involved in investigating more than five hundred cases of reincarnation and near-death experiences since 1973. In doing so, she has highlighted the fact that there are far fewer reincarnation cases reported in South India, where she is based, than in the north of the country. She worked closely with Ian Stevenson over the years, particularly during a period spent at the University of Virginia School of Medicine. Like Mills, Pasricha has documented the difficulties that can face researchers in this field. In one case, she and her colleagues had to walk sixteen kilometers to reach a village where there was no road link, but were then unable to trace the family they were looking for. "On other occasions," she writes,[9] "after the monsoons, road communications had been blocked due to the sudden collapse of the bridge; we then had to wade through water." The sight of Dr. Pasricha and her colleagues, notebooks and cameras in hand, led some young male villagers to stop working and hide, believing the group to be from a birth-control program intent on sterilizing them. For this reason, researchers often refrain from asking about the number of children in a subject's family, she reveals.

Kirti S. Rawat, PhD

The last researcher to interview Shanti Devi (chapter 5)[10] before her death, making audio and video recordings, retired philosophy professor Dr. Rawat has extensive knowledge of reincarnation, having investigated the subject for over four decades. The Indian researcher told a conference in Nepal in 2009 that he has five hundred case files at his International Center for Survival and Reincarnation Research, including that of a boy who was born circumcised into a Hindu family, and who not only knew exactly how to perform the Muslim ritual of Nawaz, but could recall the exact process of circumcision. Rawat assisted in some of Ian Stevenson's early investigations[11] and collaborated with Titus Rivas in producing a paper discussing the reported intermission period between lives.[12] Mary Roach accompanied Rawat on a couple of case investigations while researching her best-selling book, *Spook*.[13]

Marge Rieder, PhD

Like Barbara Lane, Rieder is a hypnotherapist whose research appears to have uncovered a remarkable story of group reincarnation. It began when a subject near Lake Elsinore, California, slipped into a past life and spoke of a former life in Millboro, a small town in Virginia, at the time of the Civil War. In time, more than thirty-five people sought Dr. Rieder's therapeutic help, and during regressions, also recalled a previous incarnation in Millboro, often in graphic detail and providing information that was not in the public domain. The conclusion, contained in *Mission to Millboro*,[14] was that they had lived as a group during the Civil War and had chosen to be reborn together in the twentieth century. Rieder's follow-up, *Return to Millboro*,[15] explored the group's intricate connections and relationships in even greater depth.

Walter Semkiw, MD

Trained in psychiatry and now a physician working in occupational medicine in San Francisco, Dr. Semkiw began researching reincarnation in 1995. He is president and a founder of the Institute for the Integration of Science, Intuition and Spirit (IISIS), whose primary focus is "to compile and present compelling reincarnation cases that demonstrate objective evidence of reincarnation." His interest in reincarnation began with an investigation into one of his own past lives, as he recounts in *Return of the Revolutionaries*.[16] His collaboration with medium Kevin Ryerson has led him to identify the past lives of numerous famous people, showing similarities in facial appearance from one life to the next. He argues that objective evidence of reincarnation has the potential to change the world in a fundamental way and to that end he is now focusing his efforts on the IISIS website,[17] promoting compelling case studies in multiple languages.

Francis Story

London-born during World War I and privately educated, Story's independent thinking led him into Buddhism as a teenager. Following the death of his wife six years after they married, he became a voluntary worker in India and lived in Asia for a quarter of a century, during which time, as well as promoting Buddhism,[18] he explored the concept of reincarnation, conducting careful investigations of many cases, notably in Myanmar. Ian Stevenson has acknowledged the invaluable assistance he received from Story on his first visit to Sri Lanka and second visit to India, "adding greatly to the gathering of data and their analysis."

Linda Tarazi

Intrigued by one of her patient's detailed accounts of an apparent past life in Spain, the psychologist and regression therapist decided to see how much of the data could be corroborated. It was the start of a three-year investigation, one-third of which was spent in Spain, searching through archives and checking data gathered during one thousand taped sessions with her subject. Most of the material was verified (see chapter 20). The results appeared first as a paper published by the American Society for Psychical Research's *Journal*[19] and then in narrative book form.[20]

Jim Tucker, MD

A board-certified child psychologist, Tucker is associate professor of psychiatry and neurobehavioral sciences at the University of Virginia and worked with Ian Stevenson for several years on reincarnation research, taking over from him on his retirement in 2002. The main focus of his studies has been American children, though his investigation of a Scottish boy, Cameron Macaulay, was the subject of a television documentary. Tucker has developed a method of evaluating cases—the Strength of Case Scale—to determine which offer the best evidence for reincarnation. His book *Life before Life*[21] explores current and future reincarnation research.

Paul Von Ward

A clinically trained psychologist, Von Ward describes himself as "an interdisciplinary cosmologist and independent scholar who spent three decades in public service as a US naval officer, diplomat, and international nonprofit executive, before becoming a full-time writer and lecturer." His book *The Soul Genome*[22] deals with "science and reincarnation" and he runs the Reincarnation Experiment "to determine if science can prove reincarnation." His personal belief is that "current research in the energetic/information aspects of species evolution now points to a physical genome embedded in an information-rich, energetic field that contains memories, DNA patterns, emotional profiles, and knowledge and skills honed in previous incarnations."[23]

Appendix 2

Meet the Therapists
Past and Present

Using hypnosis or similar methods to induce altered states of consciousness and explore the possibility that we possess an indestructible soul that
continues over many lifetimes is the domain of some researchers. Therapists,
on the other hand, use the same tools to help their subjects confront and
overcome problems in their current existence, though they are not unanimous in their interpretation of what precisely is happening or how their
results are achieved. Does regression reveal actual past lives or simply give
patients a scenario that enables them to come to terms with certain conditions? Here, alphabetically, are just a few of the many working in this field
who have contributed to our growing understanding of past-life therapy.

Carol Bowman

Author, researcher, and past-life therapist Bowman has her children,
Sarah and Chase, to thank for introducing her to reincarnation (see chapter
7).[1] Based in Media, Pennsylvania, Bowman holds an MS in counseling from
Villanova University. She also runs a useful website, and because of her own

experiences, part of her therapeutic focus is on children, particularly those suffering from phobias.

Edgar Cayce

Known as the Sleeping Prophet, Cayce gave past-life readings and also diagnosed his clients' medical conditions and provided remedies while in trance. Though not a traditional past-life therapist, Cayce opened many minds to the possibility of reincarnation and continues to have a very large following more than six decades after his passing.

Adam Crabtree

Canadians Adam and Joanne Crabtree have been practicing psychother- apy in Toronto, Ontario, for over thirty years, using therapeutic trance and hypnosis to explore the inner mind. Therapeutic trances, they say, are very effective in working with regression, including past-life memories. Crabtree has also written extensively about multiple personalities and possession.[2]

Janet Cunningham

· Based in Edgewood, Maryland, Cunningham is a past-life regressionist with an international reputation, having conducted training sessions and workshops throughout the world and led tours to spiritual sites, including Egypt, Thailand, China, and Turkey. She is president of the International Board of Regression Therapy, a past president of the International Associa- tion for Regression Research and Therapies (IARRT), and has written or pro- duced over fourteen books and CDs. Her book, *A Tribe Returned*, tells the story of her involvement in a group reincarnation.[3]

Hazel Denning

A founder and past president of IARRT in 1980 (when it was known as the Association for Past Life Research and Therapies), Denning was a full-time past-life regression therapist until her retirement, after which she continued to work for the association, as well as on parapsychology projects and the writing of three books, including *Life without Guilt*.[4] Denning, who made a huge contribution to regression therapy in its early days, lived in Riverside, California, where she died in 2006 at the age of ninety-eight.

Lee Everett

Mixing with celebrities came easily to Lee Everett, having once been a singer and also the partner of pop idol Billy Fury and then TV presenter and disk jockey Kenny Everett. So, having become a past-life regressionist, she had no problem persuading the likes of Elton John and tennis star Billie Jean King to recall previous existences. She recounted their experiences in *Celebrity Regressions*.[5] Today, together with husband John Alkin, Lee runs the Obsidian College for Healing and Integrated Medicine, dedicated to the pursuit of "spiritual intelligence" that introduces intuition and compassion into conventional medicine.

Adrian Finkelstein

Not only has Finkelstein apparently discovered the reincarnation of Marilyn Monroe during a series of hypnosis sessions (see chapter 9)[6] but he has also concluded that Seattle-based Valerie Franich, an "intuitive educator," is the reincarnation of Hollywood's first blonde bombshell, Jean Harlow, who died prematurely of kidney failure at the age of twenty-six. Not only that, but Finkelstein learned from the entranced Franich that in his previous existence he was her first husband, Paul Bern, one of MGM's top executives.[7] Finkelstein graduated from Hadassah Medical School, Hebrew University, Jerusalem, Israel, in 1968 and has been researching reincarnation and conducting past-life therapy since 1977.

Edith Fiore

Having completed her doctorate in psychology at the University of Miami, Dr. Fiore went into private practice, first in Miami and then in Saratoga, California. Her introduction to hypnosis at a weekend seminar at the Esalen Institute resulted in her using it increasingly, first to reduce patient anxiety, then to regress clients to events in this life, and finally to explore past lifetimes. In her book *You Have Been Here Before*,[8] Dr. Fiore tells readers: "In my work with reincarnation theory, I am finding there is not one aspect of character or human behavior that cannot be better understood through an examination of past-life events." She has also written about spirit possession and alien abductions.

Bruce Goldberg

A doctor of dental surgery, with a BA degree in biology and chemistry, California-based Dr. Goldberg has focused on past-life regression and future-life progression since retiring from dentistry. The author of twenty-one books, including *Past Lives, Future Lives*,[9] Goldberg is described on his website as "the world's foremost authority on futuristic time travelers" and says he has conducted more than thirty-five thousand regressions and progressions.

Judy Hall

An English past-life therapist, healer, and karmic astrologer, Hall is author of over forty books on a range of psychic and spiritual subjects, including *Hands across Time: The Soulmate Enigma*.[10] She believes that far from being victims of circumstance or the product of karmic consequences, we each follow a soul plan that will help us achieve spiritual growth.

Robert G. Jarmon

A woman patient, Anna, seeking to reduce her weight, changed Dr. Jarmon's life when she agreed to be hypnotized so that he could help her change undesirable habits that were leading to weight gain. His instruction, "Go back to where it began," had a surprising result, when instead of talking of an event in her current life, she announced that her name was Elizabeth, and she described a deathbed scene in an unspecified European country. Dr. Jarmon, a specialist in emergency medicine, was then a physician working at a New Jersey hospital, with an active private psychiatric counseling practice. He also had no belief in reincarnation, but the therapeutic value of Anna's past-life recall led him to use it on other patients with equally impressive results.[11]

Joe Keeton

It was the famous Bridey Murphy case that inspired Englishman Keeton to explore the possibility of reincarnation through hypnotism. In the process, he produced many impressive cases,[12] though he believed that racial memory, rather than past lives, might explain the phenomenon. He had no doubts, however, about the ability of the hypnotized mind to produce dramatic improvements in health conditions. The Liverpool hypnotherapist claimed his methods had even enabled a young woman to regrow her heel, which she had lost in a motorcycle accident.[13]

Denys Kelsey

Together with his wife, Joan Grant, the famous author of Far Memory books, English physician and psychiatrist Dr. Kelsey was a pioneer regression therapist, using a mixture of psychic insight and past-life recall to help patients. "I should like people to share my belief in reincarnation," he wrote forty years ago.[14] "I think it would cause them to be much happier, much less frightened, and very much more sane. For a psychiatrist to hold this belief, and to have made it the basis of his therapy, is still very unusual."

Ian Lawton

A proponent of evidence-based, rational spirituality, English writer and researcher Lawton's developing interest in the soul has not only led him to write several books on the subject and to propose a new theory about its nature but also to establish a regression-therapy practice. *The Holographic Soul*[15] suggests that we are individual aspects and simultaneously a full holographic representation of "the Source"—a concept that one reviewer said "brilliantly solves many spiritual conundrums."

Winafred Blake Lucas

A diplomat of the American Board of Professional Psychology, Dr. Lucas, who passed on in 2006, served on the faculty of Los Angeles State University and on the educational board of the American Institute of Hypnotherapy and was later a core faculty member of the California School of Professional

Psychology. But it was in the field of past-life regression that she made the greatest impact, as editor of IARRT's *Journal of Regression Therapy* during its early years and with the monumental two-volume *Regression Therapy: A Handbook for Professionals*,[16] which she edited and published, contributing ten chapters to the first volume, which give an overview of the history of past-life therapy and its many controversies. This is a superb introduction to the subsequent thirteen contributed papers from some of the earliest and leading practitioners in this field. Dr. Lucas also participated in a triple regression, filmed by ABC Television, together with physician Gladys T. McGarey and writer Mantosh Devji/Singh, in which all three recalled former associated lives in India. In that life, Lucas had been a daughter of Shah Juhan and his wife, Mumtaz Mahal, in memory of whom he built the Taj Mahal. Dr. McGarey had been the midwife who delivered Mumtaz's children.[17]

Morris Netherton

One of the first pioneering practitioners of past-life therapy, Netherton conducted over forty thousand sessions over a forty-five-year period before his retirement, using his own techniques to assist his clients in identifying, reliving, and releasing unresolved issues "from experiences across the vast expanses of time." He gave an early insight into his methods and conclusions in *Past Lives Therapy*,[18] published more than three decades ago. His purpose, he explains, was to create change in the current life at both the finite and infinite levels. "I have always found the answers to my own life's questions within the study and practice of this process, and it has always proven to be an effective healing process," he adds.

Julio Peres

Clinical psychologist Dr. Peres has a PhD in neuroscience and behavior from the Institute of Psychology at the University of São Paulo, is an expert on post-traumatic stress disorder, and has written a number of papers on the effectiveness of past-life regression treatment that he uses in his clinic in Brazil. In an analysis of results of sessions conducted by three psychotherapists with 610 patients between 1996 and 2002, during which they were asked to discuss the most traumatic event they could recall, without being directed as to whether it was in the current or a past life, 39 percent described a life trauma in the present life and almost the same number—38 percent—referred to an event that appeared to be in a past life. Of that second group, however, 77 percent gave no verifiable data about that previous existence, and the information provided by another 21 percent, who gave names and other data about a past life that could be checked, was found to be inaccurate. Only 2 percent provided verifiable past-life facts. But the most significant statistic for Dr. Peres and his co-researchers is that two-thirds of the subjects experienced a *total remission* from the symptoms that had led them to seek help.

Chet Snow

While working for the United States Air Force in California in 1983, Dr. Snow met pioneering regressionist Dr. Helen Wambach, and they worked together for two years until her untimely death in 1985. He then produced *Mass Dreams of the Future,*[19] based on Dr. Wambach's concept of "future-life progressions" and his own research. Snow, who has degrees from Columbia University and the Sorbonne in Paris, has given over five hundred past- and future-life lectures and seminars in English, French, and Spanish on three continents, including a lecture at the United Nations in 1994. He is a past president of the APLRT (now IARRT), and as well as being a Sedona-based regression therapist, he also leads small-group tours to sacred sites in Europe.

Dick Sutphen

As a therapist, researcher, and writer specializing in soulmates and predestined love,[20] it is only fair that Dick Sutphen eventually found the love of his life—Tara—with whom he believes he has shared many previous lives. Sutphen was one of the first hypnotherapists to conduct a past-life regression on national television in the USA, for Tom Snyder's *Tomorrow* program in 1976. He and Tara, who presents with him at workshops and seminars, believe the power of love is unlimited and is capable of transcending time and space. It's a concept that explains "love at first sight." He adds: "In all my work in this area, I have found only a few cases where I have been unable to establish a past link between present lovers." Sutphen has authored well over thirty books, a third of them metaphysical, and produced three hundred self-help tapes.

Hans TenDam

Having pioneered the "Dutch School" of past-life theory almost three decades ago, management consultant TenDam is well-qualified to be president of EARTh (European Association for Regression Therapy), which is dedicated to improving and enlarging the professional application of regression therapy, and was organizer of the First World Congress for Regression Therapy in 2003. His groundbreaking books, *Deep Healing*[21] and *Exploring Reincarnation*,[22] serve as excellent introductions to the subject for both the public and would-be therapists, as well as complementing the workshops he conducts in Japan, India, Brazil, and in various European countries.

Helen Wambach

A Berkeley, California, clinical psychologist, Wambach set out to debunk past-life therapy in the 1960s but was persuaded by the evidence and became a regression therapist, writing two books about her experiences, *Reliving Past Lives*[23] and *Life before Life*,[24] that have encouraged many others to follow in her adventurous footsteps. Chet Snow participated in her research and took over her work when she died after a third heart attack, at the age of sixty in 1985. It formed the foundation of his *Dreams of the Future*,[25] being based on "progression" sessions in which Dr. Wambach took her subjects, including Snow, into the future at specific periods between 2100 and 2500 AD. "She was an unusual lady for spiritual work," Chet recalls with affection. "She was about two hundred pounds overweight and chain-smoked, ate gargantuan meals, and enjoyed life to the fullest. If she didn't have a glass of brandy at the end of the day it wasn't a good day! Helen was very pragmatic; she knew exactly what she was doing. She had already had two heart attacks when I met her and had a bypass which involved having a piece of pig valve sewn in. When asked how she was, she would reply: 'The pig and I are OK.'"

Brian Weiss, MD

As a traditional psychotherapist, Dr. Weiss was astonished and skeptical when one of his patients began recalling past-life traumas that seemed to hold the key to her recurring nightmares and anxiety attacks. His skepticism was eroded, however, when she began to channel messages from "the space between lives," which contained remarkable revelations about Dr. Weiss's family and his dead son (see chapter 15). Using past-life therapy, he was able to cure the patient and embark on a new, more meaningful phase of his own career. A graduate of Columbia University and Yale Medical School, Weiss is Chairman Emeritus of Psychiatry at the Mount Sinai Medical Center in Miami and maintains a private practice in the city. In addition, he conducts national and international seminars and experiential workshops as well as training programs for professionals and is the author of several top-selling books, the best known of which is *Many Lives, Many Masters.*[26]

Roger J. Woolger

A Jungian analyst with degrees in psychology, religion, and philosophy from Oxford and London Universities, Woolger has been a guest professor at Vassar College and a visiting professor at the University of Vermont and Concordia University, Montreal. He describes himself as a pragmatist, explaining: "I think my position is a little unusual. I don't hold a brief for reincarnation. I don't care whether you can prove it or not. What is certain is that when the unconscious mind is given the opportunity to play stories *as if they are past lives,* it comes up with staggering solutions, releases, and spontaneous healings, which you don't get in other therapies." So how does he view his own past-life recalls—are they real or fantasy? "Oh yes, they're past-life memories," he responds, "but I don't know who 'myself' is. Instead of saying, 'I was that soldier in the thirteenth century,' I prefer to say, 'I have the remnants of that soldier in me today.'" His first book, *Other Lives, Other Selves,*[27] is regarded as a definitive work in the field of regression therapy, and he has since developed what is described as "a highly original therapeutic tool," the Deep Memory Process.

Endnotes

Chapter 1

1. "Religion in the Lives of American Adolescents: A Review of the Literature." A Research Report of the National Study of Youth and Religion. Published by the University of North Carolina (2003).
2. The Pew Research Center's Forum on Religion and Public Life provides a neutral venue for discussions of timely issues (http://pewforum.org).
3. The renowned Sir E. A. Wallis Budge said of Deveria: "No other scholar had such a wide and competent knowledge of the Book of the Dead."
4. Bonwick, J. (1878).
5. Kingsley, P. (2010).

Chapter 2

1. "Behind the Scenes at Amarna Reunion," *Reincarnation International*, No. 3, July 1994, pp. 18–19.
2. Cott, J. (1988).
3. Rogo, D. S. (1985).
4. Stearn, J. (1965).
5. In his blog: http://www.drhawass.com/blog/mark-and-me#_jmp0_.
6. January–March 2011 issue of *Venture Inward*.

Chapter 3

1. The hour-long TV documentary *Back from the Dead* was first screened in the UK by Channel 4 on May 18, 1998, and has since been shown around the world.
2. The London-based charity seeks to educate the public about the Druze culture, history, and tradition. Its founder, Salim Kheireddine, tells of his own past-life memories in an introduction to a book published by the foundation: Playfair, G. L. (2006).
3. Julia Makarem on the American Druze Heritage website (www.americandruze.com).
4. Stevenson, I. (1980).
5. Reproduced in full, with photographs by Roni Sofer, in *Reincarnation International*, No. 6, July 1995, pages 23–26.
6. April 1997.
7. *Reincarnation International*, No. 15, June 1998, p. 20.
8. Ibid., p. 21.
9. *Reincarnation International*, No. 17, July 1999, p. 25–26.
10. Ibid., p. 23–24.

Chapter 4

1. Hanzhang, Y. (1991).
2. Tayé, J. K. L. (1997).

Chapter 5

1. Lönnerstrand, S. (1998).
2. Rawat, K. S. (1997).

Chapter 6

1. Bernstein, M. (1965).
2. Story filed October 13, 2010.
3. Stevenson, I. (1966).
4. Ibid. (1974).
5. Harris, M. (1986a).
6. Ibid. (1986b).
7. "Bridey Murphy Lives—Again—In a Pueblo Living Room." *The Pueblo Chieftain,* October 27, 2005.
8. Private communication with author, 2011.

Chapter 7

1. Stevenson, I. (1990).

Chapter 8

1. Stevenson, I. and Keil, J. (2005).
2. Mills, A. (1989).
3. Stemman, R. (1997, revised 2005).

Chapter 9

1. "Tsar Memory," *Life & Soul Magazine,* No. 16, March 1999, 10–17.
2. Norsic, D. (1998).
3. www.reincarnationexperiment.org.
4. *Reincarnation International,* No. 12, July 1997, p. 5.
5. Ibid. No. 1, January 1994, p. 5.
6. *Kindred Spirit,* December–February, 1993–94.
7. *Reincarnation International,* No. 17, July 1999, p. 8.
8. www.peterteekamp.com.
9. www.johnadams.net/cases/samples/Montez-Michelangelo/index.html.
10. Harwood, B. (2006).
11. www.johnadams.net/cases/samples/laurel-hardy/index.html.
12. http://en.wikipedia.org/wiki/Sherrie_Lea.
13. www.marilynmonroereincarnated.net/.
14. www.nickbunick.com.
15. Bunick, N. (2010).
16. www.guardian.co.uk/world/2002/may/24/russia.iantraynor.
17. www.telegraph.co.uk/news/newstopics/howaboutthat/6016147/David-Shayler -transvestite-MI5-spy-turned-Jesus-Christ-faces-eviction-from-squat.html#_jmp0_.
18. Salva, R. (2009).
19. Leonardi, D. (1975).
20. Semkiw, W. (2008).
21. www.johnadams.net/cases/samples/Obama-Trumbull/index.html.
22. Barnes, W. (1999) and "Titanic Memories," *Reincarnation International,* No. 18, November 1999, pp. 11–14.
23. Karlén, B. (2000).
24. "Anne Frank Returned?" *Life & Soul Magazine,* No. 16, March 1999, pp. 224–30, and "Anne Frank's New Diary," Summer 2000, p. 34.

Chapter 10

1. Stevenson, I. (1997a) and (1997b).
2. Ibid.
3. Ibid. (1974).
4. Ibid.
5. Ibid. (2003).
6. Hall, H. F. (1898).
7. "Joan Rivers' 'Reunion' with Her Dead Mother," *Reincarnation International*, No. 10, November 1996, p. 10.
8. "They Were Born to Be Together," *Reincarnation International*, No. 10, November 1996, pp. 8–12.
9. "Keeping It in the Family," *Reincarnation International*, No. 1, January 1994, p. 6.
10. Author's blog: www.ParanormalReview.com.

Chapter 11

1. Toyne, C. (1970).
2. Ibid. (1976).
3. Percival, H. W. (1946).
4. "Taking Royal Claim at Face Value," *Reincarnation International*, No. 5, March 1995, pp. 18–20.
5. Semkiw, W. (2003).
6. www.johnadams.net/cases/samples/Semkiw-Adams/index.html.
7. Semkiw, W. (2003).
8. Myss, C. and Shealy, N. (1998).
9. Bellamy, E. (1888).
10. Free download available at: www.reincarnation2002.com/on-line_book.htm (though this website has not been updated for some years).
11. www.infinitesouls.com/page24.html#_jmp0_.
12. "Love's Déjà Vu: Married Again 125 Years Later." www.indiadivine.org/audarya/world-review/443366-loves-deja-vu-married-again-125-years-later.html.

Chapter 12

1. Stevenson, I. (1987).
2. Blavatsky, H. P. (1888).
3. "The Future of Women," *Lucifer*, Vol. 7, October 1890, p. 116.
4. Besant, A. and Leadbeater, C. W. (1949).
5. Ibid. (1924).
6. Stevenson, I. (1983).
7. Ibid. (1974).
8. Ibid. (2003).

Chapter 13

1. Interview with *Rolling Stone* magazine, November 25, 2010.
2. Dowding, H. C. T. (1945).
3. Cuban publication *Periodico 26*, September 28, 2006.
4. *San Francisco Examiner,* August 26, 1928.
5. Interview in *Jewish Telegraph*, November 27, 1998.
6. Interview in *The Times* (UK), January 30, 1999.
7. Hugo, V. (1998).
8. MacLaine, S. (1983), (1989), (2000).

9. Interview by Melvyn Bragg, *Sunday Times Magazine* (UK), June 5, 1983.
10. Rabanne, P. (1997).
11. Interview by Kala Ambrose, posted in three parts on www.examiner.com, on August 6–7, 2009.
12. "Celebrity Regressions," *Reincarnation International,* No. 13, October 1997, p. 21.
13. "Sweet Soul Music," *Reincarnation International,* No. 10, November 1996.
14. Varah, C. (1992).
15. *The Guardian,* January 25, 1996.
16. "Celebrity Regressions," *Reincarnation International,* No. 13, October 1997, p. 21.

Chapter 14

1. See appendix 2 and Jarmon, R. G. (1997).
2. Stevenson, I. (1994).
3. Denning, H. (1987).
4. Van der Maesen, R. (2006).
5. Stemman, R. (1997).
6. "Face to Face with Roger Woolger . . . and His Many Selves." *Reincarnation International,* No. 4, November 1994, pp. 21–25.
7. Woolger, R. (1988).

Chapter 15

1. Chris French is a professor of psychology and head of the Anomalistic Psychology Research Unit at Goldsmiths, University of London.
2. Hall, H. F. (1898).
3. Stevenson, I. (1997a).
4. Bose, C. S. (1952).
5. Stevenson, I. (1997a).
6. Ibid. (1997a).
7. Case contributed by Dutch researcher Titus Rivas on the website www.prebirth experience.com.
8. Weiss, B. (1988).
9. Whitton, J. L. and Fisher, J. (1986).
10. Moody, R. (1979).
11. Fiore, E. (1979).
12. Wambach, H. (1979).
13. Newton, M. (1994).

Chapter 16

1. Wambach, H. (1979 and 1981).
2. Snow, C. (1989).
3. Cockell, J. (1993).
4. Ibid. (1996).
5. "From Surrey to Roman Empire and Back . . . In an Afternoon." *Reincarnation International,* No. 11, April 1997, pp. 12–14.
6. Cannon, D. (1991, 1992, and 1994).
7. "Has Nostradamus Broken through the Time-Space Barrier?" *Reincarnation International,* No. 11, April 1997, pp. 8–11.
8. Goldberg, B. (1996).
9. www.examiner.com/metaphysical-spirituality-in-national/i-am-woman-the -invincible-spirit-of-singer-helen-reddy-part-one#_jmp0_.

Chapter 17

1. *Deccan Chronicle,* December 25, 2009.
2. *Weekly World News,* March 10, 1998.
3. "In the Pangolin Lives Their Mother, Children Believe." *Hindustan Times,* April 11, 2006.
4. *Daily Telegraph,* November 3, 2009.
5. Reported on the Indian news portal Sify.com, January 11, 2006.
6. London *Evening Standard,* April 1, 2007.
7. BBC News website, June 18, 2011.
8. *National Post,* March 13, 2006.
9. AolNews.com, July 29, 2010.
10. *Reincarnation International,* No. 3, July 1994, p. 6.
11. "Ben Johnson's Curious Tale of Reincarnation, 'The Matrix' and 'The Mystery Man,'" by John Leicester, The Associated Press, October 22, 2010.
12. Iverson, J. (1976).
13. Flournoy, T. (1900).
14. Kampman, R. (1973).

Chapter 18

1. Barnes, J. (2008).
2. *Daily Telegraph,* March 26, 2011.
3. www.sonustech.com/paravicini/.
4. www.optimnem.co.uk/.
5. Parker, E. S., Cahill, L., and McGaugh, J. L. (2006).
6. http://nhne-pulse.org/60-minutes-the-gift-of-endless-memory/.
7. Kampman, R. (1973).
8. Pearsall, P., Schwartz, G., and Russek, L. (2000).
9. Schwartz, G. and Russek, L. (2006).
10. "The Heart Remembers," *Natural Health,* March–April, 1998.
11. Tucker, J. B. (2005).
12. Review of Tucker, J. B. (2005), *Journal of Scientific Exploration,* Vol. 19, No. 4, pp. 632–636.

Chapter 19

1. Stevens, E. W. (1878).
2. Stevenson, I., Pasricha, S., and McClean-Rice, N. (1989).
3. Published in the October 2010 *Proceedings* of the Society for Psychical Research.
4. Pasricha, S. (1990).
5. Ibid.

Chapter 20

1. "Haneen: Remembers Being School Teacher before Shell Killed Her," *Reincarnation International,* No. 15, June 1998, pp. 12–14.
2. "Rabih: Famous Footballer and Singer before Dying in Explosion," *Reincarnation International,* No. 15, June 1998, pp. 16–18.
3. "Past-life Memories Inspire Hunt for Buried Treasure," *Reincarnation International,* No. 5, March 1995, pp. 28–30.
4. "Roundhead Returns to Where He Fought for Cromwell," *Reincarnation International,* No. 4, November 1994, pp. 16–17, and "Digging Up the Past," *Reincarnation International,* No. 8, March 1996, p. 23.
5. Pasricha, S. (1998).

6. Stemman, R. (2005).
7. *The Reincarnation Experiments* (1983 TV documentary) and *In Search of Past Lives* (1990) by Peter Ramster.
8. "Records Prove Corporal Existed," *Life and Soul,* Issue 17, July 1999, pp.15–16.
9. Tarazi, L. (1990 and 1997).
10. "Far Memory of Petra," *Reincarnation International,* No. 6, July 1995, pp. 33–35.
11. Obituary in *The Daily Telegraph* (UK), October 14, 2008.
12. Cockell, J. (1993) and "Past-life Search Leads to Family Reunion," *Reincarnation International,* No. 1, January 1994, pp. 10–16.
13. Haraldsson, E. (2000).
14. Haraldsson, E. and Abu-Izzeddin, M. (2002).
15. Leininger, B. and Leininger, A., with Gross, K. (2009).
16. Harrison, P. and Harrison, M. (1991).
17. "The Uncanny Case of Carl Edon," by Mike Blackburn, www.GazetteLive.co.uk, January 15, 2002.
18. Norman, B. (2008).
19. Llewelyn, K. (1991).

Chapter 21

1. Stevenson, I. (1993).
2. Ibid. (1997a).
3. Ibid.
4. Mills, A. (1989).
5. Stevenson, I. (1993).
6. Ibid. (1997a).
7. "The Shape of Things to Come," *Reincarnation International,* No. 2, April 1994, pp. 22–25.
8. Stevenson, I. (1997b).
9. "The Shape of Things to Come," *Reincarnation International,* No. 2, April 1994, pp. 22–25.
10. Pasricha, S. (1998).
11. Stevenson, I. (1997a).
12. Ibid.
13. Ibid.
14. Ibid.
15. Ibid.
16. Ibid.
17. Ibid.
18. Ibid.
19. Ibid.

Chapter 22

1. Shroder, T. (1999).
2. Angel, L. (1994b).
3. Ibid. (1994a).
4. Stevenson, I. (1995).
5. Ibid. (1995).
6. Edwards, P. (1996).
7. John Beloff's review in the *Journal* of the Society for Psychical Research, Vol. 61, No. 846.
8. James Matlock's review in the *Journal of Scientific Exploration,* Vol. 11, No. 4, Winter 1997.
9. Almeder, R. (1997).
10. Reported in Fisher, J. (1984).
11. Stevenson, I. (1984).

12. Ibid. (1974).
13. Banerjee, H. N. (1980).
14. Semkiw, W. (2003).

Chapter 23

1. Revealed in a letter to *APRT Newsletter* in 1998.
2. Gershom, Y. (1992 and 1996).
3. "Hoddle Puts His Faith in God and England," *The Times* (UK), January 30, 1999.
4. Stevenson, I. (1987).

Chapter 24

1. *Omni Magazine,* 10 (4): 76, 1988.
2. *Vanity Fair,* August 1996.
3. Tayé, J. K. L. (1997).
4. David-Néel, A. (1997).
5. Newton, M. (1994).
6. "The Spirit Constructed in the Brain," April 29, 2011: www.huffingtonpost.com/michael-graziano/the-spirit-constructed-in_b_855160.html#_jmp0_.
7. Penrose, R. and Hameroff, S. (2011).
8. Playfair, G. L. (2006).
9. Radin, D. (1997).
10. Ibid. (2006).
11. www.reincarnationexperiment.org/.
12. Guirdham, A. (1974).
13. Rieder, M. (1993).
14. Stevenson, I. (1994).

Appendix 1

1. Stevenson, I. (1960).
2. Ibid. (1997a).
3. Ibid. (1997a). The case of Henry Elkin is also featured in Stevenson, I. (1966).
4. Ibid. (1997b), pp 78–79.
5. Ibid. (1977).
6. *Journal of Scientific Exploration,* Vol. 22, No. 1, 2008, the contents of which are available online at www.scientificexploration.org/journal/articles.html.
7. Lane, B. (1996).
8. Mills, A. (1989).
9. Pasricha, S. (1990).
10. Rawat, K. S. (1997).
11. Stevenson, I., Prasad, J., Mehrotra, L. P., and Rawat, K. S. (1974).
12. Rawat, K. S. and Rivas, T. (2005).
13. Roach, M. (2005).
14. Rieder, M. (1991).
15. Ibid. (1988).
16. Semkiw, W. (2003).
17. www.iisis.net/.
18. Story, F. (1975).
19. Tarazi, L. (1990).
20. Ibid. (1997).
21. Tucker, J. B. (2005).

22. Von Ward, P. (2008).
23. www.reincarnationexperiment.org/home/authorsperspective.html.

Appendix 2

1. Bowman, C. (1997).
2. Crabtree, A. (1985).
3. Cunningham, J. (1994).
4. Denning, H. (1998).
5. Everett, L. (1996).
6. Finkelstein, A. (2006).
7. www.marilynmonroereincarnated.net/.
8. Fiore, E. (1979).
9. Goldberg, B. (1988).
10. Hall, J. (1997).
11. Jarmon, R. G. (1997).
12. Keeton, J. and Moss, P. (1979).
13. Keeton, J. and Petherick, S. (1988).
14. Grant, J. and Kelsey, D. (1968).
15. Lawton, I. (2010).
16. Lucas, W. B. (1993).
17. "Reliving Drama of Taj Mahal," *Reincarnation International,* No. 4, November 1994, pp. 18–20.
18. Netherton, M. (1978).
19. Snow, C. (1989).
20. Sutphen, D. (1976, 1978, and 1988 are of particular interest).
21. TenDam, H. (1996).
22. Ibid. (2003).
23. Wambach, H. (1979).
24. Ibid. (1981).
25. Snow, C. (1989).
26. Weiss, B. (1988).
27. Woolger, R. (1988).

Bibliography

Note: Dates quoted here reflect original publication and may differ from those quoted in the text.

Almeder, R. (1997). "A Critique of Arguments Offered against Reincarnation." *Journal of Scientific Exploration*, Vol. 11, No. 4, pp. 499–526.

Angel, L. (1994a). *Enlightenment East and West*. New York: State University of New York Press.

———. (1994b). "Empirical Evidence for Reincarnation?" *Skeptical Inquirer*, Vol. 18, 5 (Fall 1994), pp. 481–487.

Armstrong, N. (ed.) (1976). *Harvest of Light*. London: Neville Spearman.

Banerjee, H. N. (1980). *Americans Who Have Been Reincarnated*. New York: Macmillan Publishing Co.

Barnes, J. (2008). *Nothing to Be Frightened Of*. New York: Alfred A. Knopf.

Barnes, W. (1999). *I Built the Titanic*. Gillette, NJ: Edin Books.

Bauval, R. and Gilbert, A. (1994). *The Orion Mystery*. London: William Heinemann.

Bellamy, E. (1888). *Looking Backward, 2000–1887*. Boston: William Ticknor.

Bernstein, M. (1965). *The Search for Bridey Murphy*. 1990 revised and updated. London: Bantam Books.

Besant, A. and Leadbeater, C. W. (1924). *The Lives of Alcyone*. Vol. 1 & 2. Madras, India: Theosophical Publishing House.

Betts, R. B. (1990). *The Druze*. New Haven, CT: Yale University Press.

Blavatsky, H. P. (1888). *The Secret Doctrine*. London: Theosophical Publishing Co. Electronic version available on Internet as free download.

Bonwick, J. (1878). *Egyptian Belief and Modern Thought*. Oxford: Oxford University. (Also, Indian Hill, CO: Falcon's Wing Press, 1956.)

Bose, C. S. (1952). *A Case of Reincarnation*. India: Ligate, Satsang S. P.

Bowman, C. (1997). *Children's Past Lives*. Shaftesbury, UK: Element Books. (Also, New York: Bantam Books.)

Budge, E. A. W. (1895). *The Egyptian Book of the Dead*. Reprinted 1967, New York: Dover Publications.

Bunick, N. (2010). *Time for Truth*. Carlsbad, CA: Hay House.

Cannon, A. (1933). *The Invisible Influence*. London: Rider & Co.

———. (1952). *The Power Within*. London: Rider & Co.

Cannon, D. (1991, 1992, and 1993). *Conversations with Nostradamus*, Vols. 1, 2, and 3. Huntsville, AR: Ozark Mountain Publishing.

———. (1994). *Conversations with Nostradamus*, Vol. 3. Huntsville, AR: Ozark Mountain Publishing.

Cockell, J. (1993). *Yesterday's Children*. London: Piatkus Books.

———. (1996). *Past Lives, Future Lives*. London: Piatkus Books.

Cott, J. (1988). *The Search for Omm Seti*. London: Rider & Co.

Crabtree, A. (1998). *Multiple Man: Explorations in Possession and Multiple Personality*. Toronto: Somerville Books.

Cunningham, J. (1994). *A Tribe Returned*. Crest Park, CA: Deep Forest Press.

David-Néel, A. (1927). *My Journey to Lhasa.* New York: Harper & Brothers.

———. (1939). *Buddhism: Its Doctrines and Its Methods.* English trans. of 1911 book. London: The Bodley Head.

———. (1958). *Magic and Mystery in Tibet.* English trans. of 1929 book. New York: University Books.

———. (1997). *Immortality and Reincarnation.* English trans. of 1961 book. Rochester, VT: Inner Traditions International.

Delanne, G. (1904). *Evidence for a Future Life: Documents for the Study of Reincarnation.* English trans. London: G. P. Putnam's Sons.

Denning, H. (1987). "The Restoration of Health through Hypnosis." *Journal of Regression Therapy,* 2:1, p. 524.

———. (1998). *Life without Guilt: Healing through Past Life Regression.* Woodbury, MN: Llewellyn Publications.

Dowding, H. C. T. (1945). *Lynchgate: The Entrance to the Path.* London: Rider & Co.

Ducasse, C. J. (1960). "How the Case of the Search for Bridey Murphy Stands Today." *Journal of the American Society for Psychical Research,* No. 54 (January 1960): 3–22.

———. (1961). *A Critical Examination of the Belief in a Life after Death.* Springfield, IL: Charles C. Thomas.

Edwards, P. (1996). *Reincarnation: A Critical Examination.* Amherst, NY: Prometheus Books.

Everett, L. (1996). *Celebrity Regressions.* Slough, UK: W. Foulsham & Co.

Finkelstein, A. (2006). *Marilyn Monroe Returns: The Healing of a Soul.* Charlottesville, VA: Hampton Roads Publishing Company.

Fiore, E. (1978). *You Have Been Here Before.* New York: Ballantine Books.

Fisher, J. (1984). *The Case for Reincarnation.* Revised ed. 1998. Toronto: Somerville House.

Flournoy, T. (1900). *From India to the Planet Mars.* English trans. 1900. New York & London: Harper & Brothers Publishers.

Fuller, J. O. (1993). *Joan Grant: Winged Pharaoh.* USA: Theosophical History Occasional Papers, Vol. 3.

Gadit, A. M. (2009). "Myth of Reincarnation: A Challenge for the Mental Health Profession." *Journal of Medical Ethics,* 35:91.

Gay, S. E. (1890). "Theosophical-Feminist Manifesto." *Lucifer* magazine of Theosophical Society.

Gershom, Y. (1992). *Beyond the Ashes.* Virginia Beach: A.R.E. Press.

———. (1996). *From Ashes to Healing.* Virginia Beach: A.R.E. Press.

Goldberg, B. (1988). *Past Lives, Future Lives.* New York: Ballantine Books.

———. (1996). *Soul Healing.* St. Paul, MN: Llewellyn Publications.

———. (2004). *Past Lives, Future Lives Revealed.* Pompton Plains, NJ: New Page Books.

Grant, J. (1937). *Winged Pharaoh.* New York: Overlook Press (paper).

———. (2007). *Speaking from the Heart.* Edited by Nicola Bennett. London: Overlook Press.

Grant, J. and Kelsey, D. (1968). *Many Lifetimes.* London: Victor Gollancz.

Guirdham, A. (1974). *We Are One Another.* St. Helier, Jersey: Neville Spearman.

Hall, H. F. (1898). *The Soul of a People.* London & New York: Macmillan and Co.

Hall, J. (1997). *Hands Across Time: The Soulmate Enigma.* Scotland: Findhorn Press.

Hanzhang, Y. (1991). *The Biographies of the Dalai Lamas.* Beijing: Foreign Languages Press.

Haraldsson, E. (2000). "Birthmarks and Claims of Previous-Life Memories: The Case of Purnima Ekanayake." *Journal* of the Society for Psychical Research, Vol. 64.1, No. 858, January 2000.

Haraldsson, E. and Abu-Izzeddin, M. (2002). "Development of Certainty about the Correct Deceased Person in a Case of the Reincarnation Type in Lebanon: The Case of Nazih Al-Danaf." *Journal of Scientific Exploration,* Vol. 16, No. 3, pp. 363–380.

Haraldsson, E. and Samararatne, G. (1999). "Children Who Speak of Memories of a Previous Life as a Buddhist Monk: Three New Cases." *Journal* of the Society for Psychical Research, Vol. 63, No. 857, pp. 268–291, October 1999.

Harris, M. (1986a). "Are 'Past-Life' Regressions Evidence of Reincarnation?" *Free Inquiry,* Fall 1986, 18–23.

———. (1986b). *Investigating the Unexplained.* Buffalo, NY: Prometheus Books.

Harrison, P. and Harrison, M. (1991). *The Children That Time Forgot.* New York: Berkley Books.

Harwood, B. (2006). *My Truth: The Far-Memory of Christopher Marlowe.* Bloomington, IN: Authorhouse (paperback).

Hearn, L. (1897). *Gleanings in Buddha-Fields: Studies of Hand and Soul in the Far East.* London: Kengan Paul, Trench, Trübner & Co.

Hubbard, L. R. (1989). *Have You Lived before This Life?* Denmark: New Era Publications International.

Hugo, V. (1998). *Conversations with Eternity: The Forgotten Masterpiece of Victor Hugo.* Ed. John Chambers, Introd. Martin Ebon. Boca Raton, FL: New Paradigm Books.

Hulme, A. J. H. and Wood, F. H. (1937). *Ancient Egypt Speaks.* London: Rider & Co.

Iverson, J. (1976). *More Lives than One?* London: Souvenir Press.

———. (1992). *In Search of the Dead.* London: BBC Books. (Also, San Francisco: HarperSanFrancisco.)

Jarmon, R. G. (1997). *Discovering the Soul.* Virginia Beach, VA: A.R.E. Press.

Johnson, B. (2010). *Seoul to Soul.* Canada: Ben Johnson Enterprises.

Kampman, R. (1973). "Hypnotically Induced Multiple Personality: An Experimental Study." *Acta Universitatis Oulvensis,* Series D, Medica No. 6, Psychiatrica No. 3, pp. 7–116.

Kardec, A. (1857). *The Spirits' Book.* English versions still in print.

———. (1861). *The Book on Mediums.* English versions still in print.

———. (1864). *The Gospel According to Spiritism.* English versions still in print.

Karlén, B. (2000). *And the Wolves Howled.* London: Clairview Books.

Keeton, J. and Moss, P. (1979). *Encounters with the Past.* London: Sidgwick & Jackson.

Keeton, J. and Petherick, S. (1988). *The Power of the Mind.* London: Robert Hale.

Kelsey, D. (2007). *Now and Then.* Folkestone, UK: Trencavel Press.

Kingsley, P. (2010). *A Story Waiting to Pierce You: Mongolia, Tibet, and the Destiny of the Western World.* California: Golden Sufi Centre.

Lane, B. (1996). *Echoes from the Battlefield.* Virginia Beach, VA: A.R.E. Press.

Lawton, I. (2010). *Your Holographic Soul.* Dorset, UK: Rational Spirituality Press.

Leadbeater, C. W. (1949). *The Soul's Growth through Reincarnation: The Lives of Arcor.* Madras, India: The Theosophical Publishing House.

Leininger, B. and Leininger, A., with Gross, K. (2009). *Soul Survivor.* London: Hay House. (Also New York: Grand Central Press.)

Leonardi, D. (1975). *The Reincarnation of James Wilkes Booth*. Old Greenwich, CT: Devin-Adair Pub.

Llewelyn, K. (1991). *Flight into the Ages*. New South Wales, Australia: Felspin.

Lönnerstrand, S. (1998). *I Have Lived Before*. Huntsville, AR: Ozark Mountain Publishing. English trans. by Leslie Kippen of 1994 original, Sweden: Larsons Förlag.

Lucas, W. B. (1993). *Regression Therapy: A Handbook for Professionals*. Vols. 1 and 2. Crest Park, CA: Deep Forest Press.

MacLaine, S. (1983). *Out on a Limb*. New York: Bantam.

———. (1989). *Going Within*. New York: Bantam

———. (2000). *The Camino*. New York: Atria.

Mailer, N. (1948). *The Naked and the Dead*. New York: Rhinehart.

———. (1983). *Ancient Evenings*. Boston: Little, Brown.

Mills, A. (1989). "A Replication Study: Three Cases of Children in Northern India Who Are Said to Remember a Previous Life." *Journal of Scientific Exploration*, Vol. 3, No. 2, pp. 133–184.

Montefiore, H. (2002). *The Paranormal: A Bishop Investigates*. Leicestershire, UK: Upfront Publishing.

Moody, R. (1979). *Life after Life*. New York: Bantam Books.

Motoyama, H. (1992). *Karma and Reincarnation*. London: Judy Piatkus (Publishers).

Myss, C. and Shealy, N. (1998). *The Creation of Health*. New York: Three Rivers Press.

Netherton, M. (1978). *Past Lives Therapy*. New York: William Morrow.

Newton, M. (1994). *Journey of Souls*. St. Paul, MN: Llewellyn Publications.

Norman, B. (2008). *South Bank Dornier*. Guisborough, UK: Bill Norman.

Norsic, D. (1998). *To Save Russia*. Fairfield, IA: Sunstar Publishing.

Parker, E. S., Cahill, L., and McGaugh, J. L. (2006). "A Case of Unusual Autobiographical Remembering." *Neurocase*, Feb., 12:1, pp. 35–49.

Pasricha, S. (1990). *Claims of Reincarnation*. New Delhi: Harman Publishing House.

———. (1998). "Cases of the Reincarnation Type in Northern India with Birthmarks and Birth Defects." *Journal of Scientific Exploration*, Vol. 12, No. 2, pp. 259–293.

Pearsall, P. (1998). *The Heart's Code*. New York: Broadway Books.

Pearsall, P., Schwartz, G., and Russek, L. (2000). "Changes in Heart Transplant Recipients that Parallel the Personalities of Their Donors." *Integrative Medicine*, 2(2), pp. 65–72.

Penrose, R. and Hameroff, S. (2011). "Consciousness and the Universe." Special edition of *Journal of Cosmology*, Vol. 14, April–May 2011.

Percival, H. W. (1946). *Thinking and Destiny*. New York: The Word Foundation. Also available as a free download at: http://word-foundation.com/a-books.htm.

Playfair, G. L. (2006). *New Clothes for Old Souls*. London: Druze Heritage Foundation.

Rabanne, P. (1997). *Journey: From One Life to Another*. Shaftesbury, Dorset, and Rockport, MA: Element Books.

Radin, D. (1997). *The Conscious Universe*. New York: HarperEdge.

———. (2006). *Entangled Minds*. New York: Paraview Pocket Books.

Rawat, K. S. (1997). "The Case of Shanti Devi." *Venture Inward*, March/April 1997, published by the Association for Research and Enlightenment.

Rawat, K. S. and Rivas, T. (2005). "The Life Beyond: Through the Eyes of Children Who Claim to Remember Previous Lives." *Journal of Religion and Psychical Research*, Vol. 28, No. 3.

Rieder, M. (1988). *Return to Millboro.* Grass Valley, CA: Blue Dolphin Publishing.

———. (1991). *Mission to Millboro.* Nevada City, CA: Blue Dolphin Publishing.

Roach, M. (2005). *Spook: Science Tackles the Afterlife.* New York: W.W. Norton & Company.

Rochas, A. de (1911). *Les Vies Successives.* Paris: Bibliothèque Chacornac.

———. (1913). *La Suspension de la Vie.* Paris: Dorbon-aîné.

Rogo, D. S. (1985). *The Search for Yesterday: A Critical Examination of the Evidence for Reincarnation.* Englewood Cliffs, NJ: Prentice Hall.

Salva, R. (2009). *The Reincarnation of Abraham Lincoln.* Second ed. Nevada City, CA: Crystal Clarity Publishers.

Schwartz, G. and Russek, L. (2006). *The Living Energy Universe.* Charlottesville, VA: Hampton Roads Publishing Company.

Semkiw, W. (2003). *Return of the Revolutionaries.* Charlottesville, VA: Hampton Roads Publishing Company.

———. (2006). *Born Again.* New Delhi: Ritana Books.

———. (2008). *Origin of the Soul and the Purpose of Reincarnation.* New Delhi: Ritana Books.

Shirley, R. (1936). *The Problem of Rebirth.* London: Rider & Co.

Shroder, T. (1999). *Old Souls.* New York: Simon & Schuster.

Snow, C. (1989). *Mass Dreams of the Future.* Wellingborough, NY: McGraw-Hill Publishing Co.

Stearn, J. (1965). *Edgar Cayce: The Sleeping Prophet.* New York: Bantam Books.

Stemman, R. (1997). *Reincarnation: True Stories of Past Lives.* London: Judy Piatkus (Publishers).

———. (2005). *One Soul, Many Lives.* Revised, updated version of 1997 book. Berkeley, CA: Ulysses Press.

Stevens, E. W. (1878). *The Watseka Wonder.* Chicago: Religio-Philosophical Publishing House.

Stevenson, I. (1960). "The Evidence of Survival from Claimed Memories of Former Incarnations." *Journal of the American Society for Psychical Research,* 54, pp. 51–71, 95–117.

———. (1966). "Twenty Cases Suggestive of Reincarnation." *Proceedings* of the American Society for Psychical Research, Vol. 26.

———. (1974). *Twenty Cases Suggestive of Reincarnation.* Second ed. revised and enlarged. Charlottesville, VA: University Press of Virginia.

———. (1977). "The Explanatory Value of the Idea of Reincarnation." *Journal of Nervous and Mental Disease,* 164, pp. 305–326.

———. (1980). *Cases of the Reincarnation Type: Vol. 3, Lebanon and Turkey.* Charlottesville, VA: University Press of Virginia.

———. (1983). *Cases of the Reincarnation Type: Vol. 4, Twelve Cases in Thailand and Burma.* Charlottesville, VA: University Press of Virginia.

———. (1984). *Unlearned Language: New Studies in Xenoglossy.* Charlottesville, VA: University Press of Virginia.

———. (1987). *Children Who Remember Previous Lives.* Charlottesville, VA: University Press of Virginia.

———. (1990). "Phobias in Children Who Claim to Remember Previous Lives." *Journal of Scientific Exploration,* Vol. 4, No. 2, pp. 243–254.

———. (1993). "Birthmarks and Birth Defects Corresponding to Wounds on Deceased Persons," *Journal of Scientific Exploration,* Vol. 7, No. 4, pp. 403–410.

——— (1994). "A Case of the Psychotherapist's Fallacy." *American Journal of Clinical Hypnosis,* 36:3, January 1994, pp. 188–193.

———. (1995). "Empirical Evidence for Reincarnation? A Reply to Leonard Angel." *Skeptical Inquirer,* Vol. 19, 3 (May/June), p. 50–51 (and Angel's reply, p. 51).

———. (1997a). *Reincarnation and Biology: Vol. 1, Birthmarks; Vol. 2, Birth Defects and Other Anomalies.* Westport, CT: Praeger Publishers.

———. (1997b). *Where Reincarnation and Biology Intersect.* Westport, CT: Praeger Publishers.

———. (2003). *European Cases of the Reincarnation Type.* Jefferson, NC: McFarland & Company.

Stevenson, I. and Keil, J. (2005). "Children of Myanmar Who Behave Like Japanese Soldiers: A Possible Third Element in Personality." *Journal of Scientific Exploration,* Vol. 19, No. 2, pp. 171–183.

Stevenson, I., Pasricha, S., and McClean-Rice, N. (1989). "A Case of the Possession Type in India with Evidence of Paranormal Knowledge." *Journal of Scientific Exploration,* Vol. 3, No. 1, pp. 81–101.

Stevenson, I., Prasad, J., Mehrotra, L. P., and Rawat, K. S. (1974). "The Investigation of Cases of the Reincarnation Type in India." *Contributions to Asian Studies,* 5, 36–49.

Story, F. (1975). *Rebirth as Doctrine and Experience.* Sri Lanka: Buddhist Publication Society.

Sutphen, D. (1976). *You Were Born to Be Together.* New York: Simon & Schuster Pocket Books.

———. (1978). *Past Lives, Future Loves.* New York: Simon & Schuster Pocket Books.

———. (1988). *Predestined Love.* New York: Simon & Schuster Pocket Books.

Tarazi, L. (1990). "An Unusual Case of Hypnotic Regression with Some Unexplained Contents." *Journal* of the American Society for Psychical Research, Vol. 84(4), 309–344.

———. (1997). *Under the Inquisition.* Charlottesville, VA: Hampton Roads Publishing Company.

Tayé, J. K. L. (1997). *Enthronement: The Recognition of the Reincarnate Masters of Tibet and the Himalayas.* Ithaca, NY: Snow Lion Publications.

TenDam, H. (1996). *Deep Healing.* Holland: Tasso Publishing.

———. (2003). *Exploring Reincarnation.* London: Rider Books.

Toyne, C. (1970). *The Testament of Truth.* London: George Allen & Unwin.

———. (1976). *Heirs to Eternity.* London: Neville Spearman Ltd.

Tsering, D. (2000). *Dalai Lama, My Son: A Mother's Story.* London: Virgin Publishing.

Tucker, J. B. (2005). *Life before Life: A Scientific Investigation of Children's Memories of Previous Lives.* New York: St. Martin's Press, Griffin.

Van der Maesen, R. (2006). "Doctoral Dissertation: Studies on the Effectiveness and Client Satisfaction in Reincarnation Therapy." English translation available at http://www.earth-association.org/articles/by-other-authors/doctoral-dissertation-of-ronald-van-der-maesen-2006.html.

Varah, C. (1992). *Before I Die Again.* London: Constable.

Wambach, H. (1978). *Reliving Past Lives.* New York: Harper & Row.

———. (1981). *Life before Life.* New York: Bantam Books.

Weiss, B. (1988). *Many Lives, Many Masters.* New York: Simon & Schuster, A Fireside Book.

Whitton, J. L. and Fisher, J. (1986). *Life between Life.* London: Grafton Books.

Wood, F. H. (1935). *After Thirty Centuries.* London: Rider & Co.

———. (1940). *This Egyptian Miracle.* London: Rider & Co.

Woolger, R. (1988). *Other Lives, Other Selves.* New York: Bantam.

Index

Cases Index